Age Discrimination

I would like to thank two wonderful American friends for giving me some space in order to write this book. David Wright and Kendrick King are examples of how age is irrelevant to how one lives a life. It is always a pleasure to meet and spend time with them.

Age Discrimination

Ageism in Employment and Service Provision

MALCOLM SARGEANT
Middlesex University, UK

GOWER

Published by
Gower Publishing Limited
Wey Court East
Union Road
Farnham
Surrey, GU9 7PT
England

Ashgate Publishing Company
Suite 420
101 Cherry Street
Burlington,
VT 05401-4405
USA

www.gowerpublishing.com

British Library Cataloguing in Publication Data
Sargeant, Malcolm.
Age discrimination : ageism in employment and service
provision.
  1. Age discrimination in employment. 2. Age discrimination
  in employment--Law and legislation--Great Britain.
  3. Older people--Employment. 4. Age and employment.
  5. Service industries workers--Legal status, laws, etc.
  6. Ageism.
  I. Title.
  331.398133-dc22

ISBN: 978-0-566-08926-8 (hbk)
ISBN: 978-0-566-08927-5 (ebk)

Library of Congress Cataloging-in-Publication Data
Sargeant, Malcolm.
Age descrimination : ageism in employment and service provision / by
Malcolm Sargeant.
    p. cm.
  Includes bibliographical references and index.
  ISBN 978-0-566-08926-8 (hbk) -- ISBN 978-0-566-08927-5 (ebook)
  1. Age discrimination in employment. 2. Age discrimination in
  employment--Law and legislation. I. Title.
  HD6279.S368 2011
  331.3--dc23

                                                                2011025532

Printed and bound in Great Britain by the
MPG Books Group, UK

Contents

List of Tables

Preface

This book is a successor to a previous one titled *Age Discrimination in Employment* (Gower Publishing, 2007). It expands and updates the content of that book and adds a lot of material, including a consideration of the Equality Act 2010 and the possibility of measures making age discrimination in facilities, goods and services unlawful.

In 2011 the UK government announced the withdrawal of the mandatory retirement age. This book is dedicated to all those who campaigned for this event and all those who have, and continue to do so, fought to end the prejudice that causes age discrimination. There is still a long way to go to achieve this end and I hope this book is a small contribution to it.

Malcolm Sargeant, November 2011

1

Age Discrimination

Age discrimination occurs when one particular age group is treated differently to another age group on the grounds of chronological age. It is possible for this different treatment to be benign, as in giving reduced admission rates for cinemas to older persons. It is also possible for it to be less favourable treatment when, for example, a person is refused medical treatment because they are deemed to be too old to benefit from it.

Age discrimination is a practical manifestation of ageism, which is about having an essentially negative image of older people. A good definition is contained in a UN report on ageing. It states that: 'Ageism reinforces a negative image of older persons as dependent people with declines in intellect, cognitive and physical performance. Older persons are often perceived as a burden, a drain on resources, and persons in need of care'.[1] Ageism is primarily 'an attitude of mind which may lead to age discrimination'.[2] The word 'ageism' is said to have first been used by Robert Butler MD in 1969. Butler wrote a short article[3] about the strongly negative reaction of white affluent middle class residents to a proposal for a public housing project for the 'elderly poor' in their district. He described ageism as: 'Prejudice by one age group against other age groups'. Although he highlighted the issue of ageism the events that he described appeared also to be a mixture of prejudice based upon race and class.

Age discrimination has, of course, both an institutional and an individual perspective. A report by the Equality Authority of Ireland stated that: 'Ageism

---

1   'Follow-up to the second world assembly on ageing. Report of the Secretary-General'. (2009) United Nations.
2   'A literature review of the likely costs and benefits of legislation to prohibit age discrimination in health, social care and mental health services.' (2007) Centre for Policy on Ageing on behalf of the Department of Health.
3   Butler, R.N. (1969). 'Age-ism: another form of bigotry', *Gerontologist*, 9, 243–6.

involves an interlinked combination of institutional practices, individual attitudes and relationships.'

Institutional practices in this context can be characterised by:

- The use of upper age limits to determine provision or participation.

- Segregation, where older people are not afforded real choices to remain within their communities.

- A failure to take account of the situation, experience or aspirations of older people when making decisions, and a failure to seek to ensure benefit to them as a result of an over emphasis on youth and youth culture; and

- Inadequate provision, casting older people as burdens or dependents.

Institutional practices can shape, and be shaped, by individual attitudes based on stereotypes of older people as dependent, in decline or marginal. Some of these practices can also have a detrimental impact on an older person's sense of self worth.[4]

These institutional manifestations of age discrimination are based on group stereotypes. Upper age limits may be imposed for health care or for employment purposes, for example, because of a belief that it is correct to treat older people less favourably than others. This may be the result of an idea that older people have outlived the useful part of their lives and that society should somehow allocate its resources to those that have something left to contribute. Older people may be segregated and regarded as a drain on the resources of the community. There is no attempt in these practices to differentiate one older person from another. Like all discriminatory practices it can accept that there are exceptions to the general rule, but the general rule results in treatment relying upon an unacceptable criterion. There is little attempt to differentiate between one older person and another. It is a key argument in this book that age legislation tends to homogenise age groups, so that we end up talking about the problems of older people in general, rather than reflecting on the diversity within each age group.

---

4   'Implementing equality for older people' (2004).

Individuals' lives are defined by age:

> *Our lives are defined by ageing: the ages at which we can learn to drive, vote, have sex, buy a house, or retire, get a pension, travel by bus for free. More subtle are the implicit boundaries that curtail our lives: the safe age to have children, the experience needed to fill the boss's role, the physical strength needed for some jobs. Society is continually making judgments about when you are too old for something – and when you are too old.*[5]

There are many surveys that show age discrimination taking place, especially in the workplace. One survey showed that some 59 per cent of respondents reported that they had been discriminated against on the basis of the age during their careers.[6] One in three respondents to a further survey found that the over-70s were regarded as incompetent and incapable and that more people reported suffering age discrimination than any other form of discrimination.[7]

In a survey of retired trade union members, almost one third claimed to have suffered age discrimination at work and one in twelve claimed to have been harassed for reasons connected to their chronological age.[8] One of the respondents recounted this story:

> *I was a lecturer in journalism for over 11 years until I was forced to retire last year, despite having no wish to do so. I was told just before my 65th birthday that I would be compulsorily retired at the end of the summer term.*
>
> *The college, with its usual efficiency, left it too late to advertise for a replacement and they could not find a suitable applicant. At the eleventh hour, as desperation set in, I was asked to stay on. I was very happy to do so because I enjoyed my work and I was very efficient at my job.*
>
> *I would have been content to carry on for another two or three years and I assumed that, having breached their strict code of retirement at 65, the college would be pleased for me to do so. However, in April last year I*

---

5   'How ageist is Britain?' (2005).
6   'Tackling age discrimination in the workplace' (2005).
7   'How ageist is Britain?' (2005).
8   Survey carried out by Malcolm Sargeant in 2003; see Sargeant (2004).

was informed that my job was again going to be advertised and I would be forced to retire when a replacement was found. I told the personnel department that it was unfair because they had been more than ready to ignore their mandatory retirement rule when it suited them. They refused and the job was advertised, again at a late hour, and this time they found a suitable candidate although this did not happen until three weeks before the end of the summer term, so I was kept in suspense until shortly before I was due to start my holidays.

There is a sense of frustration in this letter. An experienced and active individual is ejected from employment and almost discarded as a result of the application of a rule based upon a chronological age rather than the merits of the individual.

There are sufficient surveys reported in this book to show that decisions are taken on the basis of an individual's age, in relation to employment and to the provision of goods and services. One way of reducing this discrimination is to make institutional discrimination unlawful in order to help make individual discrimination unacceptable.

Stereotypes and Discrimination

It has been suggested that the word 'stereotype' was first used in the eighteenth century to describe a printing process whose purpose was to duplicate pages of type.[9] The usage of the word later developed from the idea of producing further images from a stereotype into reproducing 'a standardised image or conception of a type of person'.[10] The problem with producing this 'standard image', or stereotyping, is that individuals are treated as members of a group, rather than being treated as individuals. It is the group to whom we attribute generalised characteristics, which clearly cannot possibly be the characteristics of every individual within that group.

One simple assumption, for example, might be that men are stronger than women. The result of this is that only men might be considered for physically demanding jobs, which in turn may be the higher paid jobs in certain types of employment. The outcome is that women are discriminated against in the selection process and end up earning less than men. The assumption is patently

---

9   Taken from 'Stereotyping' (1995).
10   This definition comes from the *Collins Dictionary and Thesaurus* 1998.

false. Not all men are stronger than all women. Some women will be stronger than many men and so on. The discrimination comes from the stereotyping of women in the first place. It is the allocation of a generalised characteristic to an identifiable group.

The result of employment policies based upon the age of employees is to reduce the participation rate of older people in the job market. These policies encourage them to leave the labour force and discourage them from re-joining it. They may also be responsible for older employees having fewer training opportunities than their younger colleagues. One of the reasons for this may be the stereotypical attitudes that employers have held towards the abilities of employees based upon their age. In one oft quoted survey of 500 companies[11] a question was asked about at what age someone would be too old to employ. Of the respondents 12 per cent considered people too old at 40, 25 per cent considered them too old at 50, 43 per cent considered them too old at 55 and 60 per cent felt they were too old at 60. The relationship of these judgements to conventional stereotypical attitudes can be shown in their answers to questions about agreeing or not agreeing with statements. Figures such as the 36 per cent who thought that older workers were more cautious, the 40 per cent who thought that they could not adapt to new technology and the 38 per cent who thought that they would dislike taking orders from younger workers suggest that stereotypical attitudes remain strong. Research indicates that there is little evidence that chronological[12] age is a good predictor of performance. An OECD study concluded:[13] 'Age has only a marginal effect on industrial productivity and the variations in productivity within a given age group are wider than variations between one age group and another.'

The willingness of employers to attach characteristics to age groups is illustrated by a New Zealand survey covering large and small employers (Table 1.1). Older workers are more reliable, more loyal, more committed and less likely to leave than younger workers. On the other hand, older workers are more likely to resist change and have problems with technology. They may also be less flexible, less willing to train and be less creative than younger colleagues.

11   Taylor, P. and Walker, A. (1994). 'The ageing workforce: employers' attitudes towards older people', *Work, Employment and Society*, 8:4, 569.
12   See McEwan (1990).
13   Demographic ageing – consequences for social policy (1988) cited in *Ageing and the Working Population* EIRO 1991.

Table 1.1   New Zealand survey of age characteristics

Older workers are more likely to:	Agree %	Neither %	Disagree %
Be reliable	83.6	11.3	5.3
Be loyal	81.2	16.0	2.9
Be committed to the job	65.9	18.5	5.6
Be willing to stay longer in the job	61.6	32.2	6.8
Resist change	60.1	22.8	17.1
Have problems with technology	55.4	28.4	16.2
Be productive	52.5	37.4	10.1
Be less flexible	39.3	33.4	27.3
Be less willing to train	32.5	36.5	30.9
Be less promotable	32.4	41.0	26.6
Be away sick	7.1	36.8	56.2
Have lower expectations	31.3	33.6	35.0
Be less creative	22.4	43.8	33.9

The argument is not whether these characteristics are largely true or largely false, it is whether they can apply to all or most workers who are of a certain chronological age. Logic suggests that such sweeping generalisations cannot be true.

The same survey asked employers to attribute characteristics to different age groups (Table 1.2).

Table 1.2   Characteristics associated with age groups: per cent responses from employers

Workers	15–29 yrs	30–44 yrs	45–59 yrs	60–75 yrs	All ages
Computer experience	66.9	19.9	1.1	–	12.1
Enthusiasm	35.2	28.5	3.3	0.4	32.6
High levels of motivation	14.9	48.0	6.4	0.3	30.3
Creativity	27.8	40.0	3.5	–	28.7
Innovation	20.0	48.4	5.1	–	26.5
Adaptability	29.8	35.3	10.8	0.3	23.8
Flexibility	24.5	33.1	16.5	1.2	24.7
Leadership	0.6	31.3	39.3	1.2	27.6
Strong work ethic	1.1	25.4	45.0	3.3	25.5
Loyalty to employer	0.3	10.7	50.3	10.6	28.1

The 45-and-over age group did not do so well. It scores highly in having leadership, strong work ethic and loyalty characteristics, but not so well in others. Similarly, young workers face prejudice based upon stereotypes. Their strengths lie in computer experience and enthusiasm, but they, according to this survey, are unlikely to have leadership qualities or a strong work ethic.

A good example of this stereotyping of older people is shown in various studies of the way that they are portrayed in the media. One study identified eight negative stereotypes. These were: (1) eccentrics; (2) curmudgeons (grouchy, angry, uncooperative, nosey/peeping toms); (3) objects of ridicule or the brunt of the joke; (4) unattractive; (5) overly affectionate or sentimental; (6) out of touch with current/modern society; (7) overly conservative; and (8) afflicted (physically or mentally deficient).[14] In a further study a number of British national newspapers were monitored[15] over a three month period from March to May 2008.[16] It appeared that very few good things ever happened to older people. One article in 20 (5 per cent) reported any sort of 'happy event' and all of these were tales of extended periods of marriage or reunions with long lost relatives. Examples of such a story include one about a couple celebrating their 80th wedding anniversary with headlines such as: 'Our 80 years of marriage' (*Daily Mail*); 'Mr and Mrs Marvel's 80 years of wedded bliss' (*Daily Express*); 'We're record breakers ... 80 years married today' (*Daily Mirror*). A second one was about a couple meeting up again after being apart for 70 years: 'Forbidden love of teenage couple has lasted 70 years' (*Times*). These happy events, of course, reflect the age of the individuals and can only happen to older people. They are an excellent example of the patronising nature of the press towards older people. The 'happy' stories are related to age and are the result of people being able to live a long time. Even 'happy' stories can be reversed into tragedy as shown by stories of long married couples who died in a suicide pact: 'Doting couple couldn't live with fear of being parted' (*Mail*); 'Suicide couple feared care home separation' (*Express*); 'Suicide pact couple were scared of being parted' (*Telegraph*) and 'Dead couple feared being separated' (*Times*). The broadsheet coverage of this story links their fears to

14 Schmidt, D.F and Boland, S.M. (1986). 'Structure of perceptions of older adults: evidence for multiple stereotypes', *Psychology and Ageing*, 1:3, 255–60 cited in T. Robinson, B. Gustafson and M. Popovich (2008). 'Perceptions of negative stereotypes of older people in magazine advertisements: comparing the perceptions of older adults and college students', *Ageing and Society*, 28, 233–51.

15 It was possible to do this as a result of a British Academy grant. The newspapers in question were: *The Times, Telegraph, Guardian, Independent, Daily Mail, Daily Express, Daily Mirror, The Sun* and *The Daily Star*. We also included their Sunday versions, including: *The Observer*.

16 See Sargeant, M. (2008). 'Age stereotypes and the media', *Communications Law*, 13:4, 119–24.

concerns about standards of health and social care. Longer interviews with local authority representatives explain that they would not have been separated and the reader is left with a rather ambiguous image of a caring and intelligent couple who are unable to understand quite simple policy statements.

There were some more positive stories about older people. A number of which concerned those who had achieved some educational or career success in later life (in other words they achieved this success despite the discriminatory barriers that society sets up): 'Age is no bar to a new skill' (*Mail*); 'The skills that only a mature worker can offer' (*Mail*) and 'Over 55? Then the job is yours' (*Express*) are stories about the discovery by employers of older workers to fill the skills shortage in their organisations. The other stories were categorised as being about:

- Elderly criminals.

- Elderly victims.

- Elderly incompetence.

- Eccentric behaviour.

- Older people with animals.

- Older people as record breakers.

- Couples with a significant age difference.

- Ageing celebrities.

The conclusions suggest that there is a particular form of illustrative image found in the coverage which serves to reinforce stereotypical images of older people whether it is as victims of poverty or ill health or in terms of their retirement aspirations.

The Scope of Age Discrimination

The population of the world is ageing, albeit at different rates. The issue of how to support this ageing population is as important to the future as the other major issues of the 21st century such as climate change.

THE AGEING POPULATION

The United Nations

According to the Population Division of the UN,[17] in July 2009, the world population was approximately 6.8 billion, 313 million more than in 2005 or a gain of 78 million persons annually. The report states that, assuming that fertility levels continue to decline, the world population is expected to reach 9.1 billion in 2050 and to be increasing by about 33 million persons annually at that time. Most of this increase comes from the growing populations of the developing countries. In contrast, without migration from these countries, the populations of the more developed regions of the world would have declined between 2009 and 2050.

The UN further reports that:

> *The population aged 60 or over is increasing at the fastest pace ever (growing at 1.9 per cent annually) and is expected to increase by more than 50 per cent over the next four decades, rising from 264 million in 2009 to 416 million in 2050. Compared with the more developed world, the population of the less developed regions is ageing rapidly. Over the next two decades, the population aged 60 or over in the developing world is projected to increase at rates far surpassing 3 per cent per year and its numbers are expected to rise from 475 million in 2009 to 1.6 billion in 2050.*

Thus ageing is a worldwide phenomenon. The population globally is both growing and ageing as a result of declining fertility rates and longer lives. There are important assumptions underlying the UN figures which relate to the continuing decline of fertility rates amongst women and the success in which the HIV/Aids epidemic in the developing world is tackled. Nevertheless

---

17   Press release 11 March 2009 concerning the 2008 revision of population statistics.

the general picture is clear. It is one of growing and ageing populations[18] in the developing world and one of declining,[19] or static, and ageing populations in much of the developed world.

Without policy changes the results of this ageing process will be serious. The UN report states that the number of people aged 60 or over is expected almost to triple, increasing from 739 million in 2009 to two billion by 2050. It is the 'older old' who will increase proportionately more as the numbers of people aged 80 or over is projected to increase four-fold to reach 395 million in 2050. Although the population of the developing world will still stay relatively young, it will also carry the weight of the biggest increases in the older population. According to the UN, already some 65 per cent of the world's older persons live in the less developed regions. By 2050 this will increase to 79 per cent. In 2009 approximately half of the older old live in developing countries but that share is expected to reach 69 per cent by 2050.

In 2002 the UN adopted the *Madrid International Plan on Ageing*.[20] This recognised the global transformation that would result from demographic change, whilst also recognising that there were different issues in the developed and the developing regions. The themes that are contained in this declaration included:

a)   The full realisation of all human rights and fundamental freedoms of all older persons.

b)   The achievement of secure ageing, which involves reaffirming the goal of eradicating poverty in old age.

c)   Empowerment of older persons to fully and effectively participate in the economic, political and social lives of their societies, including through income-generating and voluntary work.

---

18 The UN report does state, however, that the populations of the developing countries will still stay relatively young.
19 The populations of 45 countries or areas are expected to decrease between 2010 and 2050. These countries include: Belarus, Bosnia-Herzegovina, Bulgaria, Croatia, Cuba, Georgia, Germany, Hungary, Japan, Latvia, Lithuania, Moldova, Poland, the Republic of Korea, Romania, the Russian Federation, and Ukraine, all of which are expected to see their populations decline by at least 10 per cent by 2050 – see website of American Association of Retired Persons.
20 This took place at the second world assembly on ageing at Madrid in April 2002; the first assembly had been in Vienna in 1982; the UN website on the United Nations programme on Ageing can be found at <http://www.un.org/esa/socdev/ageing/un_network10.html>.

d)   Provision of opportunities for individual development.

e)   Ensuring the full enjoyment of economic, social and cultural rights, and civil and political rights of persons and the elimination of all forms of violence and discrimination against older persons.

f)   Commitment to gender equality.

g)   Recognition of the crucial importance of families, intergenerational interdependence.

h)   Provision of health care, support and social protection for older persons, including preventive and rehabilitative health care.

The document then stated that: 'Combating discrimination based on age and promoting the dignity of older persons is fundamental to ensuring the respect that older persons deserve. Promotion and protection of all human rights and fundamental freedoms is important in order to achieve a society for all ages.'

The objectives then set out include: 'Employment opportunities for all older persons who want to work', and 'health promotion and well-being throughout life'. Unfortunately the Madrid Declaration was not mandatory on the members of the UN and there are efforts by many age organisations to persuade the UN to adopt a Convention on the Rights of Older Persons.

European Union

The European Union is the only region in the world where the population is predicted to decline over the next 40 years. The EU27 currently has 495 million inhabitants.[21] Previous estimates had predicted a decline in population, in contrast to the global population which will increase from 6.4 billion to 9.1 billion in 2050.[22] This was because of declining female fertility rates and the lengthening of the lifespan of many of the population. More recent EC studies have concluded, however, that the population will increase by about ten million

21 See 'Demography report 2008 meeting social needs in an ageing society' (2009) European Commission.
22 'Europe's demographic future: facts and figures on challenges and opportunities' (2007) European Commission, Luxembourg.

people by 2060. This takes into account certain assumptions about inward migration and also a more optimistic view of fertility rates and life expectation.

The number and proportion of older people will continue to increase for the foreseeable future. It is suggested that there will be a 37.4 per cent increase between 2010 and 2030, which, in turn, requires a different approach by society to ageing, for example, the employment rate of 65–74-year-olds in the EU was 5.6 per cent in 2003 compared to 18.5 per cent in the USA (where there is no mandatory retirement age).[23]

The EU has adopted Council Directive 2000/78/EC establishing a general framework for equal treatment in employment and occupation, which makes age discrimination in employment and occupation unlawful. As is shown elsewhere this is not a comprehensive measure and, for example, still permits the adoption of mandatory retirement policies (see Chapter 7). The Community is also in the process of adopting a Directive extending this prohibition to include the provision of facilities, goods and services.

That much needs to be done in tackling age discrimination is shown by an EU-wide survey.[24] The Survey asked whether people saw various types of discrimination as being widespread or rare (Table 1.3).

Table 1.3   Perceptions of discrimination in the EU

Ground of discrimination	Widespread (%)	Rare (%)
Ethnic origin	64	30
Disability	53	42
Sexual orientation	50	41
Age	46	48
Religion or beliefs	44	47
Gender	40	53

23 European Commission communication 'Confronting demographic change: a new solidarity between generations' COM (2005) 94.
24 'Discrimination in the European Union: perceptions, experiences and attitudes' (2008). Special Eurobarometer 296, European Commission.

Thus, almost half the respondents saw age discrimination as widespread and an equal number saw it as rare. These results, of course, do not distinguish between the views of different ages in the population. The Survey established that 36 per cent of 15–24-year-olds thought age discrimination was widespread compared to 44 per cent of those aged 55 plus. Women are also more likely to see age discrimination as widespread (44 per cent) when compared to men (39 per cent).

A further question asked whether people perceived that belonging to a particular category was an advantage or a disadvantage (Table 1.4).

Table 1.4   Is belonging to one of the following groups an advantage or a disadvantage?

Group	Advantage (%)	Disadvantage (%)
Being disabled	3	79
Being a Roma	3	77
Being aged over 50	5	69
Being of a different ethnic origin	4	62
Being homosexual	2	54
Different religion	3	39
Being a woman	11	33
Being under 25	39	20
Being a man	49	4

More than two thirds of the respondents saw that being aged over 50 was a disadvantage with only 5 per cent seeing it as an advantage. Multiple discrimination is discussed elsewhere (Chapter 8) but one needs to consider what multiple disadvantage is suffered by a Roma person over the age of 50 or an older person with a disability.

The United States

The US population is changing because of the increased levels of life expectancy. The population aged 65 plus, for example, will grow from 40 million in 2010 to 55 million in 2020 and to 72.1 million in 2030; an 80 per cent increase in the

20 years from 2010.[25] The old-age dependency ratio[26] is predicted to rise from 21 per cent in 2000 to 36 per cent in 2030 and just under 40 per cent by 2050.[27]

The US was a pioneer in introducing legislation against age discrimination (see Chapter 6). It adopted the Age Discrimination in Employment Act in 1967 and the Age Discrimination Act in 1975. This latter Act prohibits discrimination on programmes that are receiving Federal financial assistance, so is limited in its scope. Nevertheless it is striking how many people continue to work. In 2008 some 6.2 million Americans age 65 and over were either working or actively seeking work. This is some 16.8 per cent of the population in this age bracket.[28]

There is much evidence that age discrimination is alive and well in the US. One survey[29] showed that more than two thirds of the workforce aged 45–74 believed that workers faced age discrimination in the workplace. Rix[30] also cites a study by Lahey,[31] in which she sent several thousand CVs to employers to study their responses to job applicants of different ages. The ages she used were between 35 years and 62 years (as indicated by high school leaving dates). The study found that the younger applicants were 40 per cent more likely to be called for interview than applicants of 50 or over.

If one looks at the figures provided by the US Equal Employment Opportunities Commission, then, in the fiscal year 2009, the EEOC received 22,718 charges of age discrimination. It resolved 20,529 age discrimination charges and recovered $72.1 million in monetary benefits for charging parties and other complainants (not including monetary benefits obtained through litigation).[32]

---

25 'A profile of older Americans: 2009'. Administration on Aging, US Department of Health and Human Services.
26 This is the ratio of the population aged 65 and over to the population aged 20 to 64 years.
27 'Ageing and employment policies: United States' (2005). Organisation for Economic Co-operation and Development (OECD).
28 'A profile of older Americans: 2009'. *supra.*
29 American Association of Retired Persons (2002) 'Staying ahead of the curve'. Cited in Sarah Rix (2006) 'Age discrimination in the United States'. Paper presented to the International Federation on Ageing conference, Copenhagen 2006.
30 Sarah Rix (2006) 'Age discrimination in the United States'. Paper presented to the International Federation on Ageing conference, Copenhagen 2006.
31 Joanna Lahey (2005) 'Do older workers face discrimination?' Boston College Center for Retirement Research.
32 <http://www.eeoc.gov/index.html>.

The United Kingdom

The estimated population of the United Kingdom in mid-2009 was 61,792,000. Children aged under 16 years made up approximately 20 per cent of the population, which was roughly the same percentage as the population over the age of 65 years. The average age of the population was 39.5 years in 2009, compared to 37.3 years some ten years earlier in 1999.[33]

For the first time there are now more people over the age of 60 years than there are children under 16 years. The change in the age population is noticeable when compared to the 1951 census. In the 50-year period following, the proportion of the population aged under 16 years fell from 24 per cent to 20 per cent. At the same time the proportion aged 60 years and over increased from 16 per cent to 21 per cent.[34]

The average age of the population in the UK as a whole is increasing as is the average age of the economically active population. Over the 25-year period between 1996 and 2021 the proportion of people over the age of 44 years will increase from 38 per cent to 46 per cent; the 45–59 age group will increase by almost one-quarter; the 60–74 age group will increase by over one-third and the 75 years and over group will increase by 28 per cent. In contrast the 16–29 years age group will fall by 5.7 per cent.[35] This process is a Europe-wide one, although the speed of the process is variable.[36] The number of people in the EU aged 50–64 years is projected to increase by 6.5 million during the next ten years.[37]

Employment[38]

In the United Kingdom the employment rate for those employees between 50 and 64 is now 65.1 per cent, compared to 81.2 per cent for the age group between 35 and 49 years and 78.7 per cent for those between 25 and 34 years. The rate drops dramatically after the age of 64 to 8.9 per cent.

---

33 Office for National Statistics <http://www.statistics.gov.uk/cci/nugget.asp?id=6>.
34 These statistics come from the 2001 census and are to be found, like the comparisons used here, on the Office for National Statistics website at <www.statistics.gov.uk>.
35 The immediate source was tackling age bias: code or law? (1998), although the original source was ONS Monitor 10.3.98.
36 See *Ageing and the Labour Market: Policies and initiatives within the European Union* (1998).
37 These and other statistics are available from demographic report, European Commission Office for Official Publications, September 1997, Luxembourg.
38 These figures are taken from Labour Market Trends, June 2011 published by the Office for National Statistics.

Labour force participation rates may be influenced by a discouragement effect and an added workers effect. The discouragement effect comes about when people who are available for work do not seek it because of the limited opportunities available. The added worker effect comes about as a result of the loss of employment by one household member resulting in another household member seeking work (ONS 2010). In the UK there is some evidence that both the discouragement effect and the added workers effect operate with regard to older workers.[39]

The ONS statistics reveal that there have been significant increases in long-term unemployment for age groups under the age of 50 years in recent years. The rate has hardly changed during the period for those aged 50 and over, although there has always been, and is, a higher proportion of older people in the long-term unemployment category than any other age group (Table 1.5).

Table 1.5   **Percentage with unemployment lasting for 12 months plus**

Year	18–24	25–49	50 and over
2008	19.6	28.1	37.9
2009	17.9	25.6	31.0
2010	25.8	33.6	37.5

Clearly the prognosis for older workers is worse than other age groups. One piece of research pointed out that: 'Once unemployed, the over 50s remain unemployed for the longest periods of time. This is largely a result of age discrimination by employers, a lack of formal educational qualifications and skill biased technological change.'[40]

The Department for Education and Employment commissioned an earlier research project with two main aims.[41] The first was to identify the effect of age on economic activity. The second was to explore the characteristics of older workers. Older workers were defined as those aged 50 years or over. The main conclusions were:

---

39 Office for National Statistics (2010) Statistical Bulletin May 2010; see <http://www.statistics.gov.uk/pdfdir/lmsuk0510.pdf>.
40 Smeaton, Deborah and Vegeris, Sandra (2009) 'Older people inside and outside the labour market: a review' Equality and Human Rights Commission, London.
41 'Characteristics of older workers' (1998).

1. Older workers were less likely to be in paid work than younger groups. When they did work they were more likely to be working as self-employed or part-time.

2. Among white-collar occupations there was a 'sharply increased' likelihood of becoming economically inactive beyond the ages of 50 and 55. An important proportion of this would be through the choice of individuals. Those in blue-collar jobs faced higher risks of unemployment and those risks became greater with age.

3. When older workers were unemployed and claiming benefit they tended to use fewer methods of job search. Once people had become unemployed, their chances of returning to paid work were much reduced if they were older than 50 years.

4. People in their 50s appeared reluctant to say that retirement represented their main economic activity. 'Only after prompting did many concede that they had, effectively, now retired.'

5. Another important reason for economic inactivity, and reduced hours, were the caring responsibilities of adults. By their late 60s, almost one woman in three had cared for an adult at some point in their life, as had more than one in five men.

6. Taking all forms of inactivity together, the chances of men leaving inactivity for paid work were sharply reduced after the age of 50 years 'and were close to zero for those over 60'. For women the chances of moving out of inactivity were much reduced after the age of 40 years and 'was particularly uncommon for those older than their late 50s'.

7. The more recently that older workers had received employer-paid training, the more likely they were to be in paid work.

The clear picture that one obtains from the research and analysis in this report is that the subject of potential disadvantages suffered by older workers is a complex one. People do not leave the workforce merely because of age discrimination, nor do substantial numbers leave involuntarily. Nevertheless the report makes clear that older workers are disadvantaged compared to younger workers. They are at a greater risk of exiting the workforce permanently and they do find it much more difficult, if not impossible, to re-enter the workforce. There is enough evidence put forward in this publication to show that one of the reasons for this are discriminatory practices used by employers. Indeed this was a conclusion accepted by the government in its subsequent consultation document and the Code of Practice on Age Diversity in Employment (see Chapter 3). The House of Lords Select Committee on Economic Affairs[42] was told,[43] in confirmation of this, that: 'Despite the research findings that age has no net effect on workers' performance, when supervisors and managers are asked to rate the performance of workers, they consistently rate the performance of older workers below that of younger workers.'

Health

Although less than 1 per cent of the older population is in hospital at any one time, 'older people tend to be stereotyped as a homogenous group characterised by passivity, failing physical and mental health, and dependency.'[44]

'There is a substantial body of evidence indicating that older people experience age discrimination in health care.'[45] One survey of general practitioners, by the charity Age Concern,[46] found that 77 per cent of the GPs surveyed said that age rationing occurs in the National Health Service and more than one-third stated that older patients do not enjoy the same quality of care in NHS hospitals as other patients. This was perhaps evidenced by the fact that 84 per cent of those surveyed stated that they had patients over the age of 50 years who had decided to go privately for treatment that they could have received on the NHS. The GPs themselves appeared, inadvertently perhaps, to assist in this discrimination by sometimes not referring older patients to other parts of the NHS because of their age.

Although the NHS is tackling age discrimination, it is clear that there are issues to be faced in the provision of healthcare, all of which may affect an individual's employability. One Department of Health report suggests that, locally, age discrimination may manifest itself in a number of different ways, including:

---

42 'Aspects of the economics of an ageing population' (2003).
43 Dr Philip Taylor Executive Director, Cambridge Interdisciplinary Research Centre on Ageing.
44 'Age discrimination in health and social care' (2000).
45 See Robinson (2003).
46 In 2000; see <www.ageuk.org.uk>.

- Low overall rates of provision of those interventions which are relatively more important to older people – for example, hip and knee replacement, cataract surgery, occupational therapy and chiropody.

- Low relative rates of access of older people to specialist services compared with younger people or refusal of particular treatments or care.

- Low referral rates to particular services.

- Unthinking and insensitive treatment from individual members of staff.[47]

This disadvantage suffered by older people is an important issue when one also considers the demographic change that is taking place in the population as a whole, which in turn affects the ageing of the general workforce. Of course much of this discrimination will have taken place against the very old who are even less likely to be part of the workforce, but there still continues to be a close relationship between healthcare and work.

Statistics on absenteeism as a result of sickness seem to be varied. One report claimed that the average annual absence rate in Europe as a whole was 7.4 days per worker.[48] Research by the Office for National Statistics in the UK showed that, in the study week, 3 per cent of employees in the public sector took at least a day off sick compared to 2.6 per cent of employees in the private sector. For large workplaces of 500 or more employees the private and public sector had the same incidence of sickness absence at 3.1 per cent. The report also showed that: 'Younger employees were more likely to take sickness absence than older employees. This was the case for both men and women. Among men, those aged 16–24 were most likely to be off sick with 2.6 per cent of employees taking at least one day off work in the reference week because of sickness. Among women, those aged 25–34 had the highest rate (3.5 per cent).'[49]

The link between health and work is also shown in statistics about early retirement. According to the Government Green Paper on 'Working and saving

---

47 'National service framework for older people: interim report on age discrimination' (2002). This extract is found on p. 19 of the report.
48 'Mercer's 2008 Pan-European health & benefit report' (2008). A summary can be found at <http://www.mercer.com/healthsurveyeurope>.
49 <www.statistics.gov.uk>.

for retirement' the mean age for men retiring in the UK is 62.6 years and for women 61.1 years. Amongst those already retired and who had retired early some 33 per cent had retired because of illness or disability. This is further evidenced by the Middlesex survey which showed that almost 23 per cent of retired members surveyed had done so because of illness or disability.[50]

These clear links might suggest that tackling discrimination in employment without providing for measures to tackle discrimination in healthcare provision leads to a regulatory provision which is incomplete.

Confusion and Contradiction

The debate about age discrimination in the UK has become confused with debates about other issues, such as the closing of defined benefits pension schemes and the demographic change that is taking place within the EU. The discussion is not only about whether discriminating on the grounds of chronological age is right or wrong, it is also about whether the present arrangements can cope with an ageing population. This is perhaps unfortunate because there is a debate to be had about age discrimination purely as a civil/human rights issue.[51]

There are perhaps two major arguments for introducing measures to combat age discrimination in employment: the demographic/economic argument and the equal treatment argument. They reveal an economic and human rights approach to the issue. It is the inter-reaction of these two approaches that causes confusion when considering the practical measures to be taken.[52]

ECONOMIC APPROACH

The demographic/economic debate is one that has concerned the European Commission for some time. The population of the EU member states is ageing, albeit at different rates. This ageing process is as a result of a combination of people living longer and a reducing birth rate. Concurrently with this process of an ageing population has been an increase in the number of older people exiting the workforce, so that there appears to be the prospect of a declining workforce with the responsibility of maintaining an increasing retired or unemployed older population.

---

50 Survey of retired trade unionists 2003.
51 See, for example, Fredman and Spencer (2003).
52 See Sargeant (2005c). See generally Sargeant (1999).

The government objectives that result from this demographic/economic process are firstly, to 'change the culture' and raise expectations about older people; secondly, to enable and encourage over 50s to stay in work; thirdly, to help and encourage older displaced workers to re-enter work; and finally, to help older people use their skills and experience for the benefit of the wider community.[53] Apart from this last objective, the measures are therefore about encouraging older people to continue working and, as part of this, to protect them from unfair treatment based on age when they are at work.

The Preamble to the Framework Directive (2000/78/EC) recognises that the prohibition of age discrimination is an essential part of meeting the aims set out in the guidelines but subsequently states (Paragraph 25), however, that differences in treatment may be justified under certain circumstances. Direct and indirect discrimination at work are to be made unlawful except where there is: 'Objective justification by a legitimate aim and the means of achieving that aim are appropriate and necessary'. Article 6 of the Directive then proposes three differences of treatment on the grounds of age that may be justifiable by: 'A legitimate aim, including legitimate employment policy, labour market and vocational training objectives'. The first difference permits some positive action for specific groups including young people, older workers and those with caring responsibilities to encourage their integration into the workforce; the second allows for the fixing of minimum conditions or the giving of advantages linked to age, professional experience or seniority; the third allows a maximum recruitment age based on the training requirements of the post or the need for a reasonable period of employment before retirement.

These exceptions seem to be in opposition to any principle of equality and suggest a contradiction between the equal-treatment approach and the latter approach which is perhaps a more functional one.[54]

A weakening of the principle of equal treatment in favour of an economic approach which is perceived to be better for business and better for employees in practice might be the result. This was reflected in the government's 2003 consultation exercise which proposed a number of specific areas for possible exceptional treatment.[55] These were:

---

53 'Winning the generation game' (2000).
54 See Sargeant (2005a).
55 'Equality and diversity: age matters' (2003).

- Health, safety and welfare – for example the protection of young workers.

- The facilitation of employment planning – for example where a business has a number of people approaching retirement age at the same time.

- The particular training requirements of the post in question – for example air traffic controllers (the government's example).

- Encouraging and rewarding loyalty.

- The need for a reasonable period of employment before retirement.

There appeared to be a willingness to compromise the principle of equality in favour of perhaps more pragmatic and functional exceptions. It is likely that these exceptions are to be treated narrowly and perhaps will not result in the contradiction illustrated here. The fact that there is a possibility however is a matter of concern. Age discrimination in employment is to be specifically allowed to continue in certain circumstances in order to encourage the employment of older people and not to place an apparently too onerous a burden upon employers. It is obviously acceptable to regard health and safety as an exception, especially perhaps the protection of young workers, as is exemplified in the special rules contained in the Working Time Regulations 1998. Phrases such as 'the facilitation of employment planning', 'the particular training requirements of the post in question', 'encouraging and rewarding loyalty' and 'the need for a reasonable period before retirement' all suggest an approach which may, in the short-term, encourage employers to employ older workers but will also limit the application of any principle of equal treatment. In the longer term, it is suggested, this may lead to a lessening of protection for such a class because there is a continued legitimisation of age discrimination in employment practices.

This debate is an economic one. It appears to have little to do with a concern about discriminatory treatment except insofar as this treatment interferes with the primary objective of keeping a greater proportion of older people in work and reducing the burden of support from the state and from a smaller workforce. If one adopts this standpoint then making age discrimination in employment unlawful makes sense unless it actually produces unwanted economic effects, for example an employer's ability to have an age diverse workforce in order to assist in long-term succession planning. Perhaps, in contrast to the treatment of discrimination on the grounds of gender, racial origin and disability, there can be justifiable exceptions to the 'principle of equality' in the treatment of age discrimination.[56]

An alternative, non-economic, justification for making age discrimination in employment unlawful is the equal treatment argument. The principle of equal treatment is mentioned in Article 1 of Directive 2000/78/EC and it is mentioned a number of times in the preamble to that Directive.[57] It is not difficult to see where this principle leads in terms of gender or race, but there is more of a problem when considering its application to age issues. Equal treatment suggests equality of treatment between parties or ensuring that one individual or group is not treated less favourably than another group. This presents real problems when considering age discrimination with the lack of a discrete group who can be judged to have been treated less favourably.

HUMAN RIGHTS APPROACH

The human rights approach provides that discriminatory treatment is wrong and such treatment cannot be justified on the grounds of age. Perhaps more is needed than just the concept of equal treatment, which requires that likes be treated as alike. The aim of equality, according to Fredman, is: 'To give all people an equal set of alternatives from which to choose and thereby to pursue their own version of the good life.'[58] In order to achieve this there needs to be some positive action that recognises the need to cope with inter-generational cultural differences. The focus might therefore be on supporting individuals rather than on some equation of relative equality.

Ageing, according to John Grimley Evans,[59] comes about because people change from how they were when they were young. All differences between young and old, however, are not necessarily due to age. An example of this

---

56 See 'Equality and diversity: age matters' (2003).
57 Clauses (1) to (6) of the Preamble; there is mention of the Community's long history of supporting the principle of equal treatment between men and women, but of course action on other issues such as racial discrimination and age are much more recent initiatives.
58 Fredman, 'The age of equality', in Fredman and Spencer (2003), p. 43; see also Dine and Watt (1996): 'If liberalism could be said … to have a central dogma it would surely include, at least at a preliminary stage, the provision that all citizens irrespective of gender, origin or other irrelevant characteristics should have an opportunity to secure for themselves, in reliance upon their own merits and endeavours, their choice from among the goods available in a given society.'
59 'Implications of the ageing process', in Fredman and Spencer (2003), p. 12.

might be what Evans calls the 'cohort phenomena' which is the result of the different experiences of people born at different times. Older people will have been through an education and training system which is different to that experienced by young people. Perhaps, in training, older people are subjected to teaching and learning techniques experienced by the young, but not by a previous generation. As a result the older worker may be faced with a greater challenge when experiencing training.

The important outcome of this debate is that the reasons for tackling age discrimination in employment are concerned with creating equality of opportunity for workers of all ages, although the principle does not necessarily require equal treatment in all circumstances. It is, however, a different debate to the functional one which derives from the economic/demographic issues.

Given that there are manifestations of discrimination based upon age and that there continues to be a stereotyping of the relative abilities of different groups of workers based on age, one might conclude that there is a case for treating such discrimination in the same way as the government has tackled discrimination based upon gender and race.

Is age discrimination different, or to be treated differently, than some other forms of discrimination. The approach does appear to be different. There might be more opportunities to *differentiate* rather than *discriminate* between persons of different ages. The US Secretary of Labor commenting in 1965,[60] prior to the introduction of the US Age Discrimination in Employment Act, on the existence of age discrimination stated that: 'We find no significant evidence of ... the kind of dislike or intolerance that sometimes exists in the case of race, color, religion, or national origin, and which is based on considerations entirely unrelated to ability to perform a job.' He did go on to say, however, that: 'We do find substantial evidence of ... discrimination based on unsupported general assumptions about the effect of age on ability ... in hiring practices that take the form of specific age limits applied to older workers as a group.'

Age discrimination took place then (and still does of course), but it may not create the strong emotions that are sometimes created in consideration of some other forms of discrimination. Perhaps it is the lack of these strong feelings that allows the economic approach to the subject to predominate.

---

60 See Eglit (1999); see also 'The older American worker-age discrimination in employment'. Report to the US Congress (1965).

2

Age Discrimination at Work

There are a number of features associated with age discrimination, in contrast to other grounds. These are that 'everyone has an age', but everyone's age is different. This is not entirely true of course, because some people are born at the same time and many are born near to each other in terms of days or months so as to make no difference. What is being suggested here is that the entire population of the UK and indeed the World has an age. The Directive and the regulation of age discrimination apply to the entire population of the UK who are in work or applying for work. There is no other ground of discrimination about which this can be said. In addition there is to be protection in the fields of facilities, goods and services.

Despite almost everyone being in this protected group, there are many subdivisions. Younger workers may have different experiences of discrimination in comparison to older workers. Although, therefore, it is correct to talk about age discrimination, it would perhaps be more useful to talk about the subgroups such as:

- Young age discrimination (16–24 years).

- Middle age discrimination (25–49 years).

- Older age discrimination (50–SPA).[1]

- Senior age discrimination (over SPA).

In the majority of cases, although sadly not all, workers will not only have an age but they will at some time in their lives be a member of each of these subgroups in turn, although never more than one at a time. It could be argued

---

1   State pension age; in 2010 this was 60 for women and 65 for men; it is due to be equalised for both by 2018 at the set age of 65 years.

that each of these subgroups has certain characteristics and might equally suffer from direct or indirect discrimination or harassment at work in relation to their age. It might be that the numerous exceptions which can be objectively justified, or currently exist, can only be understood (or properly opposed) by looking at these groups in turn and trying to consider what age discrimination they might suffer from and what measures might be needed.[2]

Young Age Discrimination[3]

Some time ago I met a distinguished labour lawyer from the US and described to him what was proposed in terms of age discrimination legislation in the UK and the EU. He was astonished that it was proposed to include young people as part of the protected group. In the US it is only those over the age of 40 years who are protected. My American colleague could not understand how young people could be thought of as being discriminated against in the same way as older people. The point is that the sort of discrimination suffered by young people, because of their age, may be different to that suffered by older people but it may still constitute direct or indirect discrimination and harassment. What is certainly true is that the outcomes of the discrimination may be different for young people in contrast to older ones. One analysis[4] looked at the 16–19 year age group and their reason for leaving their last job. The biggest reason, accounting for some 36 per cent of the group was that they resigned. Whatever the reason for the resignation, there was enough confidence among the age group to voluntarily leave their existing job. Whether it was to go to another job or not, this is not an option so readily available to older workers. The same analysis, when it looked at why people in their 50s left their last job, found that only 8 per cent did so through resignation. The problem for this latter group is that leaving a job often means leaving the workforce forever because of widespread age discrimination in recruitment practices. None of this is to say that young people do not suffer age discrimination, only to say that it might be different and might have different consequences to age discrimination suffered by some older age groups.

---

2   My inspiration for this chapter and for taking this approach comes from a publication of the Employers Forum on Age called 'Age at work: the definitive guide to the UK's workforce' published in 2005; work done in 2004.
3   See Sargeant, M. (2010a). 'Young workers and age discrimination', *International Journal of Comparative Labour Law and Industrial Relations*, 26:4, 467–78.
4   See 'Age at work' (2005).

For the sake of convenience this group is identified as everyone who is over school leaving age and under 25 years. Those of working age who are in this age group are distinguishable from other young workers because many of them are in education and, as a result, a large proportion of this group work part-time.

The 15–19-year-old group make up roughly 6–7 per cent of the population, with a slightly smaller number of 20–24-year-olds. The 2001 census also revealed the ageing population when for the first time there were more people over the age of 60 years, than there were people under the age of 16 years.[5]

The employment statistics from the Labour Force Survey in Table 2.1 reveal the following about young persons' employment:[6]

Table 2.1   Labour statistics for 16–24-year-olds[7]

Age range	Total employed	Employment rate (%)
16–17	392,000	25.8
18–24	3,425,000	58.7

There is a larger proportion of males in the 18–24-year-old group who are at work (60.1 per cent) as compared with females (57.3 per cent). All these employment rates are lower than the age groups above them.[8] This will reflect the numbers in education and not in paid work.

Many of those in employment are in part-time work. If one looks at the statistics for part-time workers, this assumption is borne out of the total of some 7.5 million part-time[9] workers in the UK, some 1.145 million were either students or pupils at school. It is even more pronounced when one looks at the figures for each sex in Table 2.2.

5   21 per cent of the population were 60 plus, while 20 per cent were under 16 years.
6   These figures do not fit into my classification of age groups, but I use them as an indicator; see <www.statistics.gov.uk>.
7   These figures are for the period March to May 2010.
8   78.1 per cent of those in the 25–34-year-old bracket for example.
9   The exact figure for March to May 2010 was 7,656,000.

Table 2.2   Young people working part-time

Category	Number
Male part-time	1,859,000
Male student or pupil part-timers	498,000
Female part-time	5,797,000
Female student or pupil part-timers	646,000

Thus, almost 30 per cent of males working part-time are students or pupils. Prior to the introduction of the Part-time Workers Regulations 2000[10] the traditional remedy for part-time workers who had been discriminated against was to claim sex discrimination, on the basis that the great majority of part-time workers are female. It is interesting to speculate whether there might be an opportunity to add a claim for indirect age discrimination to a future action in discrimination against part-time workers.

Teenage workers are concentrated in the hospitality and retail sectors where there appears to be more part-time and flexible work opportunities for students. Thus 17 per cent of 16–19-year-old workers work in the hotel and restaurant sector (compared to a national average of 4 per cent) and 39 per cent work in the wholesale, retail and motor trade sector (compared to a national figure of 16 per cent).[11]

Unemployment is an important issue for these age groups and unemployment in this age group has increased considerably in the recessionary years after 2008. In 2008 (March to May) the unemployment rate amongst 18–24-year-olds was 11.8 per cent. For the same period in 2010 the figure had increased to 17.1 per cent. In 2008 those in this age group who had been unemployed for at least 12 months amounted to a rate of 21 per cent. By 2010 this figure had increased to 26.6 per cent.

---

10   Part-time workers (Prevention of Less Favourable Treatment) Regulations 2000 SI 2000/1551.
11   'Age at work' (2005).

PERCEPTIONS OF DISCRIMINATION

A survey of a limited number of young people aged between 16 and 30 years was carried out in 2001.[12] This was part of the government's evaluation of the Code of Practice on Age Diversity in Employment.[13] It perhaps illustrates why age discrimination experienced by young workers is different to that experienced by older ones.

Respondents' perceptions, according to the report, of their treatment at work was directly related to their qualifications and experience, so those with more marketable skills seemed more protected from age discrimination. It is difficult to know how seriously to take this study because it is not clear that the treatment suffered by the young people concerned was the result of age discrimination or something else. The report states, for example, that:

> This research suggests that school leavers with few or no qualifications were more likely to experience age discrimination. In contrast, older respondents were generally more mature and confident and, having established themselves in work, were less likely to report instances of age discrimination, although some recalled such treatment in the past.

This may suggest that the adverse treatment is not just about age, but also about relevant qualifications. Despite this the survey does produce some useful illustrative information. If one looked at the employment cycle, as illustrated in the Code of Practice on Age Diversity (see Chapter 3), it is possible to recognise where age discrimination might take place:

- Recruitment – various job advertisements may contain minimum ages for jobs; these might be the result of occupational or statutory requirements (see later). The participants in focus groups in this analysis gave examples of employers wanting a secretary who was 'a bright young thing' which was a euphemism for wanting an employee who was a young attractive girl; others suggested that young people were recruited because they were cheaper; others suggested that euphemisms in recruitment advertisements such as 'mature personality' or needing experience were examples of discrimination against the young.

---

12 'Ageism: attitudes and experiences of young people' (2001); see Age Positive website <www.agepositive.gov.uk >.
13 See Chapter 1.

- Selection – being told that they were too young for a job was an example given of age discrimination in the selection process. This appeared to be true of the army, for example, with a minimum age of 18 years.

- Pay – there were examples of young people being paid less than others for doing similar work and sometimes this appeared to be justified on the grounds of age.

- Training – surprisingly the analysis reports a mixed picture on training. One would have thought that this was an area in which young workers were treated more favourably than others, but some employers seemed to want employees to prove themselves and their commitment to the organisation first before investing in training.

- Promotion – there was, amongst the group, a widespread acceptance that promotion usually came with length of service and/or experience on the job; so there were few instances of young people feeling that they were not promoted because of their age. Such instances did include a statement like 'you're still young, you've got plenty of time ahead of you'. Other statements seemed to reflect insecurity amongst the participants that maybe they did not have the experience to be promoted over older workers.

- Pensions – some employers encouraged staff to join their pension scheme as soon as possible; others had an approach which took into account length of service or age.

- Redundancy and retirement – few redundancies and little interest in retirement was reported!

The report suggested that ageism could take different forms: firstly, 'pure ageism' where age was overtly the factor influencing decisions, for example on admittance to a pension scheme; secondly, 'partial ageism' where age is interrelated with other factors, such as experience needed; thirdly, 'false ageism' where age is a euphemism for something else.

The young people surveyed were aware that older people had stereotypical views of them and that they were seen as:

- Less reliable and more likely to take days off.

- Less committed and less responsible.

- More involved in their social life than their work.

Although there were positive views held by the respondents about the benefits of working with older people, there were also views that older people could:

- Talk down to younger people and treat them like children.

- Pick on young, inexperienced recruits.

- Doubt or belittle their abilities or capacity to do a good job.

- Be a bit stuck in their ways and be reluctant to change or take advice from younger people.

- Be resentful of younger people's ability to learn new tricks and specifically to be resentful of their ability with new technology.[14]

Thus there is at least the perception of discrimination amongst young workers and undoubtedly such discrimination takes place. There are also perhaps a number of examples of occupational and statutory restrictions against young workers.

EUROPEAN COURT OF JUSTICE

A good example of a successful claim for age discrimination against a younger person took place in *Wilkinson v Springwell Engineering*[15] where an 18-year-old claimant was awarded some £16,000 in compensation for being dismissed because of her age. She was employed to replace her aunt and the employment tribunal accepted that the employer had stereotypical assumptions that capability equalled experience and experience equalled age.

---

14 This list, as with all the previous material in this section comes from 'Ageism: attitudes and experiences of young people' (2001).
15 Case number 2570420/07 Newcastle employment tribunal October 11 2007.

There have been a couple of judgements at the European Court of Justice relating to the counting of work experience of young workers, one, a referral from the German Court, and the other, a referral from the Austrian Court.

Seda Kücüdeveci v Swedex GnbH & Co. KG was a reference from the Landsarbeitsgericht, Düsseldorf. It concerned the German Law on Equal Treatment. Paragraph 10 is concerned with the permissible different treatment on grounds of age and transposes, among other matters, Article 6(1)(a) of the Directive. It states that:

> *The setting of special conditions on access to employment and vocational training, employment and occupation, including conditions of remuneration and termination of employment relationships, for young people, older workers and persons with caring responsibilities in order to promote their vocational integration or ensure their protection.*

Paragraph 622 of the German Civil Code33 (BGB) is concerned with periods of notice, which are related to the length of employment, and it stated that in: 'Calculating the length of employment, periods prior to the completion of the employee's 25th year of age are not taken into account.'

Ms Kücüdeveci joined Swedex when she was 18 years of age and was dismissed after ten years' service. The employer based the notice period, to which she was entitled, on that period of service after the age of 25 years. This gave her three years' service in all. She argued, not unreasonably, that she should be entitled to ten years' service for the calculation of her notice period. She claimed that the failure to do this amounted to age discrimination. The first question considered by the Court was whether the national legislation constituted a difference of treatment on the grounds of age and was prohibited by EU law. The Court considered that the BGB did afford less favourable treatment to employees who entered the employer's service before the age of 25 years. It used the example of two employees with twenty years' service, one who joined at the age of 18 years and one who joined at the age of 25 years – the former would have an entitlement to five months' notice, while the latter, to seven months.

Thus there was a necessity to show that there was a legitimate aim and the measure was appropriate for achieving that aim, in accord with Article 6.1 of the Directive. The 'legitimate aim' was set out as follows:

The referring court states that the second sentence of Paragraph 622(2) of the BGB reflects the legislature's assessment that young workers generally react more easily and more rapidly to the loss of their jobs and greater flexibility can be demanded of them. A shorter notice period for younger workers also facilitates their recruitment by increasing the flexibility of personnel management.

The Court pointed out, however, that: 'The legislation is not appropriate for achieving that aim, since it applies to all employees who joined the undertaking before the age of 25 whatever their age at the time of dismissal.' Thus, it would affect someone with long service who could not be classified as a young person. The legislation also affected young people unequally; those who had little vocational training and started work earlier were at a disadvantage compared to those that started at a later age.

The second judgment concerned a reference from the Oberster Gerichtshof of Austria (*David Hütter v Technische Universität Graz*). Austrian legislation contained a measure that provided for an incremental scale of pay based on the length of employment for civil servants. Employment before the age of 18 years, however, was not to count (according to the Vertragsbedienstetebgesetz, which governed such matters at the time). Mr Hütter was born in 1986 and, together with a female colleague, completed a period of apprenticeship from 2001 to March 2005. They were then recruited by the Technische Universität, Graz (TUG), for a period of three months. Mr Hütter's colleague was 22 months older than him and was therefore recruited at a higher incremental scale. This was because the period of apprenticeship completed by Hütter after the age of 18 years was just under seven months, compared with almost 29 months for his colleague. The difference in pay amounted to just EUR 29.20 per month. The TUG claimed that there was no age discrimination because the rule applied without distinction to all persons; alternatively, it argued that there was a legitimate aim and the means were appropriate and necessary. The legitimate aim was giving public services a clear and uniform structure for determining the pay of contractual public servants.

The Court stated that national legislation imposed less favourable treatment for persons whose professional experience has, at least partly, been acquired before the age of 18 years compared to those who have acquired the same experience after that age. The Court, however, considered the aim to be legitimate, that is, not to place those who pursued a general education at a disadvantage when compared to those who pursued a vocational one, also to promote the recruitment of persons with a vocational education, that is, their integration into the labour market. Partly because these two aims appeared contradictory, the Court concluded that the means were not appropriate or necessary for achieving the aim. Thus, in these two cases at least, the ECJ has protected young workers from discriminatory measures based upon age.

STATUTORY RESTRICTIONS

There are a number of restrictions imposed on young people at work by the Working Time Regulations 1998.[16] These derive from the European Council Directive concerning certain aspects of working time.[17] The purpose of the Directive is really summed up in Article 1.3 which states that:

> *Member States shall ensure in general that employers guarantee that young people have working conditions which suit their age. They shall ensure in general that young people are protected against economic exploitation and against any work likely to harm their safety, health or physical, mental, moral or social development or to jeopardise their education.*

The Directive applies to any person under the age of 18 years who has a contract of employment or an employment relationship[18] and employment of those under the official school leaving age is, with some minor exceptions, effectively eliminated.[19] The Directive assumes that young people are especially vulnerable at work and special measures are needed to protect them. It then goes on to prescribe special rules concerning working time, night work, rest periods, holidays and breaks.[20] These rules are transposed into national law in the Working Time Regulations 1998, such as limitations on working hours contained in Regulation 5A and the prohibition of employing young people to work at night is contained in Regulation 6A.[21] These measures are clearly examples of measures adopted on the basis of age, but are perhaps useful examples of positive action in favour of a subgroup with perceived special needs.

---

16 SI 1998/1833.
17 Directive 94/33/EC OJ L216/12.
18 Article 2.1.
19 Articles 1.1 and 4.
20 Articles 8–13.
21 In fact the prohibition is working during the 'restricted period' which is between 10 pm and 6 am – Article 2(1).

In contrast to these statutory measures which discriminate in favour of young workers, the measures concerned with the national minimum wage certainly discriminate against them. The full rate for the national minimum wage in October 2011 was £6.08 per hour. There are, however, differing rates for those under the age of 21 years. The development rate for those aged 18–20 years inclusive was £4.98 per hour and the rate for 16 and 17 years was just £3.68 per hour.[22] The lower rate for those under the age of 21 years of course is designed to strike a balance between helping young people into the job market and preventing exploitation. The rate for 16 and 17-year-olds was finally introduced in October 2004.

The assumption of the Low Pay Commission, who were originally opposed to a minimum wage at this level, was that 16 and 17-year-olds formed a distinct segment of the market, most of whom were in training or education. By the time of their fourth report they had become concerned about the number of full-time jobs with 'extremely low rates of pay' which provided minimal training and few development prospects.[23] The result was the recommendation for a national minimum wage for 16- and 17-year-olds 'on the assumption that it is compatible with the age strand of the European Employment Directive (2000/78/EC)'.[24] The government obviously decided that this was the case and is keeping the lower rates of pay for young people, although it is difficult to see how in some cases such a low minimum does not discriminate against young workers in comparison to others.

In contrast to keeping the measures concerning health and safety and the national minimum wage, the government did accept that the redundancy payments system did discriminate, but not only against young workers. It also discriminated against the middle age workers (see later). Firstly there was a two-year qualifying period[25] before an individual was entitled to a redundancy payment. This effectively meant that anyone under the age of 18 years could not qualify for a redundancy payment because they would not have served the two years necessary.

Of course the week's pay is subject to a statutory maximum[26] and workers of 41 years and older were entitled to a greater amount. The government initially

22 Only applies to those over school leaving age as from the last Friday in June in the school year of the 16th birthday.
23 See 'Protecting young workers: the national minimum wage' (2004).
24 Ibid., Paragraph 12.
25 Employment Rights Act 1996, Section 155 .
26 Ibid., Section 227.

was of the view that this was discrimination that could not be justified, so in the 2005 draft of the Age Regulations it proposed that although the maximum 20-years' entitlement was kept, it was to be equalised such that all received a similar amount. In the event it was not able to come to any other solution than to justify the existing discriminatory approach and just removed the upper and lower age limits.

Table 2.3   Redundancy payments to young people

Age	Amount
16–17	½ week's pay for each year of service
18–21	½ week's pay for each year of service
22–25	1 week's pay per year of service

OCCUPATIONAL RESTRICTIONS

There are other occupational restrictions which may be the result of law or the result of convention. These tend to affect workers in the young, older and senior age groups. Examples of those affecting the young are usually concerned with minimum age restrictions, such as HGV drivers, retail staff involved in the sale of alcohol or gambling activities. There may be less direct restrictions such as higher insurance premiums for younger people employed in driving or hazardous activities.[27] A further consideration of occupational and other restrictions in a number of areas of employment are considered towards the end of this chapter.

In the event of a challenge to these exceptions, the government would have to show, in the words of the Framework Directive, that they were 'objectively and reasonably justified by a legitimate aim'. Presumably they would argue justification for the exceptions contained in the Working Time Regulations 1998 and for the difference in treatment on the national minimum wage in accordance with the first exception contained in Article 6 of the Directive, namely: 'The setting of special conditions on access to employment and vocational training, employment and occupation (including dismissal and remuneration conditions) for young people, older workers and persons with caring responsibilities in order to promote their vocational integration or ensure their protection.'

---

27 'Occupational age restrictions' (2001).

The health and safety measures contained in the Working Time Regulations concern protection, while the lower rate of minimum wage concern their 'vocational integration' or at least are seen as an aid to securing them a place in the workforce. This is not presumably an argument that can be put with regard to redundancy payments. If this is correct, then this is a good example of the continuing discrimination allowed for by the Framework Directive. The justification for paying less, based on age, is to assist people into work, but we would never consider using this justification for helping people discriminated against on any of the other grounds. For example, according to the 2001 census Bangladeshi men had four times the unemployment rate of white men, so should we have an exception to the Race Relations Act 1976 which states that employers may pay Bangladeshi men a lower rate than white men to encourage their employment? The answer of course is no – it would breach totally the principle of equal treatment. Then one wonders why it is therefore permissible to discriminate against young people on age grounds to help them into employment?[28]

Middle Age Discrimination

I use this to refer to those aged between 25 and 49 years (with apologies to those at the younger end of this spectrum). It is an absurd range really because there are, as a generalisation, large differences in the life-styles and perhaps work-styles at the two ends of the range. Nevertheless it is meaningful in terms of age discrimination, because it serves to highlight the fact that many of the issues relate to workers outside this age range. This is not for one moment to suggest that age discrimination does not take place within the middle age group. It also seems apparent that the divisions are gradual so that young age discrimination issues gradually become less important at the bottom end, while discrimination against older workers becomes more of an issue towards the top end of this range. It is also clear that there are gender issues within this age range with women being perceived as becoming older workers at an earlier stage than men.

This age group is where the bulk of the workforce is. There are some 21 million people in these age groups. The employment rates are higher than for all the other age groups (Table 2.4).

---

28 See Sargeant M. (2010). 'Age discrimination and the national minimum wage', *Policy Studies*, 31:3, 1–14.

Table 2.4   Labour statistics for 25–49-year-olds[29]

Age range	Total employed	Employment rate (%)
25–34	6,306,000	78.1
35–49	10,803,000	81.0

This is the age which is characterised by the number of people who have young children. Some 68 per cent of those in their 30s and over 80 per cent of those in their 40s have children, compared to less than 20 per cent of people in their 20s. As a result some 50 per cent of women workers between the ages of 25 and 44 work part-time. This is compared to 11 per cent of men in the same age group who work part-time.[30] Interestingly, research done for the Equal Opportunities Commission suggests that it is the arrival of the second child which is most likely to trigger part-time working by the mother.[31] The EOC's research also showed that part-time women workers were earning some 40 per cent less per hour than men working full-time and because of discrimination against them, many women were not working at their full potential. The issues of part-time work and equal pay are essentially sex discrimination issues, but there may be a link to age discrimination for older women workers. Women continue to work part-time into their 50s and, according to EOC statistics, some 47 per cent of women workers in the 45–64 years age bracket work part-time compared to some 9 per cent of men in the same age group. As is suggested in Chapter 8, it may not be correct to assume that discrimination against women workers of different ages is the same and that there is a connection between age discrimination and sex discrimination which will need to be examined closely in the future.

The analysis by the Employers Forum on age[32] suggests that the 30s are the 'golden age' of recruitment. Indeed the figures suggest that this can also apply to those in their 40s. Less than 6 per cent of 30–39-year-olds and some 10 per cent in the 40–49 year age group stated that they have been put off applying for a job because of their age. This is lower than any other age group. People also reach their professional peak in their 30s and 40s (see Table 2.5).

---

29 These figures are for the period March to May 2010.
30 <www.statistics.gov.uk>.
31 'Part-time working is no crime – so why pay the penalty' (2005).
32 'Age at work' (2005).

Table 2.5   Distribution of work amongst 30- and 40-year-olds (per cent)

Occupation	20s	30s	40s
Higher managerial and professional	8	14	13
Lower managerial and professional	20	26	26
Intermediate occupations	14	11	10
Small employers and own account workers	4	8	9
Lower supervisory and technical	9	10	10
Semi-routine occupations	15	13	13
Routine occupations	11	9	9
Never worked, unemployed and other	19	9	10

Clearly there may be individual examples of direct age discrimination within this group, but it is difficult to see where one could argue indirect discrimination issues on the basis of statistics, within this group, except perhaps at the margins. The lumping together of this wide age range is a crude attempt to simplify the analysis on my part, but it is partly as a result of the way that official statistics also put these groups together. It is not possible to identify many statutory or occupational (see later) restrictions that apply to this group. There is the issue of redundancy payments which advantages those over the age of 41 years (see previously).

One conclusion is that, except perhaps for those at the younger and older age extremities, this is the group that is least likely to suffer from age discrimination, except insofar as it may relate to other grounds of discrimination. Thus discrimination against part-time workers may effectively also be discrimination against a certain age group. Similarly there is a greater likelihood of becoming disabled the older one becomes (see Chapter 8), so there may be links to certain age groups and disabilities; for example over a quarter of people who gave up a job in their 40s did so for health reasons. This compares to 13 per cent of such people in their 30s and 8 per cent of people in their 20s.[33] The Age Discrimination in Employment Act 1967 in the US only protects those employees over the age of 40 and one must wonder whether it is the Americans that have the right approach. Those over the age of 40 are more likely to suffer age discrimination and its debilitating effects than those under this age.

---

33 'Age at work' (2005).

Perhaps one can argue that if the Framework Directive and the UK Age Regulation were just about tackling age discrimination, then one might accept that regulation for much of this age group is unnecessary. However, the Directive at least is about more than this: it is also about establishing the principle of equal treatment, in which case one would have to argue that it should apply to all and that this is not just a principle that can apply to some age groups and not others.

An example of how a person in this age group can succeed in an age discrimination claim was the case of a 42-year-old banker[34] working for the Canadian Imperial Bank of Commerce. He was 'let go' in a redundancy exercise and replaced by a 38-year-old. It was said that the criteria for a replacement set out in an internal memo showed the desire for a 'younger', more entrepreneurial profile.

Older Age Discrimination

This age group begins at 50 years and ends at 65 years (State Pension Age) except for women, who still have an SPA of 60 years increasing. For these people the age range is 50–59 years. This difference in the age of pension entitlement will of course be gradually levelled upwards, so that by 2020, all people will have an SPA of 65 years (unless increased in the meantime). It is of course the disappearance of large numbers of people in this age group from the workforce and from those who would claim to be economically active that was a major motivation for governments to take action on age discrimination.

The total numbers of people in employment between the ages of 50 and the SPA are 6,609,000, representing an employment rate of 71.1 per cent. This compares to an employment rate of 81 per cent for those in the lower age group of 35–49 years.

There is ample evidence that discrimination takes place against this age group in relation to work. Older workers are more likely to lose their jobs through redundancy. This figure was one in ten workers in the 55–64 year age group according to one survey.[35]

---

34 <http://www.personneltoday.com/articles/2010/01/04/53577/42-year-old-banker-wins-age-discrimination-case.html>.

35 Age discrimination at work: survey report (2001).

Some conclusions of a DfEE report on older workers were:

- Older workers were less likely to be in paid work than younger groups and when they did work they were more likely to be working as self-employed or part-time.

- There was a greater risk of becoming economically inactive beyond the ages of 50 and 55 years.

- Taking all forms of inactivity together, the chances of men leaving inactivity for paid work were sharply reduced after the age of 50 years and 'were close to zero for those over 60'.

- For women the chances of moving out of inactivity were much reduced after the age of 40 years and 'was particularly uncommon for those in their late 50s'.[36]

This DTI consultation provided generalised definitions but, interestingly, suggested that direct discrimination can occur when a decision is made on the basis of a person's actual or *perceived* age. Examples of age discrimination given in this government consultation document are:

- Being forced to retire after reaching a certain age.

- Not being given a job they applied for because of their age.

- Being told their age was a barrier to general advancement.

- Assumptions being made about abilities due to age.

- Being selected for redundancy because of age.

There is also some evidence that individuals in this age group deselect themselves from jobs because they assume that their age will be a hindrance in applying for jobs. Some 21 per cent of the age group claimed to have been put off from applying for jobs because of their age. This is greater than any other group apart from the 16–19-year-olds.[37]

---

36 'Characteristics of older workers' (1998).
37 'Age at work' (2005).

A further survey with personal business and other advisers[38] of mostly small- and medium-sized enterprises also found that age played a significant role in the workplace. Three-quarters of business advisers said that age was a factor for employers when recruiting and most felt that employers preferred to recruit younger people. A third felt that age was important for employers when arranging training and that older workers were unable to learn new skills as a result of lacking motivation, resistance to change and inflexibility. A fifth of advisers felt that age was a consideration in promotion for organisations. As many small businesses were owner-managed, the age of the owner-manager played an important part in decision making. Generally people preferred to recruit those younger than themselves.

This perception that age is a problem when applying for jobs is an acceptance of the reality of the situation. If one looks at the occupational restrictions described in the sector summaries below, the same perception seems to be shared by employers and the public when they are involved. It is as if there is a piece of mass self-delusion taking place based on an accepted prejudice that older people are a problem when it comes to employment. It is a piece of self-delusion that is not based on animosity but on an unfounded and unproven prejudice often resulting from a total lack of contact with older workers.

Gender is also an issue, with women more likely than men to say that their age is a problem in recruitment. As over 50 per cent of women in this age group work in the public sector, there must be parts of the private sector which have no or very few female employees over the age of 50, thus having no opportunity to move away from their stereotypical view of older workers.

Health is an increasingly important issue when workers reach this age group. One in eight over-50s is economically inactive because of long-term illness (see Chapter 1 on the relationship between age and disability). Some 33 per cent gave up work for health reasons, some 15 per cent took early retirement and some 16 per cent were made redundant or took voluntary redundancy. This compares to some 13 per cent of people in their 30s, for example, who gave up work for health reasons and 11 per cent who were made redundant or took voluntary redundancy.

The major piece of discrimination based upon age that takes place against this age group has traditionally been mandatory retirement. At a certain age

---

38 Advisers working for South London Training and Enterprise Council and Business Link for London; the survey report 'Significance of age in the workplace' was completed in 2001.

many employees are ejected from the workforce, purely because they have reached the stipulated age for this event to take place. In 2011, the default retirement age in the UK was due to be abolished, but employers still had the option to justify mandatory retirement ages within their own organisations (see Chapter 7).

European Court of Justice

The European Court of Justice has considered cases concerned with maximum recruitment ages, that is, restrictions imposed because of an assumption of decline after a certain age. In *Colin Wolf v Stadt Frankfurt am Main* an applicant was turned down for a post in the fire service on the grounds of age. There was an upper limit of 30 years for the posts in question and Mr Wolf was over this limit. The case concerned, according to the Court of Justice: 'The discretion open to the national legislature to provide that differences in treatment on grounds of age do not constitute discrimination …' and, in particular:

> *Whether aims such as the concern to ensure a long career for officials, to limit the amount of social benefits paid, to set up a balanced age structure within an occupation, or to ensure a minimum period of service before retirement are legitimate within the meaning of Article 6(1) of the Directive, and whether setting the maximum recruitment age for intermediate career posts in the fire service at 30 years is an appropriate and necessary means of achieving such aims.*[39]

The Court relied upon Recital 18 of the Directive which provides that there is no requirement upon the part of the emergency services to employ persons: 'Who do not have the required capacity to carry out the range of functions that they may be called upon to perform with regard to the legitimate objective of preserving the operational capacity of those services'. Thus a concern for the operational capacity of the fire service was a legitimate aim. It also followed that the possession of 'high physical capacities' were to be regarded as a 'genuine and determining occupational requirement' within the meaning of Article 4(1). The question to be considered then was whether the setting of a maximum age of 30 years was a proportionate (appropriate and necessary) means of achieving the aim.

---

39 Paragraph 24.

Finally the Court agreed that the rule setting a maximum age of 30 years for such posts was not precluded by the Directive. The German government had produced evidence that persons over the age of 45 or 50 years did not have this capacity to carry out the required tasks. Thus, someone recruited at the age of 30 years can (after a two year training programme) carry out the activities for 15 or 20 years, whereas someone recruited at the age 40 would only have 5–10 years possible service. The Court accepted that the measure was therefore appropriate and necessary to fulfil the legitimate aim of maintaining operational capacity.

The outcome of this decision is, of course, that people of a certain age who are able to carry out the function of a job may still be rejected as the employer may not be able to maintain its operational capacity by having too many older workers who, apparently, will be unable to carry out the tasks assigned. For the purposes of this study the outcome might mean that older workers may often be at a disadvantage compared to younger workers to maintain the operational capacity of an employer.

In *Dr Dominica Petersen v Berufungsausschuss für Zahnärte für den Bezirk Westfalen-Lippe* Ms Petersen's authorisation to operate as a dentist expired when she reached the age of 68 years. The questions from the national Court concerned whether this maximum age limit was an objective and reasonable measure to achieve a legitimate aim. The legitimate aim was the health of patients as, 'based on general experience', 'a general drop in performance occurs from a certain age'. Thus although the question is about a maximum recruitment age it really aligns itself with those cases concerning a mandatory retirement age. There was also a secondary question concerning the ability to limit the numbers of dentists if there were an excess of supply. The Court pointed out that Article 2(5) of the Directive specifically states that the Directive is without prejudice to a number of measures, including 'the protection of health'. The Court considered the aims put forward by the German government in respect of Articles 2(5) and 6(1). It concluded that Article 2(5) precluded a national measure setting a maximum age for practicing as a panel dentist where the aim was the protection of patients from the effects of the decline in performance of dentists after the age of 68. The reason for not accepting this as a legitimate aim was that it only applied to panel dentists and there was no age limit for non-panel ones. In terms of Article 6(1), however, where the aim was: 'To share out employment opportunities among the generations' (if taking into account the labour market the measure was appropriate and necessary) the measure was not precluded. The outcome of course is that, in a labour market where there is a surplus in a particular profession, it seems to be acceptable to discriminate against older members of the profession in order to facilitate new members of the profession entering. This perhaps shows how limited the Court's vision is in respect of tackling age discrimination.

Senior Age Discrimination

Some people over the age of 60/65 wish to continue to work and some people under this age wish to continue working when they reach the SPA. In fact, some 34 per cent of those in their 50s, in one survey, stated that: 'The idea of retirement doesn't make sense to me.'[40]

Total numbers in employment over the SPA fall quite considerably when compared to younger age groups. Nevertheless there are quite significant numbers of people involved. Some 1,449,000 people are over SPA[41] representing an employment rate of 12.4 per cent. This compares to an employment rate of over 70 per cent for the next age group down (see previous).[42] This figure indicates an increasing trend. In the autumn of 1999, for example, the employment rate for those over SPA stood at 7.9 per cent.[43]

Some 75 per cent of women who still worked after SPA were aged 60–64 years and almost a quarter of these worked for organisations where the retirement age was 65 years. The characteristics of all over SPA, when compared to other age groups, are that they are much more likely to be self-employed and/ or working part-time for lower pay (Table 2.6).

Table 2.6   **Characteristics of older workers compared to other age groups**[44]

Percentage in employment who are aged:	16–24	25–49	50–SPA	SPA+
Self-employed	3.7	12.2	17.7	25.8
Part-time	34.7	21.1	24.9	69.8
In a permanent job	86.4	95.5	95.7	89.5
Average gross hourly wage (£)	6.15	11.23	10.92	8.40

40 'Age at work' (2005).
41 In this case all women 60 plus and all men 65 plus.
42 <www.statistics.gov.uk>. March to May 2010.
43 'Older workers; statistical information booklet' (2004).
44 Ibid.

The two biggest sectors in which senior workers are active are in 'distribution, hotels and restaurants' together with 'public administration, education and health'.[45] A significant number of people wish to continue working after SPA.[46] Important reasons for wishing to continue working are continuing job satisfaction and finance.

It is important however not to treat this group (or any of the others) as an homogenous class. There are different motivations for wishing to continue to work after SPA. This may be a result of cultural traditions or life-style or work-style adopted throughout a working life. It may be that an individual's perception of the event of retirement may depend upon that individual's approach to work and indeed the nature of the work itself. One analysis looks at groups that it calls 'workers' and 'creatives and professionals'.[47] The former consisted of the traditional working class positions such as secretary, baker, stockman, milkman and hairdresser, although there were others who perceived themselves as being in this group. The characteristic of this group was the division between work and the rest of an individual's life. In contrast to this the 'professionals and creatives' were people who saw work as part of their identity or a vocation. Work was something that they would continue to do. Often such people could not envisage not working. 'Workers' on the other hand looked at their working life as a means to an end, as a way of supporting themselves and their families. This is an over-simplified version of the analysis, but it illustrates how it is possible for different groups to have a totally different approach to retirement. For 'workers' it was a natural event, often welcomed. For the others it might represent something that has to be got round in order to carry on doing the things that are occupying one's life. The first might be characterised by a worker continuing to work in the employment they had before reaching retirement age. For the latter group it might mean developing activities on a self-employed basis. These are crude generalisations[48] but they do indicate the need not to assume that all people who reach retirement age have the same means or motivations. Clearly the amount of choice that people have depends upon a large number of financial, cultural and working life factors.

The extent to which attitudes to retirement are shaped by societal influences can be judged by surveys about the anticipated retirement age. One survey

---

45 Ibid.
46 'Age discrimination at work survey report' (2001); about one quarter of the survey expressed a desire to continue working beyond SPA.
47 'Changing priorities, transformed opportunities?' (2005).
48 These are my crude generalisations and in no way intended to reflect upon the interesting work done by Jane Parry and Rebecca Taylor in 'Changing priorities'.

showed that many people regarded the state pension age as the natural age to retire. Some 40 per cent of those working were expected to retire at the SPA. The report[49] suggested that there were two main elements to creating this expectation. The first was the state pension age itself being a set age defined by government. The second was that, at this age, a second source of income became available, thus assisting with the financial means to retire. The same report suggested that there was no hard evidence that employers' fixed retirement age had a widespread influence on whether people retired before SPA, but that there was evidence to such that fixed retirement ages may stop some people from working beyond retirement age (see Chapter 7).

Not entirely surprising is the statistic that almost 20 per cent of people in their 60s are dreading retirement and almost the same number of people have been put off applying for work because of their age.[50]

SURVEY OF RETIRED TRADE UNION MEMBERS

In 2003 a survey was conducted of the retired membership of two trade unions in the public sector, NATFHE and PCS.[51] The respondents were asked if they thought that they had been discriminated against in their career on the basis of age.[52] A significant proportion (31.7 per cent) claimed that they had been.

The two most significant areas were:

- In applying for jobs 14.9 per cent; and

- In respect of promotion 14.2 per cent.

The two other major areas were in respect of training opportunities (5.5 per cent) and on grounds of redundancy (5.2 per cent).

The next question asked whether respondents had suffered from harassment at work on the basis of their age. The questionnaire provided the definition of

49 'Factors affecting the labour market participation of older workers' (2003).
50 See 'Age at work' (2005).
51 National Association of Teachers in Further and Higher Education and the Public and Civil Service Union; the survey was carried out by Malcolm Sargeant at Middlesex University.
52 In all 1363 forms were sent out. A total of 648 responses were received. This represented a 47.5 per cent return. Not all questions were answered by all respondents. Percentages given are percentages of actual replies.

harassment put forward by the government in the consultation exercise (see Chapter 3). Some 8.6 per cent responded by saying yes.

Respondents were asked whether age discrimination should be made unlawful in all circumstances, some circumstances or not at all. The majority felt that this should be the case in all circumstances (56.2 per cent) with a substantial minority (40.9 per cent) stating that it should be made unlawful in some circumstances. Relatively few respondents preferred the not at all option (3.0 per cent).

The questionnaire then posed a number of scenarios in order to test the respondents' resolve in making such discrimination unlawful. The questions were posed in such a way as to be supportive of the government's proposed approach to allowing exceptions to the general rule of non-discrimination.

Almost one third claimed to have suffered age discrimination and one in twelve claimed to have been harassed for reasons connected to their chronological age. Generally they were opposed to age discrimination and universal mandatory retirement ages (see Chapter 7), but there seemed to be a tendency to approve of exception that might benefit the older worker, such as those associated with length of service.

SCENARIO 1

Young people should continue to receive a lower rate of national minimum wage than those over 21 years of age.

Views were divided with some 43 per cent agreeing with this statement and some 47.4 per cent disagreeing.

SCENARIO 2

At present older people receive a higher rate of redundancy pay than younger workers. This should be ended and all receive the same rate.

Interestingly a large majority (56 per cent) disagreed with this statement, with only 34.8 per cent agreeing. A much greater proportion of male respondents (38 per cent) than female respondents agreed (23.6 per cent).

SCENARIO 3

Employers should be able to stipulate the age at which workers are recruited, in order to make sure that they have a balanced and age diverse workforce.

Perhaps reflecting the numbers that thought that they had been discriminated against in applying for jobs, there was a majority who disagreed with this statement (56.4 per cent).

Female respondents were much less likely to agree (18.9 per cent) than male ones (35.8 per cent).

SCENARIO 4

There are some circumstances where the employer should be able to discriminate on the grounds of age on whether to give employee training.

A clear majority disagreed with this proposition (57.8 per cent), although again, more men were willing to agree (39.9 per cent) than women (22.4 per cent).

SCENARIO 5

There are some jobs, such as in modelling or those concerned with public safety such as airline pilots, where it is right that age should be one of the selection criteria for both recruitment and retirement, regardless of a person's capacity.

A majority agreed with the statement (57.2 per cent), although there were substantial numbers who disagreed (36.3 per cent). Significantly more men agreed (62 per cent) than women (40.6 per cent).

SCENARIO 6

Some benefits, such as longer holidays or extra privileges associated with seniority, can be justified on the basis of rewarding service, even though they inevitably mean that older workers receive more benefits than younger ones.

A large majority agreed with this statement (70.7 per cent). This was the case for female respondents (64.2 per cent) and male respondents (67.6 per cent).

PRECARIOUS WORKING

A significant feature of the older workers' employment is that, with age, there is an increasing likelihood of employment in so called precarious work, that is, work that does not consist of full-time permanent employment. The examples of precarious working used here are part-time work, flexible working, casual working and self-employment. Research also suggests that workers over SPA were twice as likely to be employed in companies with one to ten staff, and far less likely to be employed in organisations with over 50 staff. People aged 60 and over were particularly likely to be employed on a temporary basis and were more likely to work in small firms with fewer than 50 employees (Soule et al.).

PART-TIME WORK

Within the UK, in the age group 16–49 years, the part-time employment rate for women averages at some 43 per cent and for men 9 per cent. In contrast the part-time work rate for women aged 60–64 is 70 per cent and for men it is 23 per cent. There is a direct relationship between working part-time and getting older.[53]

Table 2.7   **Employment of older workers in part-time work (per cent)**

Age	Women	Men
50–54	42	6
55–59	51	12
60–64	70	23
65–69	85	64
70+	89	74
Total (50+)	52	16

FLEXIBLE WORK ARRANGEMENTS

According to analysis by Smeaton and Vegeris, older women are more likely than older men to be in flexible working arrangements.[54] It is interesting also how the proportion of both men and women working in these arrangements decreases after the age of 60; the exception being with regard to part-time working.

---

53 Whiting, E. (2005). 'The labour market participation of older people', *Labour Market Trends*, July, 285–96.
54 Smeaton, D. and Vegeris, S. (2009). 'Older people inside and outside the labour market: a review', Equality and Human Rights Commission, London.

Table 2.8   Proportion of employed men and women using flexible work arrangements 2000 and 2007

Men	Flexitime		Annualised hours		Any flexible	
Age	2000	2007	2000	2007	2000	2007
45–49	9	11	4	4	18	18
50–54	9	10	4	5	18	19
55–59	8	10	4	4	17	19
60–64	6	8	2	3	14	16

Women	Flexitime		Annualised hours		Any flexible	
Age	2000	2007	2000	2007	2000	2007
45–49	12	15	5	5	31	32
50–54	10	13	5	5	27	30
55–59	9	11	3	5	24	27
60–64	7	10	2	5	19	24

Casual employment

Older workers were also more likely to hold a temporary employment contract. Thus some 10 per cent of working men over SPA were in temporary employment compared to an average of 4 per cent for the age groups below them. Similarly some 9 per cent of women over SPA held temporary contracts compared to 6 per cent of women between the ages of 25–49 and 5 per cent of those between 50 and SPA. If one examines the type of temporary contract held then it is apparent that the oldest workers are most likely to be employed in seasonal work and casual work.[55]

Table 2.9   Type of temporary job by age

Job type	25–49	50–59/64	60/65+
Seasonal work	3	4	8
Fixed-term contract	57	57	35
Agency temping	18	15	7
Casual work	10	14	40
Other	12	11	11

---

55 Smeaton, D. and McKay, S. (2003). 'Working after state pension age: quantitative analysis'. Research Report No 182, Department for Work and Pensions.

SELF-EMPLOYMENT

Self-employment is more common amongst older workers than amongst the younger age groups. One study showed that 19 per cent of people aged 50 and over were self-employed compared with 14 per cent of people aged 25 to 49. Older men were more likely than older women to be self-employed: 26 per cent of men aged 50 and over compared with 11 per cent of women. Gender differences in self-employment become more marked after SPA – 46 per cent of men aged 65 and over were self-employed compared with 13 per cent of women aged 60–64 in 2004.[56] This is a trend that is apparent throughout the EU.

Table 2.10   Self-employed people as a percentage of total employees in the EU[57]

15–24	6.6
25–34	13.6
35–44	16.3
45–54	17.5
55+	28.8
Total	16.4

In all age groups men are much more likely to work on a self-employed basis than women. For the over 55s the figures were 72.8 per cent of the self-employed were men compared to 27.2 per cent who were women.

These figures reveal that the oldest workers are more likely to be in a non-standard contractual relationship, by working on a part-time or temporary basis and being self-employed. This pattern is not unique to the UK, but is part of a trend throughout the EU, where higher levels of part-time working and self-employment are also recorded for older workers – some 22 per cent, compared to an average of 16 per cent working part-time and almost one quarter working on a self-employed basis compared to an average of 15 per cent (Employment in Europe 2007). These are some of characteristics of a vulnerable work force, that is, one that might be more open to exploitation because it does not fulfil the criteria of being a full-time permanent contractual relationship.

---

56 Soule, A. Babb, P. Evandrou, M. Balchin, S. and Zealey, L. (eds) (2006). 'Focus on older people 2005'. Office for National Statistics.
57 European Foundation for the Improvement of Living and Working Conditions Dublin (2008) 'Working conditions of an ageing workforce'.

Occupational Age Restrictions[58]

Below is a summary of four sector reports about occupational age restrictions. They illustrate the fact that discrimination is likely to take place on the basis of people's perceptions that are related to age. This is not only about employer's perceptions, but also about how employees see themselves and often about how the public perceive them. Thus age restrictions occur in the retail and finance sector because employers perceive that the public require certain ages for certain functions, for example young people for fashion and beauty and older people for financial advice. Working practices also play a part; for example in law, where there is a tradition, especially amongst big city law firms, of working long and unsociable hours. These, it is suggested by others, effectively discriminate against older workers or those of a certain age who have dependants to look after. There is also an element of tradition about age in certain workforces which affects the way employers operate and perhaps the type of applicant who applies. Few of these restrictions are the result of law. Rather they are the result of informal work practices based upon ageist assumptions.

It is interesting to look at the different age group responses in answering the question as to whether they have been put off applying for work because of the problems they perceive arise out of being their age (Table 2.11).[59]

Table 2.11   People put off applying for a job because of age

Age	%
Teens	25
20s	17
30s	6
40s	n/a†
50s	21
60s	18

† No figure available and one must conjecture that it increases with age. It is probably the under-25s and the over-50s who are most likely to suffer from age discrimination.

58 All the information here comes from a series of sector reviews carried out for the report 'Occupational age restrictions' (2001).
59 'Age at work' (2005).

RETAIL SECTOR

Partly because of the large number of part-time and casual retail positions, many of which are occupied by students, the age group for this sector is skewed towards the young. Thus some 24 per cent of employees were aged between 16 and 24 years (compared to 14 per cent nationally); 52 per cent were aged between 25 and 49 (62 per cent nationally); and 22 per cent were aged over 50 years (24 per cent nationally). Some examples given of occupational restrictions were:

- There were some formal restrictions related to betting and the sale of alcohol by under-18-year-olds.

- Many graduate schemes had an upper age limit of 24 years. Many companies however provided less training for the young, less-skilled workers because they perceived younger workers as being disloyal and unreliable.

- There is a tendency for retailers to recruit the age group that they perceive will help sell their products; thus 'younger, attractive people' are more likely to be recruited into the fashion and beauty industry; school leavers are unlikely to be recruited in a mother and child store. One representative organisation is quoted as saying: 'You are most likely to find yourself being sold a washing machine by a woman in her early 30s and a hi-fi or mobile phone by a man in his late teens or early 20s.'

- There were few people over 50 years on British Retail Institute training courses, perhaps because of an unwillingness to train people of this age.

The sector report concluded with examples of unjustified age discrimination:

- Employers' deliberate or informal age restrictions, particularly in recruitment and training.

- Customer perceptions and stereotyping of age groups, so that some employers recruit in line with these stereotypes.

- Sector-wide traditions, which have created an image and practices that are not attractive to particular age groups.

LAW SECTOR

As a result of the way in which people qualify to become a solicitor or a barrister, there is effectively a minimum recruitment age of 23–24 years. Figures indicate that few people enter the profession in their late 30s or above and most late entries are people who have qualified through the lengthy Legal Executive route. The average age for those entering the profession as solicitors was:

- 27.8 years for those who have a qualifying law degree.

- 29.9 years for those who have completed a non-law degree.

- 33.9 years for those qualifying through the Legal Executive route.

Examples of possible discrimination are:

- There is a culture of long and unsociable hours, which may limit, in practice or by perception, the recruitment of older workers and also the retention of female solicitors in their 30s, or other ages with young children. There is also a problem for those groups with dependents with the small amount of part-time work available.

- One study[60] found that older students were 15 per cent less likely to be employed following training than younger students.

- Another study[61] found that 25 per cent of newly qualified solicitors were discriminated against because of their age and that the two most common forms of age discrimination were: 'Hostility from colleagues or employment on less favourable terms'.

FINANCE SECTOR

The age profile for the finance sector[62] showed that it is younger than that of the UK average age for the workforce. There are significantly more employees (about one-third) in the 25–34 age group and the majority of employees are in the 25–49 years group (over two-thirds of the workforce). The study did not

---

60 'Entry in the legal professions' (2000). Cited in occupational age restrictions sector review: law (2001).
61 'Part-time working is no crime – so why pay the penalty' (2005).
62 Defined here as high street and investment banks, building societies, accountancy and insurance.

find evidence of formal age restrictions within the sector and concluded that it was an industry traditionally characterised by age restrictive practices, but with many companies now adopting age diverse policies ... but ... the culture change has not reached all parts of the sector.

There were some age limitations however, although they were held not to be 'endemic across the sector'. These related mainly to a reluctance to recruit new entrants past a certain age. Other limitations included the perception held by potential employees about the fact that the sector only recruited young graduates.

Some occupations however were more interested in mature entrants. These tended to be those concerned with giving advice in building societies or in relation to insurance needs. Despite this there was anecdotal evidence from employees in the industry which suggested that there were age limitations for older workers. Indeed one chief executive of an insurance company is quoted as saying: 'Most large insurance companies claim that they look at people's skills, abilities and competence rather than their age. In reality, ageism slips into the recruitment process.'

There were though examples given of good practice by employers who had adopted age diverse policies.

TRANSPORT SECTOR

There are about 1.7 million people employed in the transport sector. The age profile is older than the UK workforce average, although there were variations between different parts of the sector; for example some 57 per cent of road transport operatives were over 40 years of age, compared to some 37 per cent for the 'inside people' such as the storekeepers and despatch clerks.

The report covers a number of areas, but only the road haulage part is considered here. The important legal restriction concerning age is that licenses to drive large vehicles are restricted to those over the age of 21 years. Most companies expressed a preference for employing those over the age of 25 years as drivers. This was partly because of the higher cost of insurance for the under-25s and a perception that younger people take more risks and are therefore less safe on the roads.

There is also an effective upper age limit of 45 years, which is related to health. After this age drivers needed a regular health check, which apparently deterred many individuals from continuing. The result is a narrow band of employment of between 25 and 45 years.

3

Age Discrimination and Facilities, Goods and Services

Although action against discrimination in employment is important, it is, of course, not the only area in which age discrimination takes place. In the UK the Equality Act 2010 continues the protection previously offered on such grounds as race and sex from discrimination in relation to facilities, goods and services. For the first time, the Act also provides the possibility of an extension of this general protection to the protected characteristic of age. There is no novel approach in this as the model used in protection from discrimination in employment is merely extended to include these other areas. There is still a need to show less favourable treatment in direct discrimination and it will still be possible to justify direct age discrimination where there is a legitimate aim and where the discriminatory act is a proportionate means of achieving that aim.

Here is one list of examples where it has been suggested that discrimination (outside employment) takes place against older people:[1]

- Car insurance: often premiums are based on age, rather than a person's driving record; people over the age of 75 may also be refused a quotation at all.

- Travel insurance: premiums can increase with age and there may be an upper age limit.

- Loans and mortgages: in some cases the provision of financial services is limited for those over a certain age.

---

1   Taken from Help the Aged Policy Statement on 'Age discrimination in facilities, goods and services' (2007).

- Disability living allowance: those aged 65 and over who become disabled are not eligible for this; instead they are entitled to an attendance allowance, which takes longer to qualify for, is less generous, and does not include any money to cover mobility costs.

- Independent living allowance: those aged over 66 are not eligible, although it is intended to enable disabled people to live at home rather than in residential care.

- Social inclusion; lack of toilets, seats in public areas.

- Health care, education, transport and the media.

- Volunteering: in 1998 a report showed that one fifth of volunteering organisations had upper age limits.

EU Action

As already stated, such discrimination in the EU and the UK is tackled in much the same way as discrimination in employment. Thus (at the time of writing) there is a proposed EU Directive on implementing the principle of equal treatment between persons irrespective of religion or belief, disability, age or sexual orientation[2] which defines direct and indirect discrimination and harassment in much the same way as they are defined in the Framework Directive protecting people from age discrimination in employment.[3]

The prohibition on discrimination on these grounds, including age, is to apply to the public and private sectors in relation to social protection (including social security and healthcare), social advantages, education and access to, and supply of, goods and other services which are available to the public, including housing (although this last category only applies to individuals insofar as they are performing a professional or commercial activity).

---

2   Proposal for a Council Directive on implementing the principle of equal treatment between persons irrespective of religion or belief, disability, age or sexual orientation. COM(2008) 426.
3   Directive 2000/78/EC Article 2.

In a Communication on non-discrimination and equal opportunities[4] the European Commission stated that there are substantive differences between the various grounds of discrimination and that their approach was not a question of creating a hierarchy between the various grounds, but 'of delivering the most appropriate form of protection for each of them'. In relation to age the Communication stated that: 'There are situations where treating someone differently simply because of their age can be justified in the general public interest. Examples include minimum age requirements for access to education or to certain goods and services, preferential tariffs for certain age groups using public transport or visiting museums.'

Thus the proposed Directive states in Articles 2.6 that: 'Member States may provide that differences of treatment on grounds of age shall not constitute discrimination, if, within the context of national law, they are justified by a legitimate aim, and if the means of achieving that aim are appropriate and necessary. In particular, this Directive shall not preclude the fixing of a specific age for access to social benefits, education and certain goods or services.' Article 2.7 also excludes the situation where age is a factor in risk assessment based upon actuarial or statistical data.

Clearly the issue of age thresholds is an important one and it would be wrong to suggest that such thresholds should not be permitted under such legislation. The issue here, however, is whether there should be the possibility of a blanket exception based upon the concept of having a legitimate aim which can be justified, or rather whether legislation should actually specify the exceptions individually. This latter approach is more likely to avoid abuse and uncertainty.

UK Action

Prior to the adoption of the Equality Act 2010 the government's Equalities Office published a study on the subject.[5] It stated that unjustifiable age discrimination is to be outlawed for those aged 18 and above. The approach is based on a number of principles:

---

4   Communication from the Commission. 'Non-discrimination and equal opportunities: a renewed commitment', SEC(2008) 2172.
5   Equality Bill: Making it work Government Equalities Office, June 2009.

- Fair: people of all ages should be treated fairly and have an equal opportunity to access services provided by public, private and voluntary sectors.

- Proportionate: it should still be possible to treat people differently where justifiable or beneficial; or for good public policy reasons. Age is a valid reason sometimes.

- Clear and transparent.

- Practical and realistic.

The document stated that: 'We are proposing a proportionate and flexible approach that does not inadvertently hurt those we are seeking to protect.'

Three main areas were to be considered. These are health and social care; financial services; and other services such as group holidays and age concessions. The report highlighted some examples of age discrimination in these areas. Firstly, in health and social care, the following examples were given:

- A survey[6] by the British Geriatrics Society which found that 47 per cent of doctors specialising in the care and treatment of older people think that the National Health Service (NHS) was institutionally ageist; 66 per cent agreed that, in their experience, older people are less likely to have their symptoms fully investigated; 72 per cent said that older people are less likely to be referred on for essential treatments.

- A study of stroke patients at Mayday Hospital found that older patients were less likely to receive diagnostic investigations and advice on how to improve their lifestyle compared to younger patients.[7]

- The Healthcare Commission found that older people were being denied access to the full range of mental health services that are available to younger adults. In particular there was poor access

6   A 2008 survey carried out on behalf of Help the Aged; now Age UK.
7   Kee, Y.K., Brooks, W. and Bhalla, A. (2009). 'Do older patients receive adequate stroke care? An experience of a neurovascular clinic', *Postgraduate Medical Journal*, 85, 115–18.

to out-of-hours and crisis services, psychological therapies and alcohol services.[8]

In relation to financial services the report expressed particular concern about motor and travel insurance. It stated that 'many older people are worried that they have a more limited choice of services and pay a higher price for them'. In some circumstances, however, different treatment would be justified and age 'used properly is a valid criterion for pricing risk'. An example of this was that 'statistics show that 75-year-olds in 2007 were around four times more likely to make a travel insurance claim than 35-year-olds; and 85-year-olds were over eight times more likely to make a claim'. Other exceptions might relate to age-related holidays and age-based discounts and benefits.

Section 29 of the Equality Act 2010 provides:

1. A person (a 'service-provider') concerned with the provision of a service to the public or a section of the public (for payment or not) must not discriminate against a person requiring the service by not providing the person with the service.

2. A service-provider (A) must not, in providing the service, discriminate against a person (B) –

    – as to the terms on which A provides the service to B;
    – by terminating the provision of the service to B;
    – by subjecting B to any other detriment.

3. A service-provider must not, in relation to the provision of the service, harass –

    – a person requiring the service, or
    – a person to whom the service-provider provides the service.

4. A service-provider must not victimise a person requiring the service by not providing the person with the service.

---

8   Healthcare Commission. 'Equality in Later Life. A national study of older people's mental health services' (2009).

5.   A service-provider (A) must not, in providing the service, victimise a person (B) –

– as to the terms on which A provides the service to B;
– by terminating the provision of the service to B;
– by subjecting B to any other detriment.

Thus there is a specific provision aimed at stopping service providers from discriminating, harassing or victimising those to whom it is providing the service; this includes the protected characteristic of age. Section 197 of the Act also provides Ministers with the power to provide that specific conduct or anything done for a specific purpose does not amount to age discrimination. The government policy is especially focused on health and financial services.[9] In health, age will continue to be a factor to be taken into account 'where appropriate'. In financial services there is to be a specific exception to allow providers of financial services to use age as a basis for different treatment. It will be possible to vary prices according to age, but only where this 'genuinely reflects risk or costs'. There will also be a general exception allowing age to be used to determine eligibility for benefits or concessions, so as to ensure that discounts and benefits such as free travel and discounted entrance to events will be able to continue. The provisions with regard to age were due to come into effect in 2012.

As suggested above there are a number of important areas in which this abolition of discrimination in relation to services is relevant. Here we are concentrating on two of them – health provision and financial services.

Health Provision

There are important issues for older people in health care around medical and other care decisions which take into account age in deciding whether treatment is to be given or whether it is worthwhile considering the age of the patient. One can imagine scenarios where an older patient might not receive expensive surgical treatment or medicine because they only have a limited lifespan ahead of them, compared to younger patients needing similar treatment.

---

9   Government Equalities Office. 'The equalities bill: making it work – ending age discrimination in services and public functions: a policy statement' (2010).

Despite the fact, that, in contrast to the stereotypes, 'older people are, on average, in good general health although the prevalence of illness and disability tends to rise steeply over the age of 80' and that two thirds of the population over 65 report no functional disability at all,[10] there is a reliance on the provision of health services by a significant proportion of older people. In 2001 older people made up 16 per cent of population but consumed 40 per cent of health care resources. Two thirds of hospital beds are occupied by those over 65.

Three examples of discrimination in the health service, given by Roberts,[11] are, firstly, explicit age limits to health services; secondly, hidden discrimination by professionals or agencies; and, thirdly indirect discrimination where a policy or practice disproportionately affects older people.

A typology of age discrimination in health care is described in the following way:

Dimension of care	Explicit age discrimination	Hidden age discrimination	Indirect age discrimination
Access	Breast and cervical cancer screening	Age related variation in 'Do Not Resuscitate'	Means testing for nursing care arranged via local
Quality	Performance indicators and targets	Neglect of older people's needs on general medical wards	Mixed sex wards

An Age Concern survey of General Practitioners (GPs) in the UK in 2006 found that some 70 per cent of GPs surveyed believed that rationing of treatment on age grounds took place in the NHS. There appeared to be informal upper age limits for a variety of services such as heart bypass operations, knee replacements and kidney dialysis. There may be lower priority given for illnesses that affect older people, such as arthritis.

There may also be explicit age barriers in some services such as upper age limits for treatment in high dependency units and coronary care units (Bowling

---

10 Roberts Emilie (2002). *Age Discrimination in Public Policy: a Review of the Evidence*, Chapter 3, Age discrimination in health Help the Aged.
11 Roberts Emilie (2002). *Age Discrimination in Public Policy: a Review of the Evidence*, Chapter 3, Age discrimination in health Help the Aged.

1999). Age is an issue recognised by the National Health Service in the UK and any criticisms here should be read within this context.

The Age report suggests there are subtler forms of discrimination. These include:

- Health promotion, where older people seem not to be offered the same preventive or primary care or advice as other patients; lifestyle advice tends to be tailored for younger patients, although evidence like exercise and giving up smoking have major benefits for older people also.

- Diagnosis – certain conditions appear to be much less commonly diagnosed in older people; depression and other forms of physical and mental illness may even be misdiagnosed as symptoms of dementia.

- Specialist services where there was a strong suspicion of discrimination in the organisation of cancer services. There was some recognition of this in the 2001 Department of Health report *The NHS Cancer Plan* which stated that: 'Frailty and age are not the same thing and some 70-year-olds are healthier than some 50-year-olds. As within any other disease treated by the health service, ageism is unacceptable in NHS cancer services.'

- Accident and emergency service; one survey in Scotland found excess mortality in older patients; they were much less likely to receive appropriate treatment such as intensive care or referral for specialist investigation (Grant P. et al. 2000). A further survey in England, Wales and Northern Ireland found that patients over 60 waited on average almost five hours before treatment and patients over 80 waited on average four and a half hours; compared to an average wait of less than three hours for patients under 40 years (*Casualty Watch 2001*). These findings are of concern because a 'high proportion of admissions of older people are made through accident and emergency departments in the UK'.

- Quality of care for older people on hospital wards – 'In 1998, an independent investigation into acute hospital care found powerful evidence of negative attitudes towards older people and dangerous inadequacies in the care provided on some general acute wards' (Health Advisory Service 1998) – failing in meeting basic nutrition standards or personal hygiene for older patients; it seems likely that high workload and staff shortages are main factors rather than any deliberate intent.

Financial Services

The issue of discrimination in financial services is inextricably linked to the issue of low incomes, for example some 800,000 single pensioners and 400,000 pensioner couples rely entirely upon the state pension.[12] In the UK this is little more than subsistence level. All together some 2.1 million pensioners live in poverty (defining poverty as living in a household with less than 60 per cent of median income after housing costs are taken into account). Some pensioner groups are more likely to be at risk of poverty according to this definition. While some 17 per cent of white pensioner households meet the definition of poverty, this figure increases to 29 per cent for black and black British households, 32 per cent for Asian or British Asian ones, and 30 per cent for those of Chinese or other ethnic groups.[13] In particular, however, pensions are a gender issue with older women disproportionately taking a larger share of the burden of poverty in old age.

PENSIONS

The first Old Age Pensions Act in the UK was adopted more than 100 years ago in 1908. It introduced a universal, albeit means tested, state pension for those of 70 years of age and over. It was a landmark in welfare reform and was intended to alleviate the worst poverty suffered by the poorest people in the country. Yet after a century of pension provision and pension reform it is possible to state that: 'The development of pensions, and of formalised pension ages have been described by some as aspects of a process of marginalising and degrading older people in the twentieth century, as they were progressively excluded from paid work and the social status assumed to be associated with it' (Thane 2002).

It is possible to view the development of state old age pension and the creation of the state retirement age which accompanies it as creating a separate

---

12 'Financial services', Help the Aged policy statement (2007).
13 'Older people in the UK: key facts and statistics', Age Concern (2008).

class of excluded older persons, many of whom were to continue to live in relative or absolute poverty. This has been especially true of women.

Two thirds of all those in receipt of state pensions are women.[14] The following sums up the situation of women with regard to pension provision in the UK:[15]

- One in five single women pensioners risk being in poverty in retirement.

- 30 per cent of women reaching state pension age are entitled to a full state pension, compared with 85 per cent of men.

- Nearly two thirds of those in receipt of means tested pension credit are women.

- By 2020 it is estimated that there will be as many divorced women aged 65 to 75 as widows; almost two thirds of divorced and separated older women have no private pension income at all.

- 37 per cent of women work full-time, compared to 60 per cent of men.

- 25 per cent of all women aged 45 to 64 are carers.

- The number of women who are saving for retirement halves when they have a baby; the figure for men remains unchanged when they become new fathers.

There are a number of reasons why this situation has come about. They include the failure of the traditional model of husband in paid work/wife in unpaid domestic work.[16] Linked to this is the abandonment of the principle of a non-contributory entitlement or an entitlement that was not based upon the

---

14 DWP Quarterly Statistical Summary November 2007; see <www.dwp.gov.uk>.

15 Taken from the web site of the Equal Opportunities Commission, now subsumed into the Commission for Equality and Human Rights <www.equalityhumanrights.com>; Parliamentary Briefing on the Pensions Bill 16th January 2007. Figures correct for 2005.

16 Ginn, J. (2003). Chapter 1 'Trends in gender relations, employment and pensions' – 'The disproportionate share of poverty borne by today's older women reflects the model of gender relations prevailing during much of their earlier lives, one in which a gender division of labour confined most married women to raising a family and homemaking – the male breadwinner-housewife model.' See also, usefully, Price, D. and Ginn, J. (2003).

amount or regularity of contributions and the reliance on a private pension system which is linked to earnings and periods of service.[17]

If one looks at average pension income for both sexes there is also an issue about the absolute level of pension income when compared to average incomes in the individual economy. The state pension in the UK is only intended to provide a subsistence income and, when compared to other OECD countries, provides the lowest income compared to average earnings. Greece and Luxembourg had the highest weighted averages with 95 per cent and 87 per cent respectively. A further five countries have an average pension level above 75 per cent (Denmark, Hungary, Iceland, the Netherlands, and Spain). Seven countries provided an income of less than 40 per cent of average earnings (Belgium, Germany, Ireland, Japan, Mexico, New Zealand, and the UK). The UK was bottom of the table of 30 countries with 30 per cent ('Pensions at a glance: public policies across OECD countries' (2007)).

In 2002 the government published a consultation entitled 'Simplicity, security and choice: working and saving for retirement'. This stated that: '... although the average pensioner has done well in recent decades, inequality in pensioners' incomes has increased dramatically. The current generation of female pensioners are over-represented in those groups of pensioners with low incomes.'

Women, because of their longer life expectancy and their lower state pension age, made up some 64 per cent of the pensioner population, but, in 2000/01, the average income for a male pensioner was £194 per week, compared to £153 for women. The document summed up succinctly why women's pensions were lower than those of men:

- Until 1978 the system did not recognise caring responsibilities.

- Prior to 1978 women were able to pay a reduced rate of national insurance contribution and rely on their husband's contributions.

- Around 70 per cent of the female pensioner population had no private pension. This was because of a lower level of participation in the labour force and the receipt, on average, of lower rates of pay and shorter working hours as most part-time workers are women.

---

17 The current situation of women with regard to pensions and how this may be changing is dicussed later.

- As a result of a longer life expectancy, retired women's savings were required to last longer and investments to produce an annuity produced less income than that received by men. It has also been calculated that the majority of annuities taken out are done so on a single life basis, so the surviving wife has little or no continuing benefit.[18]

- An absence from the labour market has a significant effect on pay levels. On average women experience a drop in pay of around 16 per cent after a year out of the labour market; double that faced by men.

There had been measures to assist women not in receipt of even subsistence level income by the introduction of a minimum income guarantee which had helped some two million people, half of whom are single women. This was replaced in 2003 by a different form of subsidy called pensions credit. It was estimated that two thirds of those entitled to pension credit would be women, and half of these would be 75 and over.

The issue of inadequate occupational pensions has, however, never been satisfactorily dealt with. In 1974 the Secretary of State for Social Services, Mrs Barbara Castle, had proposed a partnership with private pension funds. In this 2002 consultation, 'the government proposes to encourage, rather than compel, employers to provide pensions for their staff'. There can not be satisfactory progress on equalising pensions until this were to happen.

Pensions: Challenges and Choices was volume one of a document resulting from the establishment of a Commission to examine future pensions' arrangements. It again looked at the issue of women and pensions and considered why women received less. It also considered the position of women with regard to private occupational schemes and concluded that women had received a much lower income during working life because of career breaks, working part-time, lower average earnings and a tendency to work in the service sector where pension provision was less widespread. Indeed, of course, there was a tradition of women giving up paid employment on marriage, so, for example, in 1984 when today's pensioner of 65 was 42, the employment rate of 35–49-year-old women was 65 per cent, compared to 88 per cent for men.

---

18   See the 'First report of the Pensions Commission TSO' (2004).

The net effect of this historic system is that 69 per cent of women aged 65–69 received less than the full state pension compared to 15 per cent of men. Offset partially by pensions credit and two thirds of the means tested pensions credit beneficiaries were women.

The Pensions Commission believed that the situation was gradually changing as the numbers of women in employment increased and the earnings gap continued to close. In addition there were increasing numbers of women in pension schemes and the greater concentration of women in the public sector had meant that women have been less affected by decline in defined benefit pension schemes. The illustration of the change was that women now received 72 per cent of men's occupational pension income compared to 61 per cent in 1994/5, but, of course, this may be because men's position was getting worse.

There were further reforms, as a result of the 2007 and 2008 Pensions Acts, which will make a difference for future pensioners. For those who reach state pension age after April 6 2010 the contribution conditions, in order to qualify for a full state pension, for category A and B pensions are to be reduced to 30 years for men and women alike, rather than the current level of 44 years for men and 39 years for women.[19] The Act also removes the restriction which stopped those entitled to a category B pension from receiving it until their spouse or civil partner reached retirement age.[20]

Home responsibilities protection will also be extended and will become available to a maximum of 22 years for those who have been awarded child benefit for a child under 16; regularly engaged for at least 35 hours per week in caring for someone in receipt of attendance allowance; or are an approved foster parent or carer. All pension rates will be uprated annually in line with earnings – perhaps by 2012 or the end of the next Parliament, but the state pension age is to be increased to 66 years for men and women by 2020 and by one year a decade thereafter.

---

19 Category A pensions is a contributory one that entitles an individual to a state pension or additional state pension. Category B pensions are payable by virtue of a spouse's or a civil partner's contributions. Category B pensions will become available to married men and people in civil partnerships on the same basis as currently available to married women.

20 In 2010 the Coalition Government proposed to introduce a pension related to age rather than contributions.

THE FINANCIAL SECTOR

Thus many older people are also poor people and this group is often not well provided for by the financial sector. Thus older people are disproportionately affected by post office closures and bank branch closures. The issue is not just transport and social isolation, but the ability of poor people to access financial services, such as bank accounts and loans at reasonable rates. One study ('Financial exclusion among older people' (2006)) found that financial exclusion amongst older people was the product of a number of factors:

- A traditional conservative approach to money management and a resistance to change.

- The presence of one or more disabilities that limit mobility and access to financial services.

- Degrees of social isolation and a lack of trusted support.

- An inability or reluctance to use new methods of money management.

- Worries about personal security and safety on the streets.

As a result there was some evidence, according to this study, of voluntary self-exclusion from normal banking services.

MOTOR INSURANCE

Older people drive cars (see Table 3.1). The number of people in their 70s who have a driving licence is apparently due to increase from four million (in 2006) to 10 million by 2050 (insurance and age: exploring behaviour, attitudes and discrimination' a report for Age Concern and Help the Aged (2007)). The following is part of a survey for Age Concern and Help the Aged in the UK.

Table 3.1   Proportion of people with motor insurance by age group

Age group	Proportion (%)
20–24	32
30–34	60

Table 3.1   *Concluded*

40–44	65
50–54	62
60–64	59
70–74	46
80–84	29

Thus a greater proportion of people aged 80–84 have a driving licence compared to the youngest age group quoted here.

Here is a letter taken from the *Guardian* newspaper ('Money' section p. 4 Saturday 3 October 2009):

> *I am 72, have had my licence since the mid-60s and have not made a claim for 20 years. I have just paid £452 for my car insurance. Each year my quote rises and my existing insurer never seems interested in retaining me as a customer. Consequently each year I go through the same process to try to get a quote similar to my last.*

This letter speaks volumes about the discrimination that older people suffer in some aspects of financial services. Not only does the cost of insurance rise each year with age (despite the fact, for example, that this person has not made a claim in 20 years), but there appears to be a disinterest from the supplier in the customer and certainly no-one seems to be fighting over his or her custom.

TRAVEL INSURANCE

Older people travel and take holidays. According to the Age Concern and Help the Aged survey quoted above people aged 65–74 holiday at least as often as those aged 30–49. The figures drop after the age of 75 years, but, according to the survey, still some 28 per cent of people in this age group had taken a holiday at least three times in the previous year compared to 18 per cent of those aged 30–49 (see Table 3.2):

Table 3.2   Frequency of different age groups taking holidays in previous
               year (per cent)

Age group	None	Once	Twice	Three times	Four+
30–49	30	30	21	11	7
65–74	29	25	23	11	12
75+	37	19	18	14	14

It appears that obtaining a quotation for motor insurance or travel insurance
or car hire becomes more difficult the older the applicant. According to Age
Concern/Help the Aged (see Table 3.3):

> *Nearly one in five of those ages 65 plus trying to obtain a new quotation
> were unsuccessful, compared with only 3 per cent of those aged
> 30–49. The oldest respondents (75 plus) were particularly frustrated,
> the proportion being unable to get a quotation rising to 29 per cent.
> This made them nine times more likely to be refused cover than those
> aged 30–49.*

Table 3.3   Was a quotation for cover/hire obtained as requested
               (per cent)?

Age group	Yes	No
30–49	97	3
65+	81	19
65–74	88	12
75+	71	29

It is not possible to say that these difficulties were unreasonable or not
for good reasons, but it is clear that many older people believe that they are
discriminated on the grounds of age when it comes to trying to arrange insurance
cover or car hire. According to the survey some 31 per cent of people aged 80
plus felt discriminated against when obtaining such quotations, compared to
some 2 per cent of people aged 30–49 years. The survey also showed that some
75 per cent of people aged 75 plus believed that the insurance industry 'is less
willing to insure older people' (see Table 3.4):

Table 3.4 **How respondents felt when obtaining quotations**

Age group	In control	Respected	Looked down on	Annoyed	Discriminated against
30–49	65	48	1	7	2
65–69	47	46	4	8	8
70–74	39	56	7	12	10
75–79	48	50	4	16	13
80+	31	38	10	22	31

Insurance is a particularly difficult area when tackling age discrimination, because age is an important part of its assessment of risk. As a House of Commons research paper (House of Commons Research Paper 09/42 May 2009) suggested:

> *Of all the trades and professions affected by anti-discrimination insurance is one with most to concern it. Insurance is one consumer service that, on the face of it, 'embeds' discrimination into its very nature, age and gender being the most obvious examples. Older people can struggle to find affordable travel insurance. A benefit of middle age is lower car premiums whilst young people receive more favourable terms on life insurance.*

Research for the government Equalities Office ('The use of age-based practices in financial services' (2009)) showed a number of age-based practices in the provision of financial services. These were:

- Prices for motor and travel insurance differ depending on the age of the customer.

- Prices for travel insurance often stay flat within an age band, but then can jump in a step-wise manner (and often significantly) as the individual moves up the age bands.

- Providers of motor and travel insurance specialise and often target particular age groups, excluding others.

- Age is often a filter to determine how risk is assessed and a product sold, so prospective customers of different ages can be treated differently in the sales process, for example, by providing more information or by the use of method of communication (for example, telephone or internet).

The insurance industry's justification for this is, of course, that such differentiation takes place during actuarial calculations of the risk to be carried in insuring an individual. The very nature of assessing risk means that the calculations are often done on a group basis, rather than an individual one. Thus a young driver may find that he or she has a higher premium for car insurance, regardless of the individual's driving record, merely because he or she is young and therefore part of a group that is assessed as carrying a higher risk. Despite all this the Association of British Insurers is able to state that, from its own research, that more than 99 per cent of customers aged 65 or over are able to obtain motor insurance and more than 98 per cent of those aged 65 or over are able to obtain travel insurance.[21] This does not deal with the difficulties which older people perceive that they face.

Hope for the Future

There is enough evidence to show that discrimination does take place against older people on the basis of their chronological age. In the UK there is the promise of legislation to tackle this and this promises a more hopeful future. The concern must always be that, like the prohibition of age discrimination in employment, there will be the opportunity for general and unjustified exceptions to the prohibition which will allow substantial discrimination to continue.

---

21 ABI Research Paper No 12 2009 cited in Vincent Keter 'Equality Bill' House of Commons Research Paper 09/42 7th May 2009.

4

The Regulation of Age Discrimination in the UK

The process of law making can sometimes be long and complex. The Labour government which came to power in 1997 (until May 2010) had a commitment to taking some action on age discrimination, although it was not clear what this action would be. In the beginning it procrastinated by taking a voluntarist route, which few thought would succeed. At the same time the EU had been developing its own approach to a Framework Directive on equal treatment in employment and occupation.[1] This included discrimination on the grounds of age in its provisions (see Chapter 5). The Directive allowed member states to apply for a further extension on implementation of up to three years from the original implementation date of December 2003, 'in order to take account of particular conditions'. The UK took advantage of this with the result that there was to be a final implementation date in the UK of December 2006. In the event the government adopted Regulations in 2006. These were later substantially incorporated into the Equality Act 2010. The default retirement provisions, however, were left to be removed by the subsequent coalition government in 2011.

First Consultation

In May 1997 the government announced that it would consult on the best way to tackle age discrimination in employment. The results of this consultation were published in *Action on Age*.[2] A major contributor to this consultation was some research which had already been commissioned by the DfEE in 1996. The report entitled *Characteristics of Older Workers* was published in January 1998.[3]

---

1   Directive 2000/78/EC.
2   'Action on age report of the consultation on age discrimination in employment' (1998).
3   See consideration of this report in Chapter 1.

The purpose of this report was to identify the effect of age on economic activity and to explore the characteristics of older workers, using data from the Family and Working Lives Survey. The study concluded that any 'older workers effect' becomes apparent around the age of 50 years and stated that: 'Once they had become 50, the risks of leaving work to become unemployed or inactive tended to increase. And the chances of returning to paid work for those who were inactive or unemployed tended to decrease.'

The most common area raised in the consultation was the difficulties that older workers had in finding jobs. Problems encountered included the use of age criteria and language in job advertisements. This was an issue borne out by the *Middlesex Survey* (see Chapter 2) and certainly other research at the time. In the late 1980s for example, the Equal Opportunities Commission monitored more than 11,000 recruitment advertisements in a variety of journals. More than 25 per cent stipulated an upper age limit, with almost two-thirds of those stating an upper[4] limit of 35 years. In the debate on her Bill (see previous) Ms Perham MP referred to advertisements which used language which had a discriminatory effect, such as an advertisement in the *Independent* newspaper advertising for secretaries to join a 'young, fun team of surveyors'.[5]

A further issue mentioned in the 'Action on age' consultation was the pressure exercised on older employees while they were in work. There was concern about training and promotion opportunities being open to older workers and the encouragement of older workers to leave to make way for others, especially through the redundancy process when older workers, it was suggested, were more likely to be considered first.

Perhaps the most interesting part of this consultation was its incompleteness as it did not include a consideration of retirement ages or what happened to workers after normal retirement age. The issue of retirement was raised a lot during the consultation. The document, however, stated that: 'This is [retirement age] outside the scope of the consultation, as like other terms and conditions of employment, retirement ages are a matter for negotiation between individual employers and their employees, or their representatives.'

---

4   See McEwen (1990).
5   At this time the author of this book also wrote to the advertising managers of six national newspapers to ask whether they had a policy on age in recruitment advertising. None appeared to have one and, indeed, the Advertising Standards Authority confirmed that no code existed for the industry as a whole.

It is perhaps ironic that it is this lack of a national policy on retirement ages that placed the UK in the position of debating the removal of mandatory contractual retirement ages, in order to comply with the Equal Treatment in Employment Directive.

Only a limited number of measures came out of this consultation. The action plan seemed more concerned with helping older workers cope with age discrimination rather than requiring employers to end the practice. Thus there were a number of measures to help older workers find jobs[6] and some help with education and training, but little else apart from the removal of the upper age limit from job vacancies in government-owned Job Centres and a consultation on a Code of Good Practice in Age Discrimination.

VOLUNTARISM V STATUTE

The issue of whether to introduce legislation or continue on a voluntarist route was considered as part of the consultation. Arguments put forward in favour of legislation included:

- Social change would only take place against a background of anti-discrimination legislation.

- Research indicated that both managers and employees favoured legislation.

- Legislation in other countries was effective.

The majority of calls for legislation, according to the consultation report, were for a far wider piece of legislation that included more than just employment. Since legislation already existed for sex, race and disability discrimination, then it should be introduced with regard to age.

Arguments put forward against legislation included:

- Employers should be free from further labour market regulation and costs.

---

6   Extending the New Deal for unemployed people aged 25 years and over and also for disabled people.

- Employers would find ways around the legislation or 'take it underground'.

- Legislation would be so complex that it would be 'a part measure only'.

One could imagine these arguments being used against any proposed legislation on any form of discrimination. The consultation document stated however that: 'On balance, there was no consensus of opinion on legislation and a strong case for legislation was not made during the consultation.'[7] Yet it had earlier stated that: 'Research findings indicated that managers and employees favoured legislation.'[8] There were some indications that employer representatives and especially human resource professionals favoured legislation. One report of an Institute of Personnel Management conference at Harrogate some years earlier suggested the following arguments in favour of legislation:[9]

- Legislation would raise the issue of age discrimination to the same level of importance as sex and race discrimination.[10]

- Legislation would demonstrate society's disapproval of morally unacceptable behaviour such as the translation of age-related stereotypes about people into decisions which have a deep affect upon people's lives.

- Legislation would empower human resource people and others to influence their colleagues who may not find age discrimination unacceptable.

- Legislation would empower older workers.

- Legislation would help businesses by reversing the practice of encouraging older workers to exit the labour force thus stopping valuable resources being thrown away.

---

7   'Action on age' report, Paragraph 2.31.
8   Op. cit., Paragraph 2.26.
9   Handley (1993); the speech was by Professor Warr of Sheffield University.
10 This speech was made before the adoption of the Disability Discrimination Act 1995.

In a survey of the membership of the Institute of Management some two-thirds of respondents supported the introduction of comprehensive legislation to prevent age discrimination at work. An even greater number (70 per cent) supported legislation to restrict the use of age in job advertisements. Support from managers and HR professionals for legislation may, of course, indicate that arguments to end discriminatory practices in their own organisations are considerably strengthened when there is legislation in existence.

Major employer organisations, however, did not support a legislative route and it may be that this deep seated opposition still manifests itself when considering the practical aspects of the 2006 Age Regulations, for example, in the opposition of employer organisations to the abolition of the mandatory retirement as expressed in the 2003 consultation (see later). The Institute of Directors welcomed the government's decision at the time not to introduce legislation and believed that such legislation would entail an unwarranted restriction on an employer's right to organise their business. It also doubted whether legislation would be effective as there was little evidence that the problem had been eliminated in those countries which had introduced laws on the subject. The Institute did state that discrimination in all its forms was wrong and can be damaging to individual enterprises and the economy. It was legitimate, however, to discriminate on the basis of age on occasions when the job or situation demanded. The Confederation of British Industry (CBI) also supported a voluntary approach. Their Director of Human Resources was quoted as saying that the CBI believed that the eventual Code of Practice will: 'Help drive attitudinal change and achieve fair treatment for all ages in the workplace'.[11] The CBI was opposed to legislation because: 'The law is a blunt instrument to change outmoded attitudes'.[12]

In contrast there was strong support for legislation from the trade union participants in the consultation. The General Secretary of the Trades Union Congress (TUC) summed up the union point of view in a 1998 statement:

> *The TUC has long been concerned that the talents and experience of many older working people are being wasted as a consequence of prejudice and misconception. We have no wish to see all aspects of the employment relationship regulated by legislation. But in the case of*

11 Mr John Cridland, CBI Press Release June 1999.
12 CBI press briefing 16.11.1998.

*age discrimination we consider that legislation similar to race and sex
discrimination laws would be helpful in changing attitudes.*[13]

This preference for a legislative approach was supported by the trade
unions who participated in the consultation exercise,[14] such as the General
and Municipal Boilermakers Union (GMB) which stated that they were
disappointed that the government has not stuck to its manifesto commitment
of legislation against age discrimination, and have concerns that a voluntary
approach will not be sufficient to deal with this problem.

The report also stated that the fact that other countries had legislation
was not conclusive and the effectiveness of that legislation, 'was open to
interpretation'.

The outcome of all this was that the government rejected the statutory
route and decided that its role was to provide a framework in which age
discrimination could be tackled. As part of this enabling policy it proposed
to publish a non-statutory Code of Good Practice on Age Discrimination in
Employment and in June 1999 the final version of the Code was published.[15]

WINNING THE GENERATION GAME

'Winning the generation game' was a report produced in 2000[16] which suggested
that workers have been stopped from making a contribution as they grow older
by, amongst other measures:

- A view among society, employers and many older people themselves
  that they have less to offer – often based on demonstrably false
  prejudices.

- Perverse incentives in occupational pension regimes that encourage
  employees and employers to come to early retirement arrangements.

- Assumptions in the benefits and employment services, which tend
  to 'write off' older workers.

---

13 TUC Press Release 30 January 1998.
14 Including the TGWU, the GMB, MSF, UNIFI, NUT and the GMB.
15 It was further updated in 2001.
16 Performance and Innovation Unit, Cabinet Office.

This report was about helping people to remain active in later life, which meant not writing off or excluding people from work, leisure or community participation. It was part of a government project on active ageing, in which the Performance and Innovation Unit of the Cabinet Office was asked to look at the implications of the trend towards economic inactivity of people between 50 years and state pension age, and to identify whether the government should take action. The report's conclusions are revealing. It states what is perhaps obvious to many, but not to some who make such decisions:

> *The fact is that age is not a sound basis on which to judge ability to work or learn. Even though people change as they age, they do not all change in the same way, at the same speed or the same extent. Some will change for the better and some for the worse, and that judgment will in itself be different in respect of different activities. It is essential, therefore, that people should be judged on the basis of ability and not age. Moreover, insofar as it is possible (though potentially misleading) to assess older workers as a group, evidence shows that their productivity and return to employers is no different to younger ones.*

Research, according to the report, showed that British employers held views about both young and older people 'that are not supported by objective evidence'. Employers' stereotypical views about age affected decisions about recruitment, training, promotion and 'releasing workers'. It does seem an odd reflection upon later government consultations where the views of employers result in having an important effect upon decisions concerning the Age Regulations, for example, given this report's conclusions about employers' views and given the fact that the majority of private sector employers do not employ people over the age of 60 years it does seem odd that it is the employers' views about the need to keep a mandatory retirement age that have prevailed (see later).

The report then recommended more positive action by the government and also considered the issue of voluntarism or legislation. It stated that the evidence internationally was not conclusive, but also pointed out that it would be equally difficult to demonstrate conclusively the impact of other anti discrimination legislation. The conclusion was that age discrimination legislation would have a: 'Positive effect on British culture and would build, as other discrimination Acts have, on a growing sense of public interest and concern about the issue. Most importantly, the report states that 'the absence of legislation on age, when it exists for gender, race and disability, sends a powerful message that age discrimination is taken less seriously'.

The report recommended that the government should consider introducing legislation if an evaluation of the *Code of Practice* found that it had not been effective. It also recommended that this evaluation be transparent and command confidence.

The government did publish in full the results of the evaluation.[17] Substantial numbers of employers were surveyed through 1999 and 2000. These surveys revealed once again the stereotypical views held by many employers.[18]

Respondents were asked to indicate whether or not the specified attributes applied to older or younger workers, to both or neither. Stability, maturity, reliability, work commitment and good managerial skills were the most frequently stated attributes of older workers, while ambition, IT skills, creativity and a willingness to relocate were attributed to younger workers.

Encouragingly, one in three companies were aware of the Code of Practice,[19] but, of these, only 23 per cent had actually seen a copy. More alarmingly perhaps, only 1 per cent of companies expected to make changes as a result of the Code. The report stated that the main reason for no change taking place: 'Is the belief that company policy or practice is already appropriate or that it currently meets government guidelines'. Age discrimination was generally rated as less important than other types of discrimination such as race, gender or disability. According to the analysis: 'The lower rating was undoubtedly due, at least in part, to its lower profile and the fact that, unlike other areas, it is not covered by legislation'. The report suggested that there was a feeling that age discrimination at work was more acceptable or was perhaps something that was inherent in the workplace. Respondents made it clear that they expected that the Code would eventually be replaced by legislation and that much needed to be done to raise awareness of the issue. 'The Code', according to the report, 'although seen as paving the way is unlikely to achieve the effect on its own'.

---

17 'Evaluation of the code of practice on age diversity in employment final report' (2001).
18 'Evaluation of the code of practice on age diversity in employment interim summary of results' (2000).
19 Not surprisingly, awareness was much higher in large companies where almost two-thirds knew about the Code of Practice.

A good example of discrimination being inherent in the workforce is in parts of the legal profession. An article in the *Law Society Gazette*[20] suggested that: 'Many legal employers consider it unrealistic to be expected to give out training contracts to people in their forties. Training costs a lot of time, money and effort, which may not be worth only 10 or 15 years of work in return.'

One human resources director of a large city law firm was quoted in the same article as saying: 'Of course we are ageist; offering training contracts to older applicants would have serious disadvantages. Our firm likes to think we can shape trainees into our particular mould; we have a certain style, we are known for it, we have a certain way of doing things. We just can't guarantee that older trainees would espouse that style.'

The final evaluation report concluded that the Code was seen as a step in the right direction, but that respondents expected that the Code would eventually become law. The authors of the report stated that: 'The researchers therefore conclude from the research, that there is a small but growing level of support for age discrimination legislation.'

Second Consultation

In December 2001 the government published a further consultation document titled 'Towards equality and diversity'.[21] It was concerned with implementing the Race Directive[22] and the Framework Directive.

Apart from a general summary of the approach to implementing these Directives, the consultation document contained one chapter[23] on some specific issues relating to age. This began with the statement that 'we intend to legislate to tackle age discrimination at work and in training'. This, of course, was a major step forward, which was the result of the adoption of the Framework Directive in 2000. It was also clear however that the voluntarist route had failed and that the only way in which age discrimination was going to be effectively tackled was through legislation. It is impossible to know whether the UK government would have progressed to this stage without the requirement to implement the Framework Directive.

---

20 Lewis (2001).
21 'Towards equality and diversity; implementing the employment and race directives' (2001).
22 Directive 2000/43/EC of 29 June 2000 which concerned the principle of equal treatment between persons irrespective of racial or ethnic origin.
23 Chapter 15.

Towards Equality and Diversity was a document which was clear in its appraisal of what was likely to come. The justification for the proposed legislation was a business one. Diversity is good for business and anti-discrimination legislation is one part of achieving that diversity. It is this approach that consistently shaped the decisions reached by the government in its progress towards the adoption of Age Regulations. The document stated, in relation to age, that: 'We need to be clear about what we trying to achieve with legislation'. The answer was to identify and prohibit unfair practices based on discriminatory attitudes or inaccurate assumptions. There was, however, recognition that there may be differences in treatment that could be justified. These include firstly those initiatives that improve the opportunities of people to enter work or training, and secondly, those employment practices which can be 'clearly and objectively justified'. Thus 'a key goal' of the consultation was to identify which types of treatment are acceptable and which are not. The word 'acceptable' is an interesting one and perhaps identifies what objective justification is really about. It may be that it is really a concern to find such justification for practices which are held to be acceptable and can be justified in economic/business terms. The consultation was not about how to protect the human rights of workers as such, unless those human rights coincided with a business rationale.

The main issues were identified and views were invited on them. These issues were considered to be those related to direct and indirect discrimination; recruitment, selection and promotion; training; occupational requirements;[24] pay and non-pay benefits;[25] redundancy and retirement.

There were a total of 870 responses received to the consultation.[26] Of these, 583 came from organisations and 287 from individuals. The responses confirmed how widespread discrimination was, based upon age. Some 50 per cent of respondents had either suffered age discrimination at work or had witnessed others suffering such discrimination. This discrimination took a variety of forms:

- Being forced to retire at a certain age 22 per cent.

- Not being given a job they applied for 18 per cent.

---

24 The consultation document stated that: 'The Directive provides for narrowly defined exceptions to be made where it is a requirement for a post to be occupied by someone of a particular age'.
25 Excluding the operation of occupational pension schemes and the use of age criteria in actuarial calculations.
26 'Towards equality and diversity: report of responses on age' (2003).

- Being prevented from attending training courses 17 per cent.

- Being told age was a barrier to general advancement 17 per cent.

- Assumptions being made about abilities due to age 15 per cent.

- Being selected for redundancy because of age 13 per cent.

According to the Consultation report, there were a number of contrasting views about how far the government should go in implementing the legislation:

- The 'age lobby' wanted legislation to cover other areas apart from employment.

- 'Age and other equality organisations' were concerned that implementing the Directive by secondary legislation, rather than statute, would undermine the authority of the Directive.

- The 2006 deadline for implementation was too far away.

- 'Business' was concerned about the legislation undermining workforce planning and succession management.

- 'Small businesses' were concerned about potential costs and how they would get support and advice.

- Trade unions needed time to review collective agreements.

- Professional bodies were concerned about the effects on their own activities – there might be implications for providers of group life assurance, income protection and so on.

Respondents suggested that there were circumstances under which age discrimination could be justified. Examples given were:

- If a job required a minimum age, such as driving or bar work 30 per cent.

- If the return on training was not cost beneficial 30 per cent.

- If the work was of a very physical nature 21 per cent.

- Health and safety grounds 18 per cent.

- If the job needed life experience, such as social work 18 per cent.

- If peers of a similar age were needed, such as holiday reps 11 per cent.

The majority of respondents were opposed to the use of age as a criterion in recruitment and promotion, although they were not opposed when considering redundancy or training opportunities, for example when a person was nearing retirement.

It is worth noting here how this whole exercise seemed to be carried out as a consultation about the effects on employers and generally the practical implications. There is little discussion about individuals' human rights. This perhaps displays the economic approach (see Chapter 1) to the issue, despite its non-functional or human rights justification.

Third Consultation

In July 2003 the government published its next consultation, 'Age matters'.[27] Again it is interesting to consider the approach as stated in the document. The proposals aimed to:

- Strike the right balance between regulating and supporting new legislation through other measures designed to achieve culture change.

- Achieve as coherent an approach as possible across all the equality strands, since that should reduce costs for business and bureaucracy for individuals.

It would have been refreshing if one of the aims had been, in accordance with the Directive, to protect and promote individuals' human rights not to be discriminated against on the grounds of age. Instead we have a pragmatic approach that seeks to balance the effectiveness of legislation with the need not

---

27 'Equality and diversity: age matters' (2003).

to impose too much of an extra burden in terms of costs or bureaucracy. The government proposed that new regulations would protect a variety of people:

- People at work, including agency workers and some self-employed people.

- People who apply for work.

- Office holders appointed by the Crown.

- People undertaking or applying for employment-related training.

- People undertaking or applying for courses in further and higher education.

- In some circumstances, people who have left work or one of the types of training or education mentioned above.

- People who are members of, or apply to, trade unions or professional bodies.

Direct discrimination, defined as occurring when a decision is made on the basis of a person's chronological age, and indirect discrimination, defined as happening when a policy or practice applies to everyone but causes disadvantage to a certain age group unless there are good reasons for it, were to be made unlawful. It would still be possible to treat people differently on the grounds of age if the employer could justify doing so by reference to specific aims which are appropriate and necessary. These aims could be:

- Health, welfare and safety, for example the protection of younger workers.

- Facilitation of employment planning, for example where a business has a number of people approaching retirement at the same time.

- The particular training requirements of the post in question, including those that have lengthy training periods and require a high level of fitness and concentration.

- Encouraging and rewarding loyalty.

- The need for a reasonable period of employment before retirement.

Certain discriminatory laws would also be capable of objective justification; for example the national minimum wage where younger people receive a different rate can be justified because it apparently helps younger workers to find jobs in competition with older workers.

The consultation document also contained a proposal for an alternative approach to justify removing the mandatory retirement age. It is worth noting that the document quotes the Green Paper 'Simpicity, security and choice'[28] as stating that: 'Under the Directive, compulsory retirement ages are likely to be unlawful unless employers can show that they are objectively justified'.

Thus there is likely to be a need for objective justification for any rule that makes it compulsory for an individual to retire at a certain age. The majority of respondents to the consultation had been opposed to allowing employers to retire employees at a certain age. The consultation proposed that compulsory retirement age be made unlawful but that employers could require employees to retire at a default age of 70 years, without having to justify their decision. How this differs from a mandatory retirement age is difficult to comprehend. It is difficult to see how it could have been justified as a proper implementation of the Directive. How would the government have been able to justify the age of 70 years in some future legal challenge. Why 70, rather than 69 or 71? (For further discussion on retirement age issues see Chapter 7).

Other proposals in the consultation document were that the age restrictions on making a claim for unfair dismissal should be removed (except of course for the moment when an employee is retired) and that the age-related aspects of the basic award element of unfair dismissal compensation be removed. Perversely the government also then proposed to keep the 20-year limit on the length of service that counts towards the basic award, thus continuing to discriminate against younger and older people. A similar approach was also proposed for statutory redundancy payments, which contained a significant age element, where half a week's pay is given for each year of service between the ages of 18 and 21 years, one week's pay[29] for each year of service between the ages of 22 and 40 years and one and a half weeks' pay for each year of service between the ages of 41 and 65 years, although there was a steep tapering off of benefits for the year before retirement age. The age limits were to be removed, but,

---

28 'Simplicity, security and choice: working and saving for retirement' (2002).
29 Subject to the statutory maximum for a week's wage.

in an astonishing piece of parsimony the government proposed changing the payment to one week's pay per year of service for everyone. This had the effect of removing the age differential, but potentially made the situation worse for every worker over the age of 41 years who would see their entitlement cut.[30] This appeared to be in contradiction of Article 8.2 of the Framework Directive which states that: 'The implementation of this Directive shall under no circumstances constitute grounds for a reduction in the level of protection against discrimination already afforded by member states in the fields covered by this Directive.'

In addition the consultation proposed making provision for employers to be able to justify recruitment upper age limits which could be objectively justifiable (it is interesting that the document did not refer to minimum age limits) and also seniority practices which otherwise may be indirectly discriminatory. These included practices which may be based upon length of service or experience, such as longer holidays, incremental pay and long-service awards.

CONSULTATION RESPONSE

The response to this consultation was published in 2005.[31] This was the final statement of views before the publication of the Age Regulations. Generally, the 427 respondents welcomed the proposals to outlaw age discrimination, but there were clearly uncertainties and differences of opinion. This may be partly a result of the government only consulting on the economic/business case for legislation, rather than any other more fundamental approach. Difficulties generally that were listed included:

- Difficulties in understanding how one could justify direct discrimination and indeed the fact that it was possible in the first place.

- The proposed specific aims which might justify differences in treatment[32] were supported by employers and employer organisations, but opposed by the TUC, other than any concerned

---

30 See Chapter 8 for what was in the final version of the Regulations.

31 'Equality and diversity: age matters age consultation 2003 summary of responses' (2005).

32 Health, safety and welfare; facilitation of employment planning; the particular training requirements of the post in question; encouraging and rewarding loyalty; the need for a reasonable period of employment before retirement.

with the health and safety of young workers. This is a division that repeats itself elsewhere in regard to the retirement age.

- Whether there should be an upper age limit on training and education opportunities. Such upper limits were opposed by a number of organisations, including the Policy Research Centre on Ageing and Ethnicity which wanted the abolition of the upper age limit of 54 years for student loans in higher education. An opposing view was put by employers who were concerned about financing training or education within too soon a period before the employee was due to retire.

- Several trade unions expressed the view that retaining a lower rate for the national minimum wage was discriminatory.

- A number of unions and others favoured extending the legislation to include goods and services.

The document also discussed issues around the retirement age, which are further discussed in Chapter 7. A majority of respondents[33] were in favour of a default retirement age, although almost two-thirds were against having that age set at 70. Some 82.4 per cent of respondent employers opposed a higher default age.

When it came to unfair dismissal and redundancy payments, there were a large majority of respondents in favour of removing the age aspects of redundancy payments and the basic award for unfair dismissal.[34] There was also a large majority who thought that an employer who dismisses employees on grounds of retirement should be able to defend the dismissal as fair.[35]

Almost three-quarters of respondents were in favour of allowing employers to apply an upper age limit to recruitment if they could justify doing so by reference to aims set out in the legislation. A number of organisations responded by connecting the upper age limit to issues of retirement. If there were no mandatory retirement age, then it would be more difficult to justify having an upper age limit on recruitment. Lastly the document looked at pay

---

33 Yes – 51.8 per cent; no – 42.9 per cent.
34 74.3 per cent in favour of removing the age elements of the basic award; 79.1 per cent in favour of making service below the age of 18 years count for the purposes of redundancy payments.
35 66 per cent in favour; 30.5 per cent against.

and non-pay benefits where a large majority (77.7 per cent) of respondents were in favour of a justification defence for basing some pay and benefits on length of service or experience, even though it might amount to direct discrimination.

It is self-evident that if you set the agenda in a certain context, then the responses to a consultation such as this will be within that context. The government context was a business one which perhaps balanced the needs of the business community with its own longer-term programme of encouraging diversity in employment. In order to encourage this diversity there may need to be exceptions made to the general principle of non-discrimination. To do otherwise would, according to this standpoint, inhibit the development of an age diverse workforce. Sometimes exceptions are made therefore which are to the long-term benefit of the group affected by these exceptions. There is an almost irresistible attraction to this argument. There is a default retirement age in order to save the dignity of employees, so that they do not end their careers going through a disciplinary or dismissal procedure because of their failing competence. Employers are to be allowed to make exceptions to facilitate staff planning, so that young people will be able to enter workforces, albeit at the expense of the older worker. Training opportunities can be withheld from older workers because there is not enough time for the employer to gain an adequate return on their investment. How different the approach might have been if one started from a human rights perspective, where each individual has the right not to be discriminated against for reasons connected to group stereotyping.

Fourth Consultation

In 2005 the government published its draft 'Age regulations' which fulfilled all the fears of those who were unhappy with the business agenda being followed by the government. Published at a very similar time was a series of case studies of employers and the pending age discrimination legislation.[36] The report stated that many human resource managers identified a number of potential benefits from reducing age discrimination. These included 'skills and knowledge retention, organisational stability, depth of experience, better management, reduced training and recruitment costs, matching staff and customer profile, and the fact that people would no longer be written off.' Even the HR managers were of the view, however, that some discriminatory practices were acceptable. There were though mixed views about the impact of any possible abolition of the contractual retirement age, although one felt that

---

36   'The age dimension of employment practices: employer case studies' (2005).

it would help improvements in the management of older workers. Employers, according to the report, identified four areas of concern about the proposed age regulations. These were, firstly, that they should be clear so that the need for litigation was limited; secondly, that any potential conflicts between the age regulations and other areas of employment law and government policy should be eliminated (worries included the relationship with the TUPE[37] Regulations, any prohibition on age-based pay systems and the national minimum wage); thirdly, that there should be general exemption from length-of-service awards; and lastly, that there should be comprehensive guidelines.

The draft Regulations allowed for important exceptions and included a default retirement age of 65 years. It is worth recording the deep differences that existed between the employers and trade unions in response to the draft Regulations. Evidence that the government had adopted an employer's agenda in dealing with age discrimination was provided by the responses to the 2005 consultation on its draft age regulations, called 'Coming of age'. The Confederation of British Industry (CBI) stated in its response: 'The *Age Matters* and *Coming of Age* consultations, as well as the ongoing dialogue that has been conducted with employers and other parties, have been highly beneficial in producing draft regulations that take business concerns into account as well as combating age discrimination.'

The Engineering Employers Federation (EEF) also responded by saying that: 'The EEF is pleased to record its appreciation that the DTI has listened to many of the concerns of employers in formulating the draft Employment Equality (Age) Regulations.'

In contrast the Trades Union Congress (TUC) stated that the responses of the TUC and the unions to previous consultations have been effectively rejected; while another trades union, NATFHE,[38] stated that: 'Our overall response to the draft age regulations is one of great disappointment. An opportunity to right some of the historical inequalities related to age has been largely squandered in an effort to keep those employers who are not committed to age diversity from protesting.'

One of the major objections of the TUC was around the ability of employers to objectively justify continuing discriminatory practices. These were thought

---

37 Transfer of Undertakings (Protection of Employment) Regulations 1981, replaced by a revised version in 2006.
38 National Association of Teachers in Further and Higher Education.

to be too wide and that there should be a list of specific exceptions, rather than some 'sweeping general justification', which was seen to be the government taking the 'lazy option'. One of the specific exceptions that were included, namely the continuing justification of paying young workers a lower national minimum wage, was thought to, 'constitute blatant direct discrimination against young adult workers'. There was also a major concern that employers would 'level down' employee rights and benefits in order to ensure that they were not discriminating. The TUC wanted a 'no levelling down clause' in the regulations to stop this practice.

The CBI's major concern centred on the retirement age. Their view was that the right to retire staff at 65 years was a 'vital management tool'. Employees must not be allowed to challenge the decision to retire a person at the proper age. This was also the concern of the EEF who were concerned that employees should not be able to challenge the presumption of retirement. They were concerned that if an employer allowed some employees to work beyond retirement age that this would be used by other employees as evidence that their dismissal was for other reasons relating to the individual, apart from retirement. The rather strange solution proposed by the EEF was to put the onus on the employee to prove that retirement was not the principal reason for his or her dismissal.

The CBI, in contrast to the TUC, was in favour of an exception being made for the paying of lower rates to younger workers. They wanted it extended to more than the national minimum wage stating, quite correctly, that one of the odd outcomes of the regulations was that an employer who paid more than the national minimum wage but who still treated younger workers differently would be guilty of age discrimination, while the employer who stuck to the national minimum wage would not be so guilty.

The government published its summary of responses to the 2005 consultation.[39] There were altogether 392 responses. The breakdown of responses is instructive because of the government's continued use of stating how many respondents were in favour or against particular recommendations:

---

39 'Equality and diversity coming of age report on the consultation on the draft Equality (Age) Regulations 2006' (2006).

Table 4.1   **Responses to 2005 consultation by type of respondent**

Type of respondent	Number
Business organisation	162
Public body	63
Educational	34
Trade union	35
Legal	38
Member of the public	60

Generally speaking there was a welcome for the Regulations, but disappointment from some trade unions about the weakness of the Regulations. There was a really interesting point of view raised by both Age Concern and by the Chartered Institute of Personnel Management (CIPD). This was that the tone of the consultation document was essentially negative. According to Age Concern, it accentuated the things that employers will be permitted to do, rather than on what was unlawful. Similarly the CIPD suggested a list of what's not exempted rather than a long list of what is. The problem of course is that in contrast to other discrimination measures there is a long list of exemptions to be covered.

There was particular concern about the retention of the national minimum wage. According to the report: 'The unions were practically as one in their conviction that workers aged 18–21 years should be able to claim the adult rate of pay in their particular job or that age-related provisions should be done away with altogether.' This of course was not a view share by employers. Indeed the CBI argued that there should be protection for employers using age-related pay rates which were different to the levels of the national minimum wage.

Although there was a general welcome for the Regulations there was concern, according to the report, that they would 'give rise to difficulties in their implementation'. The areas of concern are shown in the summary table in the report (Table 4.2).

Table 4.2   Extent of concern about future difficulties

Question	Yes	No	No strong feelings
Will the approach to 'objective justification' cause difficulties?	136	56	46
Will the approach to service-related pay and benefits cause difficulties?	32	71	37
Will the approach to the retirement age cause difficulties?	162	55	14

In contrast the majority of respondents took a more positive view about the arrangements concerning unfair dismissal, occupational pensions and statutory redundancy payments. One statement which concludes Chapter 3 of the consultation report was: 'Employers in general thought the Regulations went too far while unions, organisations for older people and other organisations who were not primarily employers, were of the opinion that they didn't go far enough.'

The UK was one of a number of countries that were able to delay the implementation of the Framework Directive for up to three years.

The Equality Act 2010

The employment provisions of the Equality Act came into effect in October 2010. This included measures to prevent discrimination for reasons connected with the protected characteristic of age in the employment context. The Act also contained the possibility of extending this to include facilities, goods and services which, it was planned, would come into effect in 2012. The Act, in relation to age, replaced the Age Regulations of 2006, with the exception of Schedule 6 which concerned the procedure to be adopted when enforcing the default retirement age.

The Equality Act 2010 replaced a substantial part of the Employment Equality (Age) Regulations 2006[40] (the Age Regulations) with effect from October 2010. The parts not included in the Act were Schedule 6 of the Regulations which dealt with the procedure in considering employees' requests to continue working after the age of 65 (normally) and Schedule 8,

---

40 SI 2006/1031.

which dealt with amendments to other statutes and transitional arrangements. The procedure in Schedule 6 was to be phased out from April 2011.

Section 4 of the Equality Act 2010 lists the nine protected characteristics with which the Act is concerned. These are age, disability, gender reassignment, marriage and civil partnership, pregnancy and maternity, race, religion or belief, sex and sexual orientation. The age characteristic it defines as: 'A person belonging to a particular age group is protected. Age group means persons of the same age or persons of a range of ages.'

This means that an age group could be the 'over fifties' or just 'fifty-year-olds' or 'twenty-one-year-olds' and so on.

PROHIBITED CONDUCT

The Act defines the conduct that is prohibited in relation to the protected characteristics.

Direct discrimination

Section 13(1) describes direct discrimination in the following way: 'A person (A) discriminates against another (B) if, because of a protected characteristic, A treats B less favourably than A treats, or would treat, others.'

The obvious example of direct discrimination with regard to age is the placing of age limits in job advertisements. Stipulating that a person must be of a certain age or within a certain age range is likely to be direct discrimination against those of other ages, except for those nearing retirement age (see later). Less obvious examples of discrimination in recruitment might be the stipulation of a certain length of experience or of the requirement for certain qualifications which are potentially discriminatory if such requirements cannot be justified. The use of advertising media which only appeals, or is accessed by, a certain age group might also infer discrimination. In the survey[41] only 6 per cent of respondents which had recruited in the previous five years had specified an age range in the advertisements for their largest occupational group, but 46 per cent had used years of experience and 62 per cent had specified qualifications in their advertised criteria (prior to the 2006 Regulations).

---

41 See survey of employers' policies, practices and preferences relating to age (2006).

Of course direct discrimination is unlikely to be as obvious as this and the problem to be tackled might be an unwritten policy within an organisation, not to recruit outside a certain age range.[42] Nevertheless the question with regard to direct discrimination is likely to be whether the complainant would have received the same treatment *but for* his or her age, to adapt the test stipulated in a sex discrimination case, *James v Eastleigh Borough Council*. Lord Goff stated in the case that:

> *This simple test possesses the double virtue that, on the one hand, it embraces both the case where the treatment derives from the application of a gender-based [age-based] criterion, and the case where it derives from the selection of the complainant because of his or her sex (age) and on the other hand it avoids, in most cases at least, complicated questions relating to concepts such as intention, motive, reason or purpose.*

Whether age discrimination is the motive or intention is also irrelevant unless it is part of the objective justification (see later). A major issue here is also that it is possible to objectively justify direct age discrimination. There is a proviso in Section 13(2) which allows A to show that the less-favourable treatment is a 'proportionate means of achieving a legitimate aim'. The meaning of this is discussed below, but discrimination on the grounds of age is the only ground for which it is possible to justify direct discrimination apart from the limited possibility of a genuine occupational requirement.

Indirect discrimination

Indirect discrimination is defined, in Section 19(1), as taking place when: 'A person (A) discriminates another (B) if (A) applies to (B) a provision, criterion or practice which is discriminatory in relation to a relevant characteristic of (B)'s.'

Thus it occurs, according to the guidance, when a policy which applies in the same way for everybody has an effect which particularly disadvantages people with a protected characteristic. Where a particular group is disadvantaged in this way, a person in that group is indirectly discriminated against if he or she is put at a disadvantage; unless A can show that it is a proportionate means of achieving a legitimate aim. Where a *prima facie* case of indirect discrimination has been established, the employer will have to satisfy the tribunal that the

---

42 'Equality and diversity: coming of age' (2005). This consultation accompanied the draft Regulations published in 2005 and contains many examples throughout, some of which are relied upon here.

discriminatory requirement or condition (provision, criterion or practice) was justifiable. Clearly, a connection must be established between the function of the employer and the imposition of the requirement or condition (provision, criterion or practice). In addition, a tribunal must assess both the quantitative and the qualitative effects of the requirement or condition (provision, criterion or practice) on those affected by it.[43] In order to justify a requirement or condition (provision, criterion or practice) which has a disproportionate impact the employer must demonstrate that the requirement or condition (provision, criterion or practice) is designed to meet a legitimate objective and that the means chosen are appropriate and necessary (proportionate) to achieving that objective.

An example given in the government consultation on the Act was that of a business which requires applicants for a courier job to have held a driving license for five years. The requirement does not mention age, but it is likely that a higher proportion of workers over the age, say, of 40 years will meet the requirement than those aged, say, 25 years.

Victimisation

Section 27(1) of the Equality Act 2010 provides that: 'A person (A) victimises another person (B) if A subjects B to a detriment because:

1.   B does a protected act, or

2.   A believes that B has done, or may do, a protected act.'

Protected act means bringing proceedings under this Act; giving evidence or information in connection with any proceedings under the Act; doing any other thing for the purpose of or in connection with this Act; making an allegation that A or another person has contravened the Act (Section 27(2)). Giving false information or evidence is not protected if the information or evidence given, or the allegation is made, in bad faith (Section 27(3)). The important change here, compared to previous legislation, is that victimisation is no longer, according to the guidance, treated as a form of discrimination. There is therefore no need for a comparator.

---

43   See *Jones v University of Manchester* [1993] IRLR 218.

Harassment

Section 26(1) of the Equality Act 2010 provides that: 'A person (A) harasses another if –

1.   A engages in unwanted conduct related to a relevant protected characteristic; and

2.   The conduct has the purpose or effect of :

   - violating B's dignity, or
   - creating an intimidating, hostile, degrading, humiliating or offensive environment for B.'

There are three types of harassment, the first of which applies to all protected characteristics except for pregnancy and maternity, and marriage and civil partnership:

- A engages in unwanted conduct related to a relevant protected characteristic which has the purpose or effect of violating B's dignity, or creating an intimidating, hostile, degrading, humiliating or offensive environment for B.

- A engages in any form of unwanted verbal, non-verbal or physical conduct of a sexual nature that has that effect (Section 26(2)).

- Because of B's rejection of or submission to conduct (whether A's or not) related to sex or gender reassignment, A treats B less favourably than B would have been treated if B had not rejected or submitted to the conduct (Section 26(3)).

Account must be taken, in deciding whether the conduct has that effect, of the perception of B, the other circumstances in the case and whether it is reasonable for the conduct to have that effect (Section 26(4)).

Applicants and employees

Section 39 of the Equality Act sets out what an employer may or may not do in relation to employees and applicants:[44]

---

44 For a further definition of employment see notes on Regulation 10 later.

1.   An employer (A) must not discriminate against a person (B).

   – in the arrangements A makes in deciding to whom to offer
     employment;
   – as to the terms on which employment is offered;
   – by not offering B employment.

2.   An employer must not discriminate against an employee.

   – as to B's terms of employment;
   – in the way A affords B access, or not, to opportunities for
     promotion, transfer or training or for receiving any other benefit,
     facility or service;
   – by dismissing B;
   – by subjecting B to any other detriment.

3.   An employer (A) must not victimise a person (B).

   – in the arrangements A makes in deciding to whom to offer
     employment;
   – as to the terms on which employment is offered;
   – by not offering B employment.

Section 40 provides that employees or applicants must not be harassed. This includes circumstances where a third party harasses B in the course of employment and A failed to take steps that would have been reasonably practicable to prevent the third party from doing this. The latter provision does not apply unless A knows that B has been harassed in the course of employment on at least two occasions; it does not matter whether the third party is the same or a different person on each occasion. A third party is a person other than A or an employee of A's.

Objective justification

One of the areas that considerably weakens the impact of the age provisions is the wide scope for justifying exceptions to the principle of equal treatment. The tests for objective justification are, firstly, that the discrimination has a legitimate aim and, secondly, that the means for achieving that aim are proportionate. The 2005 DTI consultation document accompanying the draft Regulations stated that it will not be easy to meet the requirements for objective justification, but also admits that: 'Most other discrimination legislation only allows direct discrimination in cases of genuine occupational requirements', and that for age: 'It will be possible to objectively justify direct discrimination in the same way as indirect discrimination.'

In the 2005 draft Regulations some specific examples of treatment which 'depending upon the circumstances' may be a legitimate and proportionate aim and being justified exceptions to the rule on direct discrimination, were included. In 2003 a government consultation exercise proposed a number of specific aims and the consultees were asked whether the list should be expanded. Some 42 per cent of the respondents were against, while 40 per cent approved and suggested a number of other potentially legitimate aims.[45] The government decided not to have an exhaustive list, as this would prove 'too restrictive and prescriptive'. They then put in a statement which might perhaps have revealed the true scope of the age regulation. They stated: 'We would not want to prevent employers or providers of vocational training from demonstrating that age-related practices could be justified by reference to aims other than those in such a list.'

It would not be conceivable for the government to make this statement about sex or race discrimination, but somehow it is possible with age discrimination.

In the event these examples were left out of the final Regulations (and now the Act) but it is likely that any Court might first turn to Article 6 of the Framework Directive, which permits exceptions in a way that it does not to other forms of discrimination.[46] According to the 2005 consultation document[47] 'a wide variety of aims may be considered legitimate'. Two examples of legitimate aims are 'business needs' and 'considerations of efficiency'. In themselves, of course, these are meaningless phrases but the scope that they imply are potentially of concern. The word 'proportionate' is, it is claimed, the same as the Directive's requirement that the means of pursuing the legitimate aim are 'appropriate and necessary'.[48] The 2005 consultation document states that the requirement of proportionality has three aspects:

1.   The provision, criterion or practice must actually contribute to the pursuit of the legitimate aim; an example of this is if an employer

---

45   'Equality and diversity: coming of age' (2005).
46   Directive 2000/78/EC.
47   'Equality and diversity: coming of age' (2005).
48   Framework Directive 2000/78/EC, Article 6.1,.

or other person wants to use an age-related provision, criterion or practice to encourage loyalty, then they must show that it actually does so.

2.   The importance of the legitimate aim should be weighed up against the discriminatory effects.

3.   One should not discriminate more than is necessary; if there is a choice of means of achieving the aim, then the one with the least discriminatory effect should be used.

There are therefore likely to be a number of exceptions which allow direct as well as indirect discrimination. The specific examples in Article 6 of the Directive are:

- The setting of special conditions on access to employment and vocational training, employment and occupation, including dismissal and remuneration conditions, for young people, older workers and persons with caring responsibilities in order to promote their vocational integration or ensure their protection. It is not altogether clear what the scope of vocational integration.

- The fixing of minimum conditions of age, professional experience or seniority in service for access to employment or to certain advantages linked to employment.

- The fixing of a maximum age for recruitment which is based on the training requirements of the post in question or for a need for a reasonable period in the job before retirement. Of course there would not be a need to have this second exception if there was no mandatory retirement age contained in the contract or in law. Other justifiable exemptions are discussed below.

The issue of legitimate aims and proportionate means has been tested in a number of cases at the European Court of Justice. An early case was that of *Werner Mangold v Rüdiger Helm*. Prior to the transposition of Directive 1999/70 (on fixed-term work), German law placed two curbs on fixed-term contracts of employment, requiring an objective reason justifying the fixed-term or, alternatively, imposing limits on the number of contract renewals (a maximum of three) and on total duration (a maximum of two years). Those restrictions did not apply to contracts with older people however. German law permitted fixed-term contracts, even without the above restrictions, if the employee was aged 60 or over. That situation changed partly with the enactment of the Law on Part-Time Working and Fixed-Term Contracts of 21 December 2000, transposing Directive 1999/70 ('the TzBfG'). Paragraph 14(1) of the TzBfG re-enacted the general rule whereby a fixed-term contract must be based on an objective reason. In the absence of an objective reason, according to Paragraph 14(2), the maximum total duration of the contract was again limited to two years and, subject to that limit, up to three renewals were again permitted. According to Paragraph 14(3) of the TzBfG, however: 'The conclusion of a fixed-term employment contract shall not require objective justification if the worker has reached the age of 58 by the time the fixed-term employment relationship begins.'

In 2006 this age limit was lowered to 52 years. The aim of having less protection for older workers was to increase their employment chances, as stated by the Court of Justice: 'As is clear from the documents sent to the Court by the national Court, the purpose of that legislation is plainly to promote the vocational integration of unemployed older workers, in so far as they encounter considerable difficulties in finding work.'

The Court concluded that: 'The legitimacy of such a public-interest objective cannot reasonably be thrown in doubt.' Thus the provision in German law had a legitimate aim in seeking to promote the employment of older workers. The next question for the Court was whether the measure was an appropriate and necessary (proportionate) means to achieve that aim. The problem was that the measure applied to all workers over the age of 52 years, regardless of their individual situation, for example, whether they were unemployed or employed. The Court concluded that:

> In so far as such legislation takes the age of the worker concerned as the only criterion for the application of a fixed-term contract of employment, when it has not been shown that fixing an age threshold, as such, regardless of any other consideration linked to the structure of the labour market in question or the personal situation of the person concerned, is objectively necessary to the attainment of the objective which is the vocational integration of unemployed older workers, it must be considered to go beyond what is appropriate and necessary in order to attain the objective pursued.

Thus the measure failed the test of proportionality because it used age as the only factor and thus considerably weakened employment protection for many workers in the age range who were employed and not in need of special measures.

It appears, therefore, as if there is a real need to show that the means are appropriate and necessary, although in other cases it seems that the bar has not been set so high.

In the case of *Seldon v Clarkson Wright* a solicitor had been compulsorily retired from the partnership of his firm when he reached the age of 65 years. The firm identified three aims which were held to be legitimate. These were ensuring associates were given the opportunity of partnership after a reasonable period; facilitating the planning of the partnership and workforce across individual departments by having a realistic long-term expectation as to when vacancies will arise; and limiting the need to expel partners by way of performance management, thus contributing to the congenial and supportive culture in the firm. The first two of these were described as provisions relating to 'dead men's shoes'. The third was defined as one of 'collegiality'. The Court displayed all the ignorance and bigotry of those who favour age discrimination when it stated that:

> It seems to me that an aim intended to produce a happy workplace has to be within or consistent with the government's social policy justification for the regulations. It is not just within partnerships that it may be thought better to have a cut-off age rather than force an assessment of a person's falling off in performance as they get older.

> I have not read all the evidence put in by the Government in the Age UK litigation [see later], but my experience would tell me that it is a justification for having a cut-off age that people will be allowed to retire with dignity. To have such a policy requires a cut-off age which some when they reach it will think too low but it does not follow that it is not justified to have a cut-off age.

There is the failure to recognise that older people are not a homogenous group and that the application of uniform ages for stopping work, and so on are entirely inappropriate and not justifiable. This is a failure that is repeated in other cases described in this chapter, where the courts readily accept as legitimate the arbitrary removal of older people from the workforce to make room for others.

Exceptions

OCCUPATIONAL REQUIREMENTS

Schedule 9 of the Act provides the exception for occupational requirements if the application of the requirement is a proportionate means of achieving a legitimate aim.

The example given in the 2005 consultation is that of an actor who might need to be of a certain age, but even that would need objective justification to show that it was: 'Proportionate to apply that requirement in the particular case'.[49] The same consultation pointed out that it is unlikely to be a great issue for age discrimination. This measure is used in the other statutes and regulations concerning discrimination because it is an exception to the rule that there can be no justification of direct discrimination. As we have seen above, somewhat depressingly, this rule does not apply in the case of age discrimination, where it is permissible to justify such discrimination generally.

STATUTORY AUTHORITY

This provides that nothing in the Act shall make unlawful any act done in order to comply with a statutory provision or for the purpose of safeguarding national security. An obvious statutory example quoted in the 2005 consultation document, is the Licensing Act 1964 which prohibited the employment of persons under the age of 18 years in a bar when it is open for the sale of alcohol.

POSITIVE ACTION

Section 158 of the Equality Act 2010 allows generally for the taking of positive action measures to alleviate disadvantage suffered by people who share one of the protected characteristics. This can only be done if the participation of persons who share a particular protected characteristic is 'disproportionately low' (Section 158(1)(c)). This provision is limited in that it will need to be interpreted in accord with EU law and decisions of the European Court of

---

49 Regulation 8(2)(b).

Justice. Section 159 then deals with positive action in relation to recruitment and promotion.

In the 2005 consultation document two examples are given. The first is an employer placing a recruitment advertisement only in a magazine read by young people, in order to encourage applications from young people. This might amount to indirect age discrimination unless it can be shown to come within the terms of Section 158, by reasonably appearing to the employer that it helps compensate for disadvantage suffered by that age group within the organisation. The second example is an employer asking a head hunter to search for candidates in a particular age group which is under-represented in the workforce. According to the consultation document: 'As long as applications from people in other age groups are not excluded, this is covered by the positive action provision.'

RETIREMENT

Regulation 30(1) of the Age Regulations was concerned with the exception for retirement and stated that: 'Nothing in Part 2 or 3 shall render unlawful the dismissal of an employee at or over the age of 65 years where the reason for the dismissal is retirement.'

As shown elsewhere in this book (see Chapter 7), the mandatory retirement provisions were to be phased out from April 2011, thus ending this rather blatant piece of legislative age discrimination.

NATIONAL MINIMUM WAGE

This allows for differential rates of pay related to age. This is in relation to the hourly rate set by the Secretary of State[50] or in relation to differential pay for contracts of apprenticeship.[51]

There are, of course, two lower bands for young people: one for those aged 16 and 17 years; the other for those aged between 18 and 20 years inclusive. This measure only applies to the age bands and pay levels established by the statutory measures on the national minimum wage. Objective justification would be needed to pay a 16-year-old at a different rate to a 17-year-old. Similarly, if an employer were paying rates which were above the levels of the

---

50   National Minimum Wage Act 1998, Section 1(3).
51   National Minimum Wage Regulations 1999, regulation 12(3).

national minimum wage, they would need to justify this, even if the same age bands were used. There is also a lower band payable to apprentices.

In government evidence to the Low Pay Commission (November 2007) it was stated that: 'The government's aim is to afford very young workers some protection from poverty pay, while maintaining the incentives for 16–17-year-olds to remain in education or job-related training and build up their knowledge and future earnings potential.'

This measure does exploit young people, however, and is an example of age discrimination written into statute with a business motivation outweighing any individual rights considerations. Why should not employers be expected to provide objective justification for paying some people less according to their age. They could probably do so in a number of cases, but why is it necessary to undermine the age regulation in this way? (Sargeant 2010a).

PROVISION OF BENEFITS BASED ON LENGTH OF SERVICE

This is concerned with the issue of benefits related to length of service and seniority. It is not uncommon for employees to be given extra benefits related to length of service with an organisation. Holiday entitlement is one example of a benefit that might be linked to length of service. Without further provisions such benefits might constitute unlawful age discrimination, because it will tend to mean that older (and longer serving) employees receive greater benefits than less-experienced (and often younger) employees. Para 10(1)[52] provides that: 'It is not a contravention for a person (A) to put a person (B) at a disadvantage, when compared to another (C), in relation to the provision of a benefit, facility or service insofar as the disadvantage is because B has a shorter period of service than C.'

There is a further proviso relating to service that is longer than five years. In this case it must reasonably appear to A that the way in which the criterion of length of service is used 'fulfils a business need'.[53] It is difficult to see why the government bothered with this proviso for service over five years when it will be almost impossible to disprove.

Obvious benefits that are linked to service include pay scales and entry into health and employee discount schemes. It is for the employer to decide which

---

52 Schedule 9 Part 2 Equality Act 2010.
53 Paragraph 10(2).

formula to use to calculate length of service. It may be either the length of time a worker has been working at or above a particular level or it can be the length of time the worker has been working for the employer in total. This distinction is important because it means that the five-year rule can be used again and again. Thus if a worker is employed as a shop-floor operative for a few years, doing work of a like nature, and is then promoted to being supervisor, then the five-year period can start all over again while they do work of a like nature which is different to that done previously. The 2005 consultation gives a legal example: 'A law firm uses a four-year pay scale for trainees, a five-year pay scale for junior associates, and a five-year pay scale for senior associates. The natural progression for lawyers at this firm is to rise automatically through each of these scales in turn.'

The question arises whether, for the purposes of the five-year exemption, they should be seen as a single pay scale of 14 years (in which case the last nine years would not be covered by the five-year exemption). In order to use the five-year exemption for all three scales, the employer would have to demonstrate, if challenged, that all three apply to sufficiently different kinds of work. It might be argued for instance that the responsibilities of the trainees, junior associates and senior associates are different.

Presumably this would not be difficult for the firm to do. Thus the five-year blanket exemption would apply to each of these pay scales, allowing them to continue without the need for further justification.

THE PROVISION OF ENHANCED REDUNDANCY PAYMENTS

The subject of statutory redundancy payments has been discussed elsewhere in this book. The payments are calculated using a combination of the length of service and age. The older the redundant employee the higher the rate of payment, at least until the age of 64 years when there was a severe tapering off of benefit. The government was clearly of the view that this would be discriminatory on the grounds of age and put forward a proposal to level out the payment to one week's pay per year of service up to a maximum of 20 years. This would clearly have amounted to a regression in the rights of those over the age of 40 years who would have suffered a drop in payments as part of the implementation of the Directive and this undoubtedly would have led to an indefensible legal challenge as such regression is specifically excluded by the Directive. In the final version of the Regulations, and now the Equality Act, there is a retreat back to the standard formula, but employers are to be allowed to pay more so long as they follow the same formula. The age restrictions at either end are also removed.

There is, an apparent contradiction between the ability to take length of service into account as a criterion in selection for redundancy and a desire to end discrimination upon the basis of age (Sargeant 2009). Use of this criterion will tend to favour longer serving employees, and therefore, older employees at the expense of younger ones. The same can be said of redundancy payments schemes which provide extra money to those with longer service.

A number of cases have dealt with the issues arising from this apparent contradiction. These cases concerned redundancy schemes which were all much more generous than the state scheme but which were claimed to discriminate against individuals, on the grounds of age, in particular circumstances. The main point in all the cases is whether redundancy schemes which are related to length of service can be objectively justified as having a legitimate aim with proportionate means of achieving that aim.

Rolls Royce v Unite the Union considered two collective agreements which had an agreed matrix to be used to choose who should be selected for redundancy. There were five criteria against which an individual could score between four and 24 points. In addition there was a length of service criterion which awarded one point for each year of continuous service. Thus, older employees would have an important advantage over younger ones. *MacCulloch v ICI plc* concerned a redundancy scheme which had been in existence since 1971. The amount of payment was linked to service up to a maximum of 10 years, and the size of the redundancy payment increased with age. The claimant was 37 years old and received 55 per cent of her salary as a payment, but she claimed that someone aged between 50 and 57 years would have received 175 per cent of salary under the scheme.

Loxley v BAE Systems had a contractual redundancy scheme in which each employee received two weeks' pay for the first five years of employment, three weeks' for each of the next five years and four weeks' pay for each year after 10 years. There was also a further age related payment of two weeks' pay for each year after the age of 40 years. All this was subject to a maximum of two years' pay. The scheme was amended for older workers approaching retirement when the retirement age was raised, but essentially the claimant, who was 61 years of age, was not entitled to any enhanced payments for voluntary redundancy as he had an entitlement to a pension.

The essential feature of all these cases concerned whether it was possible to have general justification for taking into account length of service or whether it should be justified in each particular case. In fact the general justification argument won, relying substantially on European case law.

THE PROVISION OF LIFE ASSURANCE COVER FOR RETIRED WORKERS

Para 14[54] provides that: 'Where a person arranges for workers to be provided with life assurance cover after their early retirement for ill health, it will be permissible to end that cover when they reach normal retirement age or, if none, then 65 years.'

These extra exceptions for age, of course, could be just a reflection of an increased complexity when compared to other grounds of discrimination. It is part of the argument of this book, however, that the numbers reflect a greater willingness to countenance exceptions which are based upon a pragmatic and business approach rather than an individual human rights one.

CHILD CARE

Para 15 of Schedule 9, Part 2, of the Act creates an exception for benefits which relate to the provision of child care where the benefit is limited to children of a particular age group. This includes natural parents and others who have parental responsibility for a child. This was a provision newly introduced in 2010 and resulted from the European Court of Justice decision in *Coleman v Attridge Law*[55] which held that discrimination by association with a person with a disability was included within the protection of the Framework Directive on Equal Treatment in Employment and Occupation. The same principle could be applied to all the other protected characteristics, so this measure ensures that apparent discrimination in favour of a parent or someone with parental responsibility because of the age of the child does not amount to age discrimination.

---

54 Schedule 9 Part 2 Equality Act 2010.
55 Case C-303/06.

Burden of Proof

Proving that discrimination has taken place can be very difficult. In order to assist complainants, Section 136 provides that it will be the respondent's task to show that discrimination did not take place, rather than the respondent having to prove that it did so. In any claim where a person is alleging discrimination, harassment or victimisation under the Equality Act, the burden of proof may shift to the respondent. Section 136(2) provides that if there are facts from which the Court could decide, in the absence of any other explanation, that a person (A) contravened the provision concerned, the Court must hold that the contravention occurred. Section 136(3) provides that this does not apply if A is able to show that A did not contravene the provision. Thus, once the complainant has established the facts from which the Court could conclude that a contravention had taken place, the onus switches to the respondent to show that there was no such breach.

Remedies on Complaints to Employment Tribunals

In a complaint to an employment tribunal the proceedings or complaint may not be brought after the end of three months starting with the date to which the complaint relates, unless the employment tribunal thinks that some other period is 'just and equitable' (Section 123(1)). There is a mechanism for the complainant to obtain information by asking questions by using the prescribed form or otherwise. The questions and answers are admissible as evidence and the Court or tribunal may draw inferences from a failure of the respondent to answer within eight weeks or from evasive or equivocal answers.

If the employment tribunal finds that there has been a contravention of a provision, then it may:

- Make a declaration as to the rights of the complainant and the respondent in relation to the complainant.

- Order the respondent to pay compensation to the complainant.

- Make an appropriate recommendation.

There is no statutory upper limit for compensation in discrimination claims or those concerned with a breach of the equality clause.

The ability to make an appropriate recommendation was introduced by the Equality Act 2010. It is a recommendation that within a specified period the respondent takes specified steps for the purpose of obviating or reducing the adverse effect of any matter to which the proceedings relate, either on the complainant or more generally, such as the wider workforce. A tribunal could, for example, recommend the introduction of an equal opportunities policy, recommend the re-training of staff or recommend the making public of the selection criteria for transfers and promotions.

The Future

In 2010 the newly elected coalition government also declared its intention to amend the Regulations and phase out the default retirement age from April 2011 and embarked on a consultation to achieve this in July 2010.[56] The government stated in the document that this was one of the steps that it was taking to enable and encourage people to work for longer. The consultation was about the best way of doing this and one concern was how to enable employer and employee to discuss retirement and flexible working without it being construed as age discrimination. The policy was still to leave the possibility of an employer-justified retirement age (EJRA), where the employer could justify this by showing a legitimate aim and that an EJRA was the most appropriate way of achieving that aim. Given the broadness of the exception allowed for in Article 6 of the Framework Directive (see Chapter 5), it remains to be seen whether employers are willing to justify mandatory retirement at any particular age.

---

56 Phasing out the Default Retirement Age Consultation document July 2010 Department for Business, Innovation and Skills plus the Department for Work and Pensions <http://www.bis.gov.uk/Consultations/retirement-age>.

5

Age Discrimination and the EU

There is ample evidence that discrimination takes place in the EU. One EU-wide indicative survey[1] of people's perceptions of discrimination[2] found that the most often cited ground for discrimination was age (5 per cent) followed by racial or ethnic origin (3 per cent), religion or belief, physical disability, learning difficulties or mental illness (2 per cent each). A 2008 survey by Eurobarometer[3] (already referred to in Chapter 1) reveals further levels of discrimination. One question asked was how, using a scale from 1 to 10 (with 10 being the highest approval rating), you would feel about someone from each of the following categories in the highest political position in your country? The average scores were as follows:

Category	Score
A person from a different religion than the majority of the population	9.0
A woman	8.9
A disabled person	8.0
A homosexual (gay man or lesbian woman)	7.0
A person under 30	6.4
A person from a different ethnic minority than the majority of the population	6.4
A person aged over 75	5.4

There is clearly an issue with people under 30 and those over 75, although such questions inevitably encourage the respondents to think in terms of

---

1 Marsh and Sahin-Dikmen (2003).
2 In relation to racial or ethnic origin, religion or beliefs, disability, age and sexual orientation.
3 Special Eurobarometer 296; 'Discrimination in the European Union: perceptions, experiences and attitudes' (2008) European Commission, Luxembourg.

stereotypes and generalise in a way which might not apply to a particular person. The survey generally found that age was the most common self-reported discrimination with 6 per cent of respondents experiencing this over the course of the year. There was, of course, much variation between the member states. The highest annual rate of self reported discrimination was in Austria, with age discrimination making up a large share of this. Some 11 per cent of Austrians said that they had experienced age discrimination. Another high figure was in the Czech Republic where 12 per cent reported experiencing such discrimination.

One of the really interesting questions asked was: 'When a company wants to hire someone and has the choice between two candidates with equal skills and qualifications, which of the following criteria may, in your opinion, put one candidate at a disadvantage?' The responses were as follows:

Criteria	%
The candidate's look, dress-sense or presentation	50
The candidate's age	45
The candidate's skin colour or ethnic origin	42
A disability	41
The candidate's general physical appearance	38
The candidate's way of speaking, his or her accent	34
The expression of a religious belief	26
The candidate's gender	22
Whether the candidate is a smoker or not	18
The candidate's name	14
The candidate's address	9

So age is seen as a critical factor in recruitment and there is plenty of evidence in this book and elsewhere that supports this view.

Demographic Change

The European Commission has been concerned about the demographic change that is taking place and its impact upon the labour market and future plans for growth of the European economy. In 1995 the Commission produced a report on the demographic situation.[4] Its opening title sums up some of the prejudices about ageing, when it stated: 'Demographic ageing must not be confused with a decrepit society.' This process resulted from two major trends:

1.   The scope for couples to decide how many children they have and when they should have them.

2.   Social and medical progress which has resulted in a longer lifespan and a drop in mortality.

Improvements in life expectancy was initially achieved by reducing infant mortality. Now it was being improved by people living longer, so that children who reached their first birthday were unlikely to die before the age of 60. The result of this was that just lumping together people over a certain age as 'the elderly' was unsatisfactory. There were now two distinct groups: firstly the retired who are in full possession of their mental and physical abilities and who are well integrated into the economy; secondly those who are really 'biologically aged' with reduced independence and high dependence upon external resources for their support. The increase in numbers in both of these groups has important outcomes. The result of this in number terms was that the number of young people aged under 20 will fall by 9.5 million (11 per cent), the number of working age people will decline by 13 million (6.4 per cent) and the number of retired adults will increase by over 37 million (50 per cent). This, of course, is partly explained by the arrival of the 'baby boomers' (born from the late 1940s to the middle 1960s) into retirement. This change will have an effect on the economy of the EU and the individual member states.

One astonishing indicator of the economic burden resulting from demographic change internationally is to look at the ratio of the retired to workers. In the OECD area[5] the ratio in 2000 was about 38 retirees for every 100 workers. This is projected to grow by 2050 to just over 70 retirees per 100 workers. 'In Europe, this ratio is projected to be close to one retiree for every worker.'[6]

One solution for maintaining, or increasing growth, is to increase the level of employment. The 1995 report illustrated the issues in relation to employment in what was a clear precursor of the Lisbon strategy adopted in 2000 (see later):

---

4   'The demographic situation in the European Union' (1995).
5   Some 35 countries in the Organisation for Economic Co-operation and Development.
6   'Live longer, work longer' (2006).

- The proportion of active women over the age of 15 is significantly lower than the equivalent figure for men, especially amongst older age groups.

- The young are particularly affected by unemployment.

- The impact of early retirement means that there are only half as many workers in the 60–65 year age group as in the 55–59 year age group.

The population change for the EU was not uniform in each country, although the overall trend is common:

Table 5.1   Population growth in the EU (per cent) between 1995 and 2025

Country	Under 19 years	20–59 years	60+ years
Austria	−11.4	−3.1	+56.4
Belgium	−9.8	−6.1	+46.1
Denmark	+2.6	−3.0	+41.5
Finland	−5.2	−4.1	+66.6
France	−6.1	+0.2	+57.7
Germany	−12.1	−13.5	+51.2
Greece	−2.06	+0.5	+41.4
Ireland	−25.1	+2.7	+67.7
Italy	−19.4	−15.2	+40.7
Netherlands	−1.2	−1.2	+79.5
Portugal	−8.8	+5.0	+34.1
Spain	−17.2	−4.4	+45.3
Sweden	+1.2	+3.7	+38.1
UK	−8.2	−2.8	+43.6

For the EU as a whole the number of young adults (25–39 years) started to decline in 2005 and the decline will accelerate (to 16 per cent between 2010 and 2030). The number of 40- to 54-year-olds will start to decline from 2010 whilst the number of people aged over 55 will grow by 9.6 per cent between 2005 and 2010, and by 15.5 per cent between 2010 and 2030.[7]

---

7   Green Paper: 'Confronting demographic change: a new solidarity between the generation', (2005), p. 94.

Clearly the effects of the demographic change will be felt at different times in different parts of the EU. Some countries were expecting a short-term gain in the population of working age, such as Ireland and Portugal. Other countries have a much more serious short-term problem, such as Italy and Germany where there are significant falls in the youngest age group and the working age population, combined with large increases in the older age group.

The European Commission later summed up the concerns posed by the ageing population.[8] There was:

- A relative decline of the population of working age and the ageing of the workforce.

- Pressure on pension systems and public finances resulting from a growing number of retired people and a decline in the working-age population.

- A growing need for old-age care and health care – the big increase in numbers of the very old will lead to a growth in demand for formal care systems.

- A growing diversity among older people in terms of resources and needs – there will be differences in the family and housing situation, educational and health status and income and wealth which will determine the quality of life of older people.

- The gender issue – women account for almost two thirds of the population above 65 years.

Thus there were to be significant policy issues concerned with, firstly, the European employment strategy in order to bring about an increase in the employment rate of older workers; secondly, with social protection policies, including reversing the trend towards early retirement; thirdly, health policies which include giving special attention to medical and social research relating to ageing; and fourthly, policies concerned with discrimination and social exclusion.

---

8   'Towards a Europe for all ages', Communication from the Commission COM (1999) 221.

The Lisbon Strategy

In March 2000 the EU Council of Ministers at the Lisbon Spring Council Meeting adopted a strategy to raise the rate of growth and employment. A major factor in this was the poor performance of the EU economy compared to that of the US as well as a concern with the emerging economies of Asia. The Community set itself the target of becoming, 'the most dynamic and competitive knowledge-based economy in the world, capable of sustainable economic growth with more and better jobs and greater social cohesion, and respect for the environment'.

The key challenges for the EU were global competition, the forthcoming enlargement and the ageing population. Europe was more likely to be successful if it worked together rather than tackling the issue from an individual member states perspective. It was a policy of combining economic growth with a concern to advance social cohesion. The EU wanted to be a high-productivity, high-value-added, high-employment economy, rather than a low-pay, low-productivity one, in order to maintain its commitment to social and environmental Europe.

The Lisbon Strategy called for:

- Increasing the total employment rate to 67 per cent by 2005 and 70 per cent by 2010; increasing the female employment rate to 57 per cent by 2005 and 60 per cent by 2010; increasing the employment rate of older workers to 50 per cent by 2010.

- Defining a multi-annual programme on adaptability of business, collective bargaining, wage moderation, improved productivity, lifelong learning, new technologies and the flexible organisation of work by 2002.

- Removing disincentives for female labour force participation.

- Adapting the European social model to the transformation towards the knowledge economy; facilitating social security in cross-border movement; temporary agencies directive; sustainability of pension schemes; open method of coordination in the field of social protection.

- Eradicating poverty; social inclusion; specific target groups.

Despite a relaunch in 2005, the Lisbon strategy, in respect of older workers, failed to achieve its objectives. The overall employment rate for older workers (55–64) was 46 per cent.[9] Only 12 member states had an employment rate which met the target of 50 per cent. Nine member states were more than ten percentage points short. These were: Malta, Hungary, Poland, Slovenia, Luxembourg, Italy, Belgium, France and Slovakia. Malta, in 2008, had the lowest rate with just 30 per cent of the age group in employment.[10] Table 5.2 provides a breakdown of the EU average employment rates by age.

Table 5.2   Employment rates by age in the EU 2008

Age	Rate (%)
15–19	19.1
20–24	55.2
25–29	75.8
30–34	80.4
35–39	81.9
40–44	82.4
45–49	81.1
50–54	75.5
55–59	59.0
60–64	30.2
65+	4.8

There is a steep fall in the employment rate after the age of 55 years and the level of employment for those over 65 is really very low. This is partly, of course, a reflection of national policies on retirement and social security systems. While the UK, for example, is proposing to raise the state pension age to 66 years in the near future, the French government faced opposition when it proposes to raise its pension age from 60 to 62 years.

In the light of the failure of this aspect of the Lisbon strategy the European Commission concluded that raising participation rates will not be easy, partly because it will depend on changes in cultural and socio-psychological factors, in particular attitudes to older people in employment, and partly because it

9   Communication from the Commission Europe 2020: 'A European strategy for smart, sustainable and inclusive growth', COM(2010) 2020.
10   'The social situation in the European Union 2009', European Commission, (2010).

will require important changes in policy instruments to achieve changes in behaviour of employers and workers.

In a newer policy document, *Europe 2020,*[11] the Commission describes some of Europe's structural weaknesses. These included:

> *Demographic ageing is accelerating. As the baby-boom generation retires, the EU's active population will start to shrink as from 2013/2014. The number of people aged over 60 is now increasing twice as fast as it did before 2007 – by about two million every year compared to one every million per year previously. The combination of a smaller working population and a higher share of retired people will place additional strains on our welfare systems.*

Perhaps more realistically than the Lisbon targets, the new target relates to the working population aged between 20 and 64. The target is to increase the employment rate for this group to 75 per cent by 2020, 'through greater involvement of women, older workers and the better integration of migrant workers in the work force'. It is disappointing that there is an upper age limit and no targets for those over 64.

Immigration

One way of mitigating the effects of an ageing population is to, at least partially, fill the gaps in the labour market with immigrant workers. Many of the statistics that one reads about the ageing population do not appear to take into account the effects of inward migration. The EU's perspective is that although managed immigration will help, it will not solve the problems associated with demographic change.

Immigration is thus unlikely to solve the problem, but it may mitigate it. As the European Commission Green Paper on 'Confronting demographic change'[12] stated: 'Immigration from outside the EU could help to mitigate the effects of the falling population between now and 2025, although it is not

---

11 Communication from the Commission Europe 2020: 'A European strategy for smart, sustainable and inclusive growth', COM(2010) 2020.
12 Green Paper 'Confronting demographic change: a new solidarity between generations' (2005); see also Green Paper on 'An EU approach to managing economic migration' (2004).

enough on its own to solve all the problems associated with ageing, and it is no substitute for economic reforms.'

The same Green Paper points out that there has never been economic growth without population growth. Ways of increasing population growth include a higher birth rate and inward migration. Immigration has clearly mitigated the effects of population decline or ageing in some countries, but from an EU perspective the migration of workers from the post 2004 member states to the rest of the EU may help some member states like the UK, but only adds to the population decline in those migrant exporting states and makes no difference at all to overall EU statistics. Indeed one analysis showed that about one-third of all non-nationals living in member states were citizens of other member states of the EU.[13]

Using immigration as the sole means of reducing the impact of ageing on the labour market is not a realistic choice. Massive increases in immigration until 2030 would be required. Estimates suggest that the annual net migration into the EU was of the order of 850,000 per annum during the 1990s. The annual inward migration necessary to keep the support ratio (4.3 persons of working age to one person aged 65 plus) at the same as in 1995 would be 15 times greater than the 1990s level. Indeed, according to the UN estimates, by 2040–2050 in some scenarios there would be a need by the EU for net immigration equivalent to half the world's annual population growth.[14]

As the migrant population would also be ageing, it may only put off the problem rather than solve it.[15] In any case there would be other social and economic issues concerned with integration that would need to be tackled if there were to be such an increase.

The Framework Directive

The justification for Directive 2000/78/EC establishing a general framework for equal treatment in employment and occupation was Article 13 of the EC Treaty, introduced by the Treaty of Amsterdam 1998. This states simply: 'Without prejudice to the other provisions of this Treaty and within the limits of the powers conferred by it upon the Community, the Council, acting

---

13 'First annual report on migration and integration' (2004).
14 'Replacement migration: is it a solution to declining and ageing populations?' (2000).
15 'Immigration, integration and employment' (2003).

unanimously on a proposal from the Commission and after consulting the European Parliament, may take appropriate action to combat discrimination based on sex, racial or ethnic origin, religion or belief, disability, age or sexual orientation.'

It is interesting to note that Article 13 does not confine the 'appropriate action' to that of employment only. The Framework Directive, however, only applies to 'employment and occupation' with regard to discrimination on the grounds of religion or belief, disability, age or sexual orientation. In contrast Directive 2000/43/EC implementing the principle of equal treatment between persons irrespective of racial or ethnic origin, introduced at much the same time, was not restricted to employment. This latter Directive included such matters as social security and healthcare, and access to and supply of goods and services, including housing.[16]

Sex discrimination was excluded from the Directive, because the Commission believed that the appropriate legal basis for such action was Article 141 EC Treaty,[17] from which a number of Directives dealing with equal treatment had already been adopted.[18]

The Framework Directive has been subject to some criticism for having an outdated approach. Professor Hepple[19] stated that:

> The main defects are that it lacks clarity and perpetuates a fragmented and inconsistent approach to different grounds of discrimination; it is limited to employment and occupation so placing a burden on employers which they cannot be expected to discharge unless corresponding duties are placed on providers of education, healthcare and transport; it is based only on negative prohibitions against direct and indirect discrimination and harassment rather than positive duties to promote equality; and it focuses on individualised retrospective fault finding rather than a strategic approach.

It is difficult not to agree with these criticisms in relation to action on age discrimination. The Framework Directive is part of a fragmented approach

---

16   Article 3 Directive 2000/43/EC.
17   See 'Proposal for a Council Directive establishing a general framework for equal treatment in employment and occupation' (1999).
18   Such as Directive 76/207 EEC on the implementation of the principle of equal treatment between men and women; subsequently amended by Directive 2002/73/EC.
19   Hepple (2001) at the Nuffield Foundation.

to discrimination as it is essentially one of three Directives (race and equal treatment Directives) making such discrimination unlawful. These Directives are inconsistent in their scope, but sometimes search for consistency where it may not be needed. It does not impose a positive duty to end discrimination. The Directive also distinguishes between those aspects of age discrimination which are undesirable, and should therefore be made unlawful, and those aspects which are desirable, and should therefore be permitted. One study sympathetic to this approach stated:

> ... *age distinctions based upon unfair assumptions and stereotypes are undesirable but other distinctions upon the grounds of age are rooted in rational considerations that are not incompatible with the recognition of individual dignity, serve valuable social and economic objectives, and often are designed to benefit of particular age groups.*[20]

This, of course, is true. The difficulty is where to draw the line between those distinctions which are desirable and those which are undesirable. It is also important to accept that both sides of the dividing line consist of discriminatory measures. It is just that, according to this view, some discriminatory measures are 'rational', 'serve valuable economic and social objectives' and benefit 'particular age groups'. This illustrates the different approach to age when compared to other grounds of discrimination. It is unlikely that it would be acceptable to use terms such as these when referring to gender or race.

Despite this, the Directive was a huge leap forward and, as a result of its adoption, at least 27 countries in Europe have made some aspects of age discrimination unlawful, as well as taking action on the other grounds of disability, religion or belief and sexual orientation. As a result of this Directive the UK has regulations which outlaw some aspects of age discrimination, only a few years after the government firmly adopted a voluntarist and non-coercive approach.

THE PREAMBLE

In Chapter 1 there was some discussion about the contradictory approaches to age discrimination contained in the Directive. On the one hand there is a human rights/equal treatment/fundamental rights justification contained in Paragraphs 1–6 of the preamble. There is then a more functional/economic/ business rationale which dominates much of the rest of the preamble. This is

---

20 O'Cinneide (2005).

clearly stated in Paragraph 11 which relates that discrimination on the various grounds 'may undermine the objectives of the EC Treaty'. These objectives are 'a high level of employment and social protection, raising the standard of living and the quality of life, economic and social cohesion and solidarity and the free movement of persons.'

In the rest of the preamble there are a number of specific areas that are excluded[21] from the scope of the Directive and it is worth noting these. They are:

- Social security and social protection schemes whose benefits are not treated as pay, nor any other form of state payment related to providing access to employment or maintaining employment (Paragraph 13).

- National provisions laying down retirement ages (Paragraph 14); the UK, unlike some other member states, did not have such provisions. Apart from the state pension age, most retirement ages are a matter of individual contracts (see Chapter 5).

- The recruitment, promotion, maintenance in employment or training of an individual who is not competent, capable and available to perform the essential functions of the post concerned or to undergo the relevant training (Paragraph 17).

This was a major issue for employers in the 2003 government consultation. There was a lot of concern that it would be difficult to dismiss older workers whose competence was failing. Indeed keeping a default retirement age was seen as a way of not having to tackle this issue as older employees would automatically leave when this age was reached.

- The armed forces, the police, the prison or emergency services are not required to recruit or keep in employment people who do not have the required capacity to carry out the range of functions required of them (Paragraph 18).

- In addition all or part of the armed forces. Each member state is left to decide whether to apply the rules to all or part of their armed forces (Paragraph 19).

---

21 Only those that are relevant to age are listed here.

- Where there is a genuine and determining occupational requirement (Paragraph 23) (see later).

- Differences in treatment which can be justified in relation to 'legitimate employment policy, labour market and vocational training objectives' (Paragraph 25) (see later).

Most of the other provisions of the Preamble are reflected in the individual Articles of the main text. It is worth noting that Paragraph 28 states that the provisions in the Directive lay down the minimum requirements and that member states have the option of introducing or maintaining more favourable provisions. The European Commission believes that some member states have introduced more favourable measures and indeed, 'this has involved the introduction of an entirely new, rights-based approach to anti-discrimination legislation and policy'.[22] The UK however had introduced its Age Regulations in accordance with the European Communities Act 1972. Section 2(2) of this Act, of course, only permits the use of Regulations to implement Community law and there are no provisions for such Regulations to go beyond the provisions of that law. Paragraph 28 also states that: 'The implementation of this Directive should not serve to justify any regression in relation to the situation which already prevails in each member state.'

This was an issue with the government's proposals to equalise the amount of statutory compensation given for redundancy to one week's pay (subject to the statutory maximum) for each year of service, regardless of age. This replaced an age-based system which gave workers over the age of 40 more compensation than their younger colleagues, namely one and a half weeks' pay per year of service over that age. The government's initial proposal to reduce it to one week for everyone appeared to be a regression as far as older workers made redundant were concerned.

Direct and Indirect Discrimination

The purpose of the Directive is set out in Article 1 as being to lay down a general framework for combating discrimination and putting into effect the principle of equal treatment. This is virtually identical to Article 1 of the Race Directive (2000/43/EC). It is interesting that the Commission's original proposal for Article 1 copied the model set out in the Equal Treatment Directive

---

22 'Equality and non-discrimination in an enlarged European Union' (2004).

(76/207/EEC) and spelt out the areas to which the principle of equal treatment would apply; namely, 'access to employment and occupation, including promotion, vocational training, employment conditions and membership of certain organisations'. These specific areas were moved into a separate Article (Article 3) covering the scope of the Directive in the final version and replaced with a general commitment to anti-discrimination and the principle of equal treatment here. As has been suggested elsewhere[23] it is important to realise that the Framework Directive only provides a minimum level of protection. This minimalist approach is especially evident with regard to age.[24]

The principle of equal treatment here means, according to Article 2, that there should be no direct or indirect discrimination on the grounds of age.[25] Thus Article 2.2(a) states that direct discrimination shall be taken to occur where one person is treated less favourably than another in a comparable situation. When one relates this to age, of course, there may be a variety of problems:

- There may be an issue where one may not be comparing like with like. Is the treatment of a 20-year-old to be compared to the treatment of a 65-year-old in all circumstances (except where a legitimate exception can be objectively justified)? Perhaps the answer is yes, but there must be a certain unease that maybe the 20-year-old requires more development, training, protection and so on when compared to someone who may have been at work for 40 years plus. On the other hand perhaps this view is the result of ageist thinking and they are both employees who should not be discriminated between, provided they are, in the Directive's words: 'In a comparable situation'.

---

23 See Whittle (2002).
24 With regard to disability there is also, of course, an important duty on employers in Article 5 to make reasonable accommodation.
25 Another aspect to this, of course, is that the principle of equal treatment can justify the equally bad treatment of a class of employees. In *Zafar v Glasgow City Council*, for example, an employment tribunal held that an individual had been treated less favourably than others because the individual had been subject to treatment falling far below that of a 'reasonable employer'. This presumption of less favourable treatment was not allowed to stand because, hypothetically, if the employer was not a reasonable employer, then he or she may treat all employees in an unsatisfactory way, so that it was not possible to state therefore that an individual had been treated less favourably. This approach to equal treatment requires employers to be consistent in their treatment of employees, not to treat them 'better' as a result of any anti-discrimination legislation. As long as all employees are treated in a similar manner, then it may not be possible to show less favourable treatment.

- Another aspect is that age groups are changeable and that during a normal lifetime one may expect to progress through a whole range of different age groups and experience different amounts and types of discrimination. As a result of this it might be difficult to assume that the interests of all in any particular age group are similar or that the experiences of those in any particular age group are similar. It may be that the 'less favourable' approach might have been better replaced with a test of someone suffering some detriment as a result of actual or perceived age.

- Age is also closely linked with other grounds of discrimination (see Chapter 8) and there may be issues concerning whether a person has been treated less favourably on the grounds of age or whether other reasons might act as a cover for age, or indeed whether age might act as a cover for something else or might act as a re-enforcer of discrimination on some other ground. It may be difficult at times to isolate an inference of age discrimination.

Examples of situations where other courts have accepted an inference of direct age discrimination have been:[26]

- A marked statistical difference in success rates for different age groups in apparently similar circumstances.

- Comments that indicate an intention to discriminate.

- Mismatch between formal selection criteria and those criteria applied in practice.

- Language in advertisements.

- Discriminatory questions asked at interview.

These, of course, are indications of discrimination that apply to other areas apart from age.

There is no need for a comparator to actually exist. Article 2(a) refers to comparison with another who 'has been or would be treated in a comparable

---

26 O'Cinneide (2005); drawing upon information about the Irish, Dutch and Slovakian experiences.

situation'. Thus it is possible to use a hypothetical comparator. Deciding who or which group is to be the hypothetical comparator may not be as straightforward as in gender or race cases.

Indirect discrimination is a more complex subject and has been an issue around which the effects of the mandatory retirement age in relation to sex discrimination has been considered by the courts in Great Britain (see later). Article 2.2(b) states that indirect discrimination is: 'Taken to occur where an apparently neutral provision, criterion or practice would put persons having a particular age at a particular disadvantage with other persons', unless: 'That provision, criterion or practice is objectively justified by a legitimate aim and the means of achieving that aim are appropriate and necessary.'

This is the same approach as in the Race Directive (2000/43/EC).

This definition is different to the original one proposed by the Commission in the 1999 document. According to the Commission this definition was a result of the case law of the European Court of Justice in cases involving the free movement of workers,[27] in particular the decision in *O'Flynn v Adjudication Officer*. In this case the complainant was a migrant worker who was refused a funeral grant because such grants were only available to those which took place in the UK. The Court stated:

> *Unless objectively justified and proportionate to its aim, a provision of national law must be regarded as discriminatory if it is intrinsically liable to affect migrant workers more than national workers and if there is a consequent risk that it will place the former at a particular disadvantage. It is not necessary in this respect to find that the provision in question does in practice affect a higher proportion of migrant workers. It is sufficient that it is liable to have such an effect.*

Relying upon this the European Commission had proposed a definition which had said that indirect discrimination had been taken to occur when an: 'Apparently neutral provision, criterion or practice is liable to affect adversely a person, or persons to whom the grounds ... applies'. This definition was the subject of some debate before the House of Lords Select Committee of the EU where the Commission representative defended it as removing the need to demonstrate statistically that indirect discrimination had occurred.[28] This

---

27 See 1999 proposals for the Directive.
28 'EU proposals to combat discrimination' (1999).

was a view supported by others in their evidence to the Committee.[29] There were also critics of this view. Professor Hepple argued that it: 'Completely misunderstands what indirect discrimination is … indirect discrimination is practiced against a group … but cannot apply to an individual'. Mr Robin Allen is also reported as stating that the Commission had: 'Lost the comparative element that needs to be in there'. As a result of its deliberations the House of Lords Select Committee stated that 'the definition of indirect discrimination as it stands is unacceptable'. They urged the Commission to adopt a definition based on that found in the Burden of Proof Directive.[30] This referred to a provision, requirement or practice which disadvantages a 'substantially higher proportion of one sex'.[31] Thus the group element and the comparative requirement are included. In the event the Commission did change the definition to include these elements, so the definition in the Framework Directive refers to 'persons' having a particular age compared to the singular version of 'a person'.

A further issue arises because the definition of indirect discrimination refers to persons of 'a particular age'. Colm O'Cinneide[32] questions how this meaning relates to an 'age group' for the purposes of indirect discrimination. He gives the example of a claimant alleging that a requirement that applicant's possess a particular skill (for example computer skills) puts persons of his particular age at a disadvantage. In such a situation should the relevant age group be:

- All those persons of the same chronological age.

- All those of a similar age.

- All those of a similar/identical age who are potential applicants for the job.

- All those of a similar/identical age with a similar educational background.

- All those of a similar/identical age resident in a particular geographical area; or

---

29 According to the report the Council for Racial Equality described it as: 'Broader, more workable and more accessible'.
30 Council Directive 97/80/EC on the burden of proof in cases of discrimination based on sex OJ L14/6, 20 January 1998.
31 Article 2.2 Directive 97/80/EC.
32 O'Cinneide (2005); drawing upon information about the Irish, Dutch and Slovakian experiences.

- Some other group?

These questions, of course, arise in decisions on comparisons concerning other grounds for discrimination. What makes age different is 'the fluid nature of age groups and the constantly shifting comparisons that can be made between different age groups, presenting difficulties in identifying suitable comparators.'[33]

JUSTIFICATION

Article 2.2(b)(i) provides a defence of justification. This can be where the provision, criterion or practice is 'objectively justified by a legitimate aim and the means of achieving that aim are appropriate and necessary'. This is further discussed below, but it is worth noting that the Commission, in its 1999 proposals, further explained the situation:

> The emphasis on objective justification in cases of indirect discrimination is put on two elements. Firstly, the aim of the provision, criterion or practice which establishes a difference in treatment must deserve protection and must be sufficiently substantial to justify it taking precedence over the principle of equal treatment. Secondly, the means employed to achieve this aim must be appropriate and necessary.

Thus there can be objective justification for a difference in treatment between groups if the difference in treatment:

- Deserves protection.

- Is sufficiently substantial for it to take precedence over the principle of equal treatment.

- The means for achieving this difference in treatment are both appropriate and necessary.

It is for the employer to justify the difference in treatment, if necessary, in accordance with Article 9 of the Directive on the Burden of Proof.[34] In the case of *Werner Mangold*[35] the European Court of Justice considered a situation

---

33 Ibid.
34 Directive 97/80/EC.
35 *Mangold v Helm.*

where German law allowed for the employer to conclude, without restriction, fixed-term contracts of employment with employees over the age of 52 years.[36] There were issues connected to the Fixed-term Workers Directive, but also with regard to the age aspects of the Framework Directive on Equal Treatment. The purpose of the German legislation, according to the national government, was to encourage the vocational integration of unemployed workers. The Court agreed that such a purpose could be 'objectively and reasonably' justified. The question then was whether this legitimate objective was 'appropriate and necessary'. The problem was that the national legislation applied to all people over the age of 53 years and not just to those who were unemployed. The Court concluded:

> Insofar as such legislation takes the age of the worker concerned as the only criterion for the application of a fixed-term contract of employment, when it has not shown that fixing an age threshold, as such, regardless of any other consideration linked to the structure of the labour market in question or the personal situation of the person concerned, is objectively necessary to the attainment of the objective pursued. Observance of the principle of proportionality requires every derogation from an individual right to reconcile, so far as is possible, the requirements of the principle of equal treatment with those of the aim pursued.

Thus it was on the grounds of proportionality that the Court held the measure to be not in accord with Community law and it seems difficult to disagree with that conclusion. Taking away the employment protection rights from employed older workers was not appropriate and necessary when introducing a measure to help unemployed older workers. What is alarming about this case is the easy acceptance by the Court that the measure was objectively justifiable in the first place. It is possible to take away the rights to employment protection of older workers who become employed for some social objective, however laudable. It is a reflection of the fault with Article 6 of the Framework Directive which allows age discrimination when it is necessary for some other legitimate objective.

The Court also stated that the Framework Directive did not in itself lay down the principle of equal treatment in the field of employment and occupation. Its purpose was, according to Article 1, to lay down a general

---

36 This is, of course, a simplification, but the purpose here is to concentrate on the aspects of the decision concerning age discrimination.

framework for combating discrimination on the various grounds. The source of the underlying principle was to be found in other international instruments and the 'constitutional traditions common to the member states' and the principle of non-discrimination on the grounds of age must thus be regarded as a general principle of Community law.

HARASSMENT

Article 2.3 provides that harassment is another form of discrimination. Harassment has a similar meaning to the definition in the Equal Treatment Directive (76/207/EEC as amended)[37] and the Race Directive. It occurs when there is unwanted conduct which takes place for the purpose or effect of violating a person's dignity or of creating an intimidating, hostile, degrading, humiliating or offensive environment.

There is also, of course, the possibility of protection under the Protection from Harassment Act 1997. Section 7(2) states that: 'References to harassing a person include alarming the person or causing the person distress'. It is clear that this needs to happen on more than one occasion.[38] *Majrowski v Guy's and St Thomas's NHS Trust* concerned an allegation that an employee was bullied, intimidated and harassed by his departmental manager. He took proceedings on the grounds that the treatment amounted to harassment under the Act and that the Trust was vicariously liable for the actions of the manager. The Court of Appeal agreed that the employer was vicariously liable but the judgment also raises another intriguing issue. The Court stated that:

> The issue arises not only where one employee in the course of his employment, harasses another employee, but where an employee, in the course of his employment, harasses an outsider, such as a customer of his employer or some other third party with whom his work brings him into regular contact. It is thus likely to be a risk incidental to employment.

It is an interesting piece of speculation to imagine a customer or supplier bringing an action for harassment against an employer because an employee has harassed them on the grounds of their age.

---

37 Articles 2.2 and 2.3.
38 Section 7(3) Protection from Harassment Act 1997; see also *Banks v Ablex Ltd.*

INSTRUCTION TO DISCRIMINATE

An instruction to discriminate against persons on the grounds of age will be deemed to be a form of direct or indirect discrimination.[39] This is intended to stop discrimination by third parties on behalf of the employer. One example might be with employment agencies used by employers to supply permanent and/or temporary staff. An express or implied instruction to only supply candidates within a particular age range will effectively discriminate against others on the grounds of age. Presumably also instructing an advertising agency only to place recruitment advertising in certain journals, which appeal to a particular age group, might also be seen as an instruction to discriminate.

FURTHER EXCEPTIONS

Article 2.5 provides that the Directive is without prejudice to, 'measures laid down by law which, in a democratic society, are necessary for':

* Public security.

* The maintenance of public order.

* The prevention of criminal offences.

* The protection of health.

* The protection of the rights and freedoms of others.

It is not altogether clear why this clause was included. It does not appear in the Race Directive. One can imagine however some parts of this being used to justify discrimination on the grounds of age. The first is with regard to 'public security and the maintenance of public order'. Age limits on membership of the armed forces, the police and the fire service might be justified, although the armed forces exception is included in Article 3.4. Whether it might be possible to only justify 'active' roles in these professions, rather than all roles, remains an issue. There are also serious issues perhaps in relation to the private sector. Will it be possible, for example, to restrict the employment of older workers in the private security sector because of the perceived need to have younger workers to deal with issues related to the 'prevention of criminal offences'.

---

39 Article 2.5.

The exception that might be of greatest concern is that linked to 'the protection of health'. This can mean the protection of young workers with exceptions being made to their working hours, breaks and so on, as in the Working Time Regulations 1998.[40] It might also justify discrimination against younger workers for the same reasons. Older workers might also be vulnerable as generalised employer concerns about competence and age lead to such workers being prevented from carrying out their work, thus restricting their employment opportunities.

SCOPE

The Directive applies to both the public and the private sector and has a wide scope, albeit limited to the areas of employment and vocational guidance and training. In particular it applies to:

- Conditions for access to employment, self employment or to occupation, including selection criteria and recruitment conditions.

- All types of activity and at all levels of the professional hierarchy, including promotion.

- Access to all types and all levels of vocational guidance and vocational training, including practical work experience.

- Employment and working conditions.

- Pay.

- Dismissals.

- Membership of, or involvement in, workers' and employers' organisations, including any benefits provided.

- Any organisation whose members carry on a profession, including any benefits provided.

The Directive also specifically excludes:

---

40 SI 1998/1833.

- Payments of any kind made by state schemes, including social security or social protection schemes.

- The armed forces, at the member state's discretion.

Thus, the scope is wide, but it is still limited to the fields of employment and vocational training. Age discrimination has a more limited scope than those measures concerned with sex and race. The Race Directive, for example, includes all the areas of application as for age, but also includes social protection, such as social security and healthcare, social advantage, education and access to and supply of goods and services which are available to the public, including housing.[41]

The argument as to whether age discrimination is different to other forms of discrimination, such as those concerned with gender or race, is an interesting one. It is clear that age is to be treated differently, and more negatively, than the other grounds of unlawful discrimination, such as sex, race and disability. Advocate General Mazák stated in the Age UK case,[42] that: 'The possibilities of justifying differences of treatment based on age are more extensive'.

In *Palacios*[43] the same Advocate General (AG) stated:

> *So far as non-discrimination on grounds of age, especially, is concerned, it should be borne in mind that prohibition is of a specific nature in that age as a criterion is a point on a scale and that, therefore, age discrimination may be graduated. It is therefore a much more difficult task to determine the existence of discrimination on grounds of age than for example in the case of discrimination on grounds of sex, where the comparators involved are more clearly defined.*

This view that age is to be treated in a different way is re-enforced by the addition of Article 6 to the Directive (see later), which lists, in broad terms, occasions when the use of age criteria might be a legitimate aim and also allows for the possibility of justifying both direct and indirect discrimination; and by the existence of Recital 14 which expressly states that the measure is: 'Without

---

41 Article 3.1 Race Directive 2000/43/EC.
42 Case C-388/07 *The Incorporated Trustees of the National Council on Ageing (Age Concern England) v Secretary of State for Business, Enterprise and Regulatory Reform.*
43 Case C-411/05 *Félix Palacios de la Villa v Cortefiel Servicios SA.*

prejudice to national provisions laying down retirement ages'.[44] AG Geelhoed stated in *Sonia Chacon Navas*[45] (a disability discrimination case) that:

> *The implementation of the prohibitions of discrimination of relevance here* [disability and age] *always requires that the legislature make painful, if not tragic, choices when weighing up the interests in question, such as the rights of disabled or older workers versus the flexible operation of the labour market or an increase in the participation level of older workers.*

OCCUPATIONAL REQUIREMENTS AND JUSTIFICATION OF DIFFERENCES OF TREATMENT ON GROUNDS OF AGE[46]

Articles 4 and 6 of the Framework Directive provide for the exceptions to the principle of equal treatment as they apply to age. Article 4.1 provides that member states may provide that a difference of treatment which is based on a characteristic related to age shall not constitute discrimination where such a characteristic 'constitutes a genuine and determining occupational requirement, provided that the objective is legitimate and the requirement is proportionate'.

The House of Lords Select Committee[47] pointed out that it was strange to say that a difference of treatment based on such a characteristic did not constitute discrimination. Such a difference of treatment is discrimination, but it is permissible discrimination because it can be justified within the terms of this definition. It has been pointed out that this might benefit the protected group in some cases.[48] One example might be in the travel business where those operating 18–30 holidays would prefer their reps to be in the same age group. In the same way those operating holidays for those over the age of 50 might also prefer reps in this age group. The problem with applying this sort of logic to age is that one person's discrimination is another person's justification. Both of these age group justifications discriminate against the other group on the basis of age.

Article 6 then takes this further. It actually provides for specific exceptions to the principle of equal treatment. Firstly it again states that differences

---

44 See later for further consideration of Article 6 and Recital 14.
45 Case C-13/05 *Sonia Chacon Navas v Eurest Colectividades SA*.
46 Article 5, which is missed out here, is concerned with reasonable accommodation for persons with disabilities.
47 Ninth Report.
48 Whittle (2002).

of treatment on grounds of age shall not constitute discrimination under certain circumstances. The reality is that these differences of treatment do constitute age discrimination but such discrimination is to be allowed under certain circumstances. They must be 'objectively and reasonably justified by a legitimate aim, including legitimate employment policy, labour market and vocational training objectives'.

In addition, the means of achieving the aim must be 'appropriate and necessary'. It is not clear what 'legitimate employment policy' means. The result is that the ultimate boundaries of age discrimination legislation are to be left to the courts with, one suspects, a large amount of litigation and uncertainty while the courts search for the boundary definitions.

Article 6 then continues to give some specific examples of differences in treatment which could be justified. Age discrimination is the only ground of discrimination in the Framework Directive that receives this special attention of having its own specified lists of areas where discrimination is to be justified. The list is:

- The setting of special conditions on access to employment and vocational training, employment and occupation (including dismissal and remuneration conditions) for young people, older workers and persons with caring responsibilities in order to promote their vocational integration or ensure their protection.

These differences in treatment could, of course, be positive as well as negative; so extra protection for young workers in terms of working hours, health and safety and so on might be justifiable here. What is perhaps most interesting, apart from the lack of definition, is the groups affected, namely young workers, older workers and those with caring responsibilities. Who is a young person? Who is an older worker? Those aged in between are not a subject of these allowable exceptions. There is no interpretive Article in this Directive, so it will be left to the courts to decide in each circumstance presumably, somewhat adding to future uncertainties:

- The fixing of minimum conditions of age, professional experience or seniority of service for access to employment or to certain advantages linked to employment.

One wonders what the effect of removing the word age from this area of justified discrimination would be. Clearly there are some jobs which require certain levels of experience or seniority of service, but why cannot these be quantified without the use of age in the criteria. There are some jobs which might just require some 'life experience', but this needs to be justified. The inclusion of a minimum age must be wrong because it assumes that experience and knowledge is gained at a uniform rate amongst the population, which is self-evidently untrue:

- The fixing of a minimum age for recruitment which takes into account the training period and the need for a reasonable period of work before the individual retires.

This difference of treatment assumes a retirement age which will limit a person's working life and therefore limit the return that an employer might receive in return. This rule might become more complex if mandatory retirement ages did not exist.

When discussing similar proposals before the House of Lords Select Committee (see previous) EurolinkAge stated that this Article would 'not produce any clear benefits for older workers in Europe who currently suffer from age discriminatory practices'. The list is non-exhaustive.[49]

The Commission representative stated that this Article was designed to fix clear limits, to insist on the principles of objective justification, necessity and proportionality, and to give some indicative examples in order to clarify the type of exception which is envisaged, and provide certainty concerning the most widespread and clearly justified examples.

The UK government had a similar vision. The Minister for Employment told the House of Commons European Standing Committee, reviewing the proposed Directive, that:

> The Government have welcomed the proposal. It is important to establish minimum standards to combat discrimination at work throughout the whole European Community. The key to tackling discrimination, however, is not just the aspiration to end it ... It is essential to ensure workable and proportionate mechanisms that deliver redress

---

49 The list is headed by the statement: 'Some differences of treatment may include, among others ...'.

effectively. Otherwise we risk introducing a parody of proper standards and unnecessary litigation. Such an outcome would undermine the confidence of the public, employers and employees, whose support is essential to the effectiveness of the measures.

It is difficult not to interpret this as a statement of minimalist standards and that it is a result of considering age discrimination differently to the other grounds contained in the Directive and elsewhere.

Article 6.2 provides that retirement ages can be fixed for the purposes of admission to or retirement from social security and invalidity benefits, and the use of ages for actuarial purposes in such schemes.

Professor Hepple has argued for the provision of a non-exhaustive list by the British government of specific exceptions to the principle of equal treatment. He quoted examples of a genuine occupational qualification; minimum age requirements for training or employment and maximum age limits for training.[50] This was a point argued by Age Concern in their challenge to the UK government's implementation of the Directive.[51] It was argued that Article 6(1) did not permit member states to introduce a general defence of justification for direct age discrimination. It permitted them to make specific provisions listing the grounds which could constitute a legitimate aim and the means are proportionate. This was not accepted by the Court.

POSITIVE ACTION

Article 7.1 provides that the principle of equal treatment will not stop member states from maintaining or adopting specific measures 'to prevent or compensate for disadvantages' linked to age.

Positive action is not positive discrimination of course. The limits for the latter have been drawn by the European Court of Justice in relation to other grounds of discrimination. A good example of this was in *Badeck*[52] where a rule, introduced by a regional authority in Germany, to ensure equal access for men and women in public sector jobs was considered. The European Court of Justice held that the Equal Treatment Directive (76/207/EC) and the principle of

---

50 Hepple (2001).
51 Case C-388/07 *The Incorporated Trustees of the National Council on Ageing (Age Concern England) v Secretary of State for Business, Enterprise and Regulatory Reform.*
52 Application by Badeck and others.

equal treatment did not preclude such a rule. It was acceptable to take positive action so that where male and female applicants had equal qualifications, then priority could be given to the female applicant. Positive discrimination would have, of course, enabled the employer to select female candidates with lesser qualifications than men.[53]

Positive action is a term that includes measures designed both to counter the effects of past discriminatory practices and to assist members of the protected group to compete on an equal basis with those not in the protected group. This may include, for example, the encouragement of applications from the disadvantaged group, through extra advertising; or the provision of special training opportunities for employees in the disadvantaged group.

This is not a positive obligation upon member states but only a discretionary option which might be taken up in particular circumstances. It is therefore a weak power which may not be an important factor in tackling age discrimination. This is because, in contrast to other forms of discrimination, there is much age discrimination to be allowed, some of which may be positive discrimination by favouring one group over another.[54] In relation to age where the whole working population is the protected group, positive action for one age group may result in negative effects for other age groups. Thus a decision to only recruit younger employees in the interest of long-term staff planning will have an effect on older applicants. This will not be a case of helping the protected group in contrast with those not in the protected group; it is a case of advantaging one part of the protected group against another part of the same group.

REMEDIES AND ENFORCEMENT

Article 8 is concerned with access to justice and ensuring that there are adequate judicial and administrative procedures to allow persons, who consider themselves affected by a failure to apply the principle of equal treatment to them, to enforce their rights under the Directive. National provisions on time limits for initiating action are not affected by this.

---

53 See also *Marschall v Land Nordrhein-Westfalen* Case.
54 The duty on employers to make adjustments for disabled employees and applicants is, of course, an exception to this and is an example of using positive action to combat historic discrimination.

The Directive[55] also provides that member states shall ensure that associations, organisations or other legal entities which have, in accordance with the criteria laid down in national law, a legitimate interest in ensuring that the provisions of this Directive are complied with, may engage, either on behalf or in support of the complainant, with his or her approval, in any judicial and/or administrative procedure for the enforcement of obligations under this Directive.

This is an expansion of the proposal in the Commission's 1999 document and provides for the possibility of organisations taking up and pursuing cases on behalf of an individual or individuals. This is important because it excludes the possibility of class actions being taken on behalf of unnamed individuals or groups. The Human Rights Commission will be able to intervene and pursue cases, as will presumably other bodies that have a 'legitimate interest', such as trade unions. The TUC's spokesperson[56] before the House of Lords Committee[57] stated that it would be useful: 'In circumstances when it was a difficult case and an individual might find it too stressful, or when it was a case that tested a particular point in law'.

Once cases have been initiated, then the burden of proof[58] is as that provided for in the approach of the Burden of Proof Directive,[59] namely that the complainant need only establish facts 'from which it may be presumed that there has been direct or indirect discrimination'. It is then for the respondent to show that there has been no breach of the principle of equal treatment. The wording used is identical to that used in Article 4.1 of the Burden of Proof Directive.

This is a powerful weapon when trying to show that discrimination has taken place. In *Igen Ltd v Wong* for example, the Court of Appeal stated that employment tribunals were required to go through a two-stage process. The first was for the applicant to prove facts from which the tribunal could decide, in the absence of an adequate explanation, that the respondent had committed, or is to be treated as having committed, an act of discrimination. The employment tribunal is being asked to make assumptions which may not subsequently turn out to be true when the second stage is reached. The fact that there is no adequate explanation is enough to shift the burden of proof to the

---

55 Article 8.2.
56 Kay Carberry.
57 See previous.
58 See Article 10.1.
59 Directive 97/80/EC, which applied to sex discrimination.

respondent. Thus, in the second stage, the respondent needs to show that they did not commit, or are not to be treated as having committed, the unlawful act. If they fail to do this then the tribunal will decide in the complainant's favour. There is a high standard for the respondent as in order to discharge the burden of proof, they have to show, on the balance of probabilities, that the treatment was 'in no sense whatsoever' on the grounds of sex.[60] The Court stated that: 'No discrimination whatsoever' was compatible with the Burden of Proof Directive.

It is clear that a consistent approach to the burden of proof on all grounds of discrimination is to be encouraged, so it is likely that cases such as *Igen* will be used in age discrimination cases, thus placing a significant task on employers to show that their treatment was 'in no sense whatsoever' on the grounds of age. Hypothetically, this might require employers to show dramatic changes of policy as a result of the Regulations. If an employer has a long history of making employment decisions on the basis of age quite lawfully, then, unless there has been an overt change in policy, that history presumably will be a contributory factor in showing evidence that the employer has committed an unlawful act.

Victimisation of individuals as a result of making a complaint or bringing an action on the protected ground is also unlawful. Member States are required to introduce measures that ensure the protection of employees against dismissal or any 'other adverse treatment' by the employer, as a reaction to a complaint or any legal proceedings that have been concerned with enforcing compliance of the principle of equal treatment.[61] The wording in the Race Directive is not quite the same as that in the Framework Directive. Article 9 of that Directive requires the introduction of measures to ensure protection 'from any adverse treatment or adverse consequences'. This may be a result of the wider scope of the Race Directive, in that it applies to more than just employment matters. Certainly, the European Commission guide to their 1999 proposals on the Framework Directive pointed out that fear of dismissal was one of the major obstacles to employees taking action or making a complaint, which is why it is specifically mentioned in Article 11.

Sanctions for failure to comply with the national measures are to be 'effective, proportionate and dissuasive'. These may include, according to the Framework Directive, payment of compensation to the victim.[62]

---

60 The Burden of Proof Directive concerned sex discrimination.
61 Article 11.
62 Article 17, which is identical to Article 15 of the Race Directive.

In respect of other measures, the Directive states that any laws, regulations or administrative provisions contrary to the principle of equal treatment are abolished. Also any provisions contrary to this principle which are contained in contracts or collective agreements, or internal rules for trade unions, employers' organisations and so on are to be declared null and void.[63] The reference to contracts presumably includes contracts of employment. Thus any provisions of a contract of employment that are contrary to the principle of equal treatment as regards to age are to be declared null and void. This is a potentially important tool for challenges against inadequate implementation of the Directive by the UK government.

INFORMATION AND DIALOGUE

Article 11 of the Framework Directive requires the member states to ensure the provisions of the national rules 'are brought to the attention of the persons concerned by all appropriate means, for example at the workplace'. There is therefore a need to publicise and disseminate information about the Age Regulations. The Commission regards this as important because the principle of equal treatment needs to be fully understood and accepted as desirable for society, ensuring that decisions are taken on an objective basis, thereby promoting stability and social coherence. The more effective the system of public information and prevention is, the less need there is for individual remedies.[64]

So it is not just about disseminating information; it is also about making sure that the principle of equal treatment is both understood and accepted. This requires a much more positive approach by government. The benefit, according to this quote, is that this acceptance will lead to less need for individual complaints and presumably litigation because employers and employees will accept that the principle of equal treatment applies to age as well as the other grounds in the Directive!

Somewhat unsurprisingly the government representatives at the House of Lords European Committee[65] objected to this and another Article[66] in the Directive which requires national governments to promote a dialogue with the social partners[67] with a view to fostering equal treatment in such matters as

---

63 Article 16.
64 Taken for the 1999 consultation on the proposed Framework Directive.
65 See previous.
66 Article 13.
67 Employers and trade unions.

monitoring workplace practices, collective agreements and codes of conduct. The escape clause for the British government is that this dialogue should take place in accordance with national traditions and practice. For the UK this might mean minimal social dialogue on these issues. This attitude was exemplified by the Home Office spokesperson at the House of Lords Committee who stated that the Directives: 'Should not prescribe in so much detail in terms of how we … go about, for example, negotiation with the social partners which would cut across well-established practices that we have in this country'.

The spokesperson for the Department for Education also stated that matters concerning dissemination and information were 'best decided at the national level'. In addition to the above there is an obligation to encourage dialogue with appropriate non-governmental organisations which have a 'legitimate interest' in the fight against discrimination.[68]

Implementation of the age aspects of the Framework Directive has presented a particular challenge to some member states as most did not have any existing general legislation concerning age discrimination.[69] There are two contrasting 'models or patterns' that have emerged in the way that member states have faced up to these difficulties.[70] One pattern or model has been to directly enact the provisions of the Directive, using the same or very similar words. This has happened in Italy, Cyprus and Greece as well as Denmark, Austria, Slovakia and Slovenia. The alternative model or pattern is to indulge in elaborate debate as to how the age aspects of the Directive might be fully integrated into national law. This debate tends to be difficult and complex as in Belgium, Germany, Netherlands and the UK.

---

68 Article 14.
69 Cormack and Bell (2005).
70 Ibid.

6

International Perspectives

The purpose of this chapter is to examine the operation of age discrimination legislation in a number of different States. It is not intended to be a comprehensive analysis, but seeks to highlight some of the issues that have resulted from the introduction of legislation and the resulting litigation in the countries concerned.[1]

Australia

It is at State level, rather than at the Commonwealth level, that measures against age discrimination have traditionally been initiated. The first legislation making it unlawful was adopted by the State of South Australia by an amendment in 1990 to the Equal Opportunity Act 1984. Queensland followed suit in 1992, Western Australia in 1993 and New South Wales in 1994. Other states followed, with the exception of the Northern Territory, with the last one being Tasmania in 1999.

The Equal Opportunity Act in South Australia covered discrimination on sex, race, disability, sexuality, pregnancy and sexual harassment. The amendment concerning age came into effect in June 1991. The Act follows the UK Sex Discrimination Act and Race Relations Act to include provisions relating to direct and indirect discrimination. Discrimination in the areas of recruitment and selection, terms and conditions offered, training, promotion and transfer opportunities, and subjecting the employee to dismissal or some other detriment are all forbidden.[2] There was also an exception for a genuine occupational requirement as well as for retirement ages.[3] Specific exceptions, apart from the genuine occupational requirement, are employment in a private

---

1   See also Hornstein (2001).
2   Section 85b.
3   Section 85f.

household and where a person may not be able to perform adequately, given as a person is not being able:

- To perform adequately, and without endangering himself or herself or other persons, the work genuinely and reasonably required for the employment or position in question; or

- To respond adequately to situations of emergency that should reasonably be anticipated in connection with the employment or position in question.

The mandatory retirement age also came within the provisions of the Act when it was effectively abolished from 1 January 1994. Legislation to abolish the mandatory retirement age was also adopted by New South Wales in 1993, Queensland in 1994, Western Australia in 1995, and the Northern Territory removed it for public sector workers in 2003.

Legislation generally has followed the model of the UK Sex Discrimination Act 1975 (now replaced by the Equality Act 2010). An exception to this is contained in the State of Victoria where their Equal Opportunity Act 2010, which replaced the Equal Opportunity Act 1995. Section 6 refers to the 'attributes', on the basis of which discrimination is unlawful. Age is one of these attributes. Direct discrimination is defined in Section 8 in the following way: 'Direct discrimination occurs if a person treats, or proposes to treat, a person with an attribute unfavourably because of that attribute.'

Thus the model of treating someone less favourably on the grounds of a protected ground, as in the Federal legislation, is not followed.

In 2004 the Federal government adopted the Age Discrimination Act (ADA). As an illustration of the similarity of concerns with the UK experience, the explanatory memorandum accompanying the Australian legislation stated that:

> The proposed new age discrimination bill will be an integral part of a wide range of key Government policy priorities to respond to the ageing workforce and population ... Age discrimination is clearly a problem for both younger and older Australians. In relation to older Australians, in particular, many recent reports have emphasised the negative consequences of age discrimination on the wellbeing of older

Australians and the broader consequences for the community. There is also evidence that the ageing of Australia's population will lead to an increase in the problem of age discrimination if Government action is not taken to address this issue. Government action is needed to address the generally unfounded negative stereotypes that employers and policy makers may have about both younger and older Australians, which limit their contribution to the community and the economy.

Indeed by 2051 over 25 per cent of Australians will be aged 65 years plus. The key features of anti-discrimination laws in Australia are summed up as follows:[4]

- Such protection derives from Commonwealth, State and Territory statute.

- Both direct and indirect discrimination are covered.

- Discrimination on certain grounds, such as sex, race, disability and age, are prohibited in 'key areas of public life' such as work, access to goods, services and facilities, access to premises, places and transport, and education.

- Provides for a range of exceptions to allow for legitimate distinctions.

- Public awareness and education are important elements in overcoming discrimination.

- Creates various institutions to consider infringements.

FEDERAL ACTION

The Workplace Relations Act 1996 contains some provisions concerning discrimination in employment, including discrimination on the grounds of age. Section 3j of the Act states that its principal objective is: 'Respecting and valuing diversity in the workforce by helping to prevent and eliminate discrimination on the basis of race, colour, sex, sexual preference, age, physical or mental disability, marital status, family responsibilities, pregnancy, religion, political opinion, national extraction or social origin.'

---

4   Taken from the explanatory memorandum accompanying the Commonwealth Age Discrimination Bill 2003, p. 3; now the Age Discrimination Act 2004.

Complaints about discrimination in employment can be made to the Human Rights and Equal Opportunity Commission (HREOC). Complaints included:

- Age requirements in agency job vacancies.

- Age requirements for vacancies in the defence forces.

- Complaints from those over 65 refused employment.

- Age discrimination and trade union membership.

- Older people being treated less well in redundancy packages.

In 2008–09, 43 per cent of complaints received by the Commission were lodged under the Disability Discrimination Act, 24 per cent under the Sex Discrimination Act, 18 per cent under the Racial Discrimination Act, 8 per cent under the Human Rights and Equal Opportunity Commission Act and 7 per cent under the Age Discrimination Act. The Commission reported that employment was the main area of complaint under the federal legislation. In 2008–09, complaints regarding employment made up 54 per cent of complaints under the Racial Discrimination Act; 91 per cent of complaints under the Sex Discrimination Act; 40 per cent of complaints under the Disability Discrimination Act; and 59 per cent of complaints under the Age Discrimination Act.[5]

A precursor of the 2004 Federal legislation was a major report by the HREOC called 'Age matters; a report on age discrimination'. This report was presented in May 2000. It considered issues of age discrimination where: 'An opportunity is denied to a person solely because of his or her chronological age and age is irrelevant to the person's ability to take advantage of that opportunity.'

The report is not dissimilar in its scope to the UK government's consultations on the age discrimination regulations. This included the question of job-related exceptions to the anti-discrimination legislation. One such is a part of the Workplace Relations Act 1996 which provides an exemption when the age distinction is based on the inherent requirements of the job. The HREOC had received complaints about age distinctions in the Australian defence forces. In one case cited, *Bradley's Case*, the complainant claimed that he was discriminated against when he was denied access to the Specialist Service Officer Scheme.

---

5   'Australian human rights commission annual report' (2008/09).

Entry was limited to the age range of 19 to 28 years. Mr Bradley was 37 years old. The army argued that older officers would not have the required level of fitness nor would they be able to cope with the stress. The Commission did not accept that there was a direct correlation between the applicant's age and the ability to meet the entrance criteria, so it was held to be discriminatory.

The report found evidence of continuing age discrimination, such as a Drake Personnel survey of the top 500 Australian employers, which indicated that none would choose to employ managers or executives in their 50s and 65 per cent said that this group would be the first to go in the event of redundancies.[6] Amongst its recommendations it concluded:[7]

> *All Australian States and Territories now have legislation making age discrimination unlawful, although the scope of the legislation differs significantly in some respects such as compulsory retirement. Federal law is now the weakest and most inadequate. It does not make age discrimination unlawful. It deals only with employment and then very narrowly and ineffectively.*

More effectively, the Commonwealth could enact a broader Age Discrimination Act comparable in its scope and application to the existing federal anti-discrimination Acts.

The Age Discrimination Act 2004 covers more than just work. It also applies to access to goods, services and facilities; access to premises and transport; federal laws and programmes; education; accommodation and land. Its objects are contained in Section 3, some of which are in stark contrast to the UK Age Regulations. These objects of the Act include:

- To eliminate, as far as possible, discrimination against persons on the grounds of age in the areas of work, education, access to premises, the provision of goods, services and facilities.

- To ensure, as far as practicable, that everyone has the same right to equality before the law, regardless of age, as the rest of the community.

---

6   p. 12.
7   pp. 116–17.

- To allow appropriate benefits and other assistance to be given to people of a certain age, particularly younger and older persons, in recognition of their particular circumstances.

- To promote recognition and acceptance within the community of the principle that people of all ages have the same fundamental rights.

- To respond to demographic change by removing barriers to older people particularly in the workforce and changing negative stereotypes about older people.

There are a number of exceptions of course. One of these is contained in Section 6 of the Act and stops claims for both age discrimination and disability discrimination. It is recognised that there is a significant overlap between these two and, somewhat distressingly, the answer for the Australian legislature is to make sure that claims cannot be made on the two grounds, unless, of course, the cause of complaint is distinguishable. Other exemptions are the inherent requirements of the job[8] (see later); youth wages;[9] superannuation, insurance and credit;[10] and positive discrimination[11] (this is to be permitted to allow measures for the benefit of a particular age group, or to prevent or reduce a disadvantage that might be suffered by a particular age group).

DEFINITIONS

The ADA provides that direct discrimination occurs where a person (the *discriminator*) *discriminates* against another person (the *aggrieved person*) on the ground of age of the aggrieved person if:

1. The discriminator treats or proposes to treat the aggrieved person less favourably than, in circumstances that are the same or not materially different, the discriminator treats or would treat a person of a different age; and

---

8   ADA 2004 , Section 18(4).
9   Ibid., Section 25.
10 Ibid., Section 37; Superannuation relates to the accumulation of retirement savings and life assurance calculations. Insurance and credit relate to non-employment law issues, but it is interesting to speculate how we in the UK would deal with these issues if age discrimination legislation were to spread to other fields. The Australian proposals will exempt actuarial calculations used to work out insurance risk and credit ratings.
11 Ibid., Section 33.

2.   The discriminator does so because of:

   a. The age of the aggrieved person; or
   b. A characteristic that appertains generally to persons of the age of the aggrieved person; or
   c. A characteristic that is generally imputed to persons of the age of the aggrieved person.[12]

Indirect discrimination occurs where a person (the *discriminator*) *discriminates* against another person (the *aggrieved person*) on the ground of age of the aggrieved person if:

- The discriminator imposes, or proposes to impose, a condition, requirement or practice; and

- The condition, requirement or practice is not reasonable in the circumstances; and

- The condition, requirement or practice has, or is likely to have, the effect of disadvantaging persons of the same age as the aggrieved person.[13]

The burden of proof that the condition, requirement or practice is reasonable in the circumstances rests with the discriminator.[14] A further important feature is that the legislation applies to a much wider framework than just employment.

In employment terms the Act specifically makes unlawful age discrimination in relation to:[15]

- The arrangements made for the purpose of determining who should be offered employment.

- In determining who should be offered employment.

- In the terms and conditions offered and made available.

---

12 Ibid., Section 14.
13 Ibid., Section 15.
14 Ibid., Section 15(3).
15 Ibid., Section 18.

- Denying or limiting access to opportunities for promotion, transfer or training.

- Dismissals.

- Subjecting the employee to any other detriment.

The Act contained a dominant reason test and may be the reason why it has not been effective. It provided that where an act is done for two or more reasons, that act will only be discriminatory if the person's age was the dominant reason for the doing of the act (it is interesting to compare this approach with that of the Supreme Court in the US to the issue of 'mixed motives'; see later). This test was withdrawn by an amendment to the the Act contained in the Disability Discrimination and Other Human Rights Legislation Amendment Act 2009.

The ADA 2004 also provides an exemption for positive discrimination.[16] Provided the act is consistent with the purposes of the ADA, then positive discrimination is permitted in relation to acts which:

- Provide a bona fide benefit to persons of a particular age. An example of this might be a hairdresser giving a discount to senior citizens.[17]

- Are intended to meet a need that arises out of the age of the persons of a particular age, such as the provision of extra welfare services for the young such as helping with homelessness.

- Are intended to reduce a disadvantage experienced by persons of a particular age, the provision of additional notice entitlements for older workers.

As in the UK, there is also an exemption for youth wages, in this case for those under the age of 21 years. This is designed to aid the recruitment of young people.

Attitudinal change is an objective of the Australian legislation so that 'people are judged on their actual capacity, rather than age being used as a

---

16 ADA 2004, Section 33.
17 The examples are taken from the explanatory memorandum to the Act.

blunt proxy for capacity'.[18] This Act is part of that process and has the specific objective of reducing the incidence of age discrimination.

INHERENT REQUIREMENTS OF THE JOB

There is an exemption in the ADA 2004 which allows an employer to discriminate on the grounds of age if the person: 'Is unable to carry out the inherent requirements of the particular employment because of his or her age'. This reflects the State and Territory laws on this subject. The term seems to be a general catch-all for jobs which require people of a certain age to perform the duties of a particular job.

Qantas Airways Ltd v Christie concerned an airline pilot who worked for Qantas Airways. His employment had ended when he reached the age of 60 years. He claimed that his employment had been terminated in breach of Section 170DF(1)f of the Industrial Relations Act 1988,[19] which prohibited termination of an employee's employment on the grounds of age. Section 170DF(2) provided for an exception to this rule: '2) Subsection (1) does not prevent a matter referred to in Paragraph (1)(f) from being a reason for terminating employment if the reason is based on the inherent requirements of the particular post.'

The Court observed that just because an employer requires employment to come to an end when an employee reaches a certain age, this does not necessarily mean that one should automatically conclude that the termination of employment at that age is by reason of age. This issue was also considered in *Stanley Edward Griffin v Australian Postal Corporation*.[20] Mr Griffin was retired at the age of 65 years against his will. He wished to continue working and claimed that he had been terminated on the grounds of his age and that this amounted to age discrimination contrary to the New South Wales Anti Discrimination Act 1977. The issue for the Court was whether it had jurisdiction. The *Australian Post* argued that it did not terminate Mr Griffin's employment, but rather it came to an end as a result of an agreement or the operation of law. In other words the term of the contract of employment had expired. This is an interesting concept which suggests that everyone who has a contract of employment which stipulates a retirement age is really on a fixed-term contract and that there is no such concept of permanent employment in these circumstances.

---

18   See Guide to the Employment Bill 2003, p. 10.
19   Now the Workplace Relations Act 1996.
20   Industrial Relations Court of Australia 980001 September 15 1998.

Qantas argued that it did not terminate Mr Christie's appointment. It argued that his employment also came to an end by 'the effluxion of time'. This was because there was a term in his contract, or a condition of his employment relationship, that his employment would terminate not later than his 60th birthday.[21] The only argument in favour of its retirement policy put forward by Qantas when this case reached the High Court was the 'Rule of 60', incorporated into the Convention on International Civil Aviation, which allows states to exclude from its airspace any aircraft flown by a pilot over the age of 60 years. This would severely limit the number of flights that Mr Christie could operate.[22] The earlier Court had, as a result of this, concluded that being under the age of 60 was an inherent requirement of the job as an airline captain. The Court had adopted the definition of 'inherent requirements' as meaning that there must be a clear and definite relationship between the inherent or intrinsic characteristics of the employment and the disability in question, the very nature of which disqualifies the person from being able to perform the characteristic tasks or skills required in the specific performance.[23]

The problem in this case was that Mr Christie could perform the 'characteristic tasks or skills required', but was unable to do so because of the international nature of the job. The argument was whether, therefore, the 'inherent requirement' rule should be interpreted narrowly or widely.

The High Court did not favour the narrow interpretation and suggested that a practical method of deciding whether there was an inherent requirement was to ask whether the position would be essentially the same if that requirement was dispensed with. In this case the issue was whether he could continue to do the job without flying the international routes and that this would not have been possible without creating a special position for him vis-à-vis the way that work for pilots was organised.

The issue was also considered in the Federal Court in *Commonwealth of Australia v Human Rights and Equal Opportunity Commission* (the HREOC). This concerned an application for judicial review of a finding by the HREOC that the Australian Defence Force had discriminated against Mr Bradley on the grounds of age (see previous) when they refused to consider his application for appointment to a helicopter pilot training scheme on the grounds of his age. The

---

21 The retirement issue was covered by an agreement between the employers and the Australian Federation of Airline Pilots which seemed to have been incorporated into the contract of employment.
22 The Court stated that this left just flights to New Zealand, Denpasar (Indonesia) and Fiji.
23 *X v Department of Defense.*

army argued that the age range was a result of the inherent requirements of the job which included medical fitness, physical performance, training failures (of other mature pilots), peer-group integration and obtaining a sufficient return on their investment. In an obvious stereotypical argument the army stated that:

> *Experience in Australian and overseas armed forces has shown that mature aged qualified pilots encounter a high incidence of difficulty in 'unlearning' acquired habits and skills to adapt to the unique requirements of military aviation. Also the physical, psychological and social stresses encountered during training are such that an older entrant would be a very high risk of failure.*

The HREOC had concluded that the rule was discriminatory and that the selected age range was not an inherent requirement of the job. The army's concerns could have been met by the other criteria, including medical fitness. It was the connection between these inherent requirements and the age range that was the problem. As Tamberlin J. stated: 'The consequences of using a broad criterion such as age to correlate with the inherent requirements of the job is that the broader the criterion, the greater will be the number of cases in which discrimination is allowed to occur.'

Canada

Canada, like Australia, has a federal system of government. Age discrimination measures are provided by the human rights legislation at both federal level and within the ten provinces (and three territories). Generally speaking this protection is part of a wider protection against discrimination in a number of different areas apart from employment.[24] In this human rights sense the purpose of anti-discrimination laws: 'Is to prevent the violation of human dignity and freedom through the imposition of disadvantage, stereotyping, or political or social prejudice.'[25]

In addition, the Canadian Charter of Rights and Freedoms was adopted in 1982 and is an important factor in the regulation of discrimination issues in government and the public sector. Section 15(1) states: 'Every individual is equal before and under the law and has the right to the equal protection and equal benefit of the law without discrimination and, in particular, without

---

24   See Gunderson (2003), pp. 318–28; also Gunderson (2001).
25   Policy on discrimination against older persons because of age (2002); see <www.ohrc.on.ca>.

discrimination based on race, national or ethnic origin, colour, religion, sex, age or mental or physical disability.'

These rights are limited by Section 1, which states: 'The Canadian Charter of Rights and Freedoms guarantees the rights and freedoms set out in it subject only to such reasonable limits prescribed by law as can be demonstrably justified in a free and democratic society.'

Thus the freedom from discrimination in Section 15 is subject to reasonable limitation as set out in Section 1. This has had an effect on the Canadian approach to protection from age discrimination, especially with respect to the rules on mandatory retirement.

The approach to the Section 1 restriction was originally set out in *R v Oakes*. The 'Oakes test'[26] was subsequently set out in *McKinney v University of Guelph*.[27] The Court held that there were a number of steps:

- An assessment of the objectives of the law to determine whether they are sufficiently important to warrant the limitation.

- The challenged law is then subject to a proportionality test to balance the objectives against the nature of the right, the extent of its infringement, and the degree to which the limitation furthers other rights or policies of importance.

McKinney concerned a number of academics who objected to being retired and based their claim upon Article 15. LaForest J. was, however, quite clear that mandatory retirement was justifiable in this situation and was a reasonable limitation on Charter rights:

> *Mandatory retirement ... ensures continuing faculty renewal, a necessary process to enable universities to be centres of excellence. Universities need to be on the cutting edge of new discoveries and ideas, and this requires a continuing infusion of new people. In a closed system with limited resources, this can only be achieved by departures of other people. Mandatory retirement achieves this in an orderly way that permits long-term planning both by universities and the individual.*

---

26 *R v Oakes* [1986] 1 S.C.R. 103.
27 (2001), 206 D.L.R. (4th) 220.

This is a somewhat dated approach and might be difficult to prove. The case was somewhat limited by *GVRD Employees' Union v GVRD*,[28] which suggested that the approach in *McKinney* and similar cases did not imply that mandatory retirement was always justified and that it had to be considered on a case-by-case basis. In this case the individual concerned was offered a position which was then withdrawn when it was discovered that he was over 65 years of age. The British Columbia Court of Appeal suggested that in the eleven years since *McKinney* 'the demographies of the workplace have changed considerably' and 'the social and legislative facts now available may well cast doubt on the extent to which the courts should defer to legislative decisions made over a decade ago.' In fact, of course, now the mandatory retirement age has effectively been eliminated throughout Canada.

Ontario

Ontario is used here as an example of the activities at Provincial level. The Ontario Human Rights Commission (OHRC)[29] was established in 1961 to administer the Ontario Human Rights Code. The Code has undergone subsequent revisions; the last major one being in 2006, which came into effect in 2008. At this time a separate Human Rights Tribunal was created. Section 5(1) of the Code records that: 'Every person has a right to equal treatment with respect to employment without discrimination because of race, ancestry, place of origin, colour, ethnic origin, citizenship, creed, age, record of offences, marital status, same-sex partnership status, family status or disability.'

Section 1 applies the same statement to the provision of facilities, goods and services.

The Commission's functions are set out in Section 29 of the Code. This includes the promotion and advancement of respect for human rights. Specifically this means, amongst other matters:

- To forward the policy that the dignity and worth of every person be recognised and that equal rights and opportunities be provided without discrimination that is contrary to the law.

- To develop and conduct programs of public information and

28 *Greater Vancouver Regional District Employees' Union v Greater Vancouver Regional District.*
29 <www.ohrc.on.ca>.

education to (i) promote awareness and understanding of, respect for and compliance with this Act, and (ii) prevent and eliminate discriminatory practices.

• To undertake, direct and encourage research into discriminatory practices and make recommendations.

Part IV of the Code establishes the Human Rights Tribunal of Ontario. If a person believes that their rights under the Code have been infringed (Section 34(1)), he or she may apply within a year of the infringement, to the Tribunal for an order to be made under Section 45(2). This permits the Tribunal to award monetary compensation or other restitution to the complainant, as well as make orders to ensure that the offending party complies with the Act in future.

Age means being 18 years or more. There is no upper limit. The right to equal treatment in employment includes discrimination that takes place in applying for posts and applies to employment agencies. There are certain exceptions with regard to bona fide qualifications because of the nature of the employment and those attending to the personal or medical needs of an individual, child, spouse or same-sex partner.

Most of the complaints on the grounds of age are related to employment, although they were only a small proportion of the total. Some 69.03 per cent of all complaints received related to employment matters (Table 6.1).

Table 6.1   New complaints to the OHRC 2008–2009[30]

Type	Number
Age	81
Ancestry	41
Citizenship	10
Creed	36
Disability	388
Ethnic origin	118
Family status	58
Marital status	19
Race and colour	277
Sex	143
Sexual orientation	21

30 Ontario Human Rights Commission annual report 2008–2009.

The average settlement for all complaints amounted to $8,495.48, and the average settlement for age complaints was $8,560.99.

MANDATORY RETIREMENT

In 2004 the Ontario government held a consultation exercise on whether to end the mandatory retirement age. The Ontario Human Rights Commission, as part of that consultation, submitted that mandatory retirement is a form of age discrimination because it involves making an employment decision solely on the basis of age, and not the person's ability to do the job; it undermines older Ontarians' independence, participation, and ability to make choices, which is contrary to the values of the Code; and, it can have serious financial impacts on certain groups, such as women, recent immigrants, racialized communities and persons with disabilities.

In 2005 the Ontario government introduced legislation to amend the definition of age in the Ontario Human Rights Code. The Code defined age as meaning ages between 18 and 65 years. The new legislation has the effect of removing the upper limit, so as to effectively make many mandatory retirement ages unlawful.

There is still to be a bona fide occupational requirement which may justify the retention of some compulsory retirement ages. In such cases the employer must show that:

- An age-based job requirement or qualification is a bona fide occupational requirement.

- The employee does not meet the job requirement or qualification; and

- The employee could not be accommodated without causing undue hardship to the employer.

The Minister of Labour at the time stated: 'Ending mandatory retirement would allow workers to retire based on lifestyle, circumstances and priorities. We listened to the needs and concerns of business, labour and others who have consulted with us and are doing this in a way that protects existing rights to pension, early retirement and benefit plans.'

This is a refreshing attitude which the British government might have considered emulating, rather than introducing a national mandatory retirement age through the concept of the 'default retirement age' (see Chapter 7).

Ireland

The Equality Authority in Ireland produced a report in conjunction with older peoples' groups which distinguished between biological ageing and social ageing:[31]

> *Biological ageing is a continuous process. However, societal attitudes, assumptions and barriers create social ageing, which is the subject of much of this report. For instance, the link between chronological age and what is and is not expected of a person at that age is socially conditioned. These social constructs can be taken as the received wisdom by people generally because they have not been examined reflectively or critically or remain unchallenged. In this kind of setting it may be very hard for individuals to see how their actions are in fact ageist rather than 'plain common sense'. Where people cannot see that there is something ageist in their assumptions and principles it may be hard to bring about change in behaviour or practice.*

The Employment Equality Act 1998, as amended by the Equality Act 2004, includes age discrimination in employment within its scope. The Equal Status Act 2000 covers certain other areas apart from employment. Section 6(1) of the 1998 Act provides that discrimination shall be taken to occur where: 'A person is treated less favourably than another person is, had been or would be treated in a comparable situation on any of the grounds specified in Subsection (2).'

Subsection 6(2) then refers to a number of discriminatory grounds, as between any two persons, including 'that they are of different ages'. The lower age limit is the statutory school leaving age (16 years), although employers may set a minimum recruitment age of 18 years if they so wish.[32]

A number of specific areas are contained in the Act[33] which provides protection against discrimination in relation to:

---

31 'Implementing equality for older people' (2004).
32 Employment Equality Act 1998, Section 6(3).
33 Ibid., Section 8.

- Access to employment.

- Conditions of employment.

- Training or experience for or in relation to employment.

- Promotion or re-grading.

- Classification of posts.

A non-discriminatory equality clause is implied into every contract of employment (excluding pensions), unless the employer can show that there are non-discriminatory reasons for the differences.[34] The Act also provides protection from indirect discrimination[35] and harassment in the workplace.[36]

A number of exceptions to the principle of non-discrimination are permitted:

- A provision that permits the setting of different retirement ages, whether voluntarily or compulsorily, of employees or any group of employees.[37]

- A provision that permits the setting of a maximum recruitment age when taking into account the period of time involved in training and the need for a reasonable period of time prior to retirement age when the recruit will be effective in the job.

- The setting of different rates of remuneration or different terms and conditions if the difference is based on relative seniority or length of service in a particular post.[38]

The retirement age in the public sector for people who joined before 1 April 2004 is 65 years. Some occupations such as the police, firefighters and the armed forces have provisions for earlier retirement. The minimum retirement age is now 65 for people who joined the public sector after 1 April 2004. This

---

34 Ibid., Section 30.
35 Ibid., Section 31.
36 Ibid., Section 14A.
37 According to ibid., Section 6(3)(c), the offering of a fixed-term contract to a person over the compulsory retirement age shall not be taken as constituting discrimination on the age ground.
38 Ibid., Section 34(3)–(5).

means that new entrants to the public sector will not have to retire at 65 but can continue working, subject to suitability and health requirements.

Section 38 of the Act also provided for the continuation of the previously existing Employment Equality Agency and renamed it as the Equality Authority. The Authority has four main functions:

1.   To work towards the elimination of discrimination in relation to employment.

2.   To promote equality of opportunity in relation to matters to which the Act applies.

3.   To provide information to the public and keep under review the relevant Acts.

4.   To keep under review the working of the Pensions Act 1990 as regards the principle of equal treatment.

The Equality Tribunal's Legal review for 2009 showed the range of complaints referred to it (Table 6.2).[39]

Table 6.2   Equality tribunal statistics 2009

Grounds	Employment status and pensions
Gender	95
Age	41
Disability	117
Race	289
Traveller community	2
Marital status	2
Family status	8
Sexual orientation	6
Religion	0
Multiple grounds	209
Total	769

---

39   See the Equality Tribunal website at <www.equalitytribunal.ie>.

If there is sufficient information to infer discrimination on the basis of age, then the burden of proof is with the employer to show that the action complained of was for a non-discriminatory reason.

Ireland, of course, is the nearest jurisdiction to the UK, which has had age discrimination legislation for some years. Some of the issues raised are those connected with the following.

PROMOTION

In *Gillen v Department of Health and Children*,[40] Mr Gillen claimed that he had been discriminated against on the grounds of age during two competitions for promotion within the Department. He was 54 years old. In the first competition there were six successful candidates chosen from 23 applicants. There were five other applicants who were also over the age of 50 years and none of them were selected. In the second competition there were twenty applicants, including seven who were aged 50 years or more. The successful candidate was 35 years old. Mr Gillen claimed to have more appropriate experience than the successful candidates. He had also been told on a number of occasions that he was suitable for promotion. Two other internal competitions also resulted in no one of 50 or above being appointed. The Equality Officer, who was investigating, secured information about the respondent's promotion statistics since 1998 and was also influenced by the fact that no records of the interviews were kept. The outcome was a finding that the employee had established a prima facie case of age discrimination and that the employer had failed to rebut it. Apart from recommendations to reform its selection processes the Department was ordered to pay the complainant €40,000 as compensation for the consequences of discrimination.

Carroll v Monaghan Vocational Guidance Education Committee also concerned a complaint of age discrimination in a public body's promotion process. Mrs Mary Carroll applied for one of six Special Duties Teacher Posts in the College for which she worked. There were twelve applicants and all the successful candidates were younger than her. The employer should have followed Department of Education and Science advice about the weight to be given to experience and service. They purported to do so, but it was clear that teachers with less experience had been awarded higher scores against these criteria than Mrs Carroll. In fact the candidates with the longest experience received the lowest marks. Again there were no interview notes available so the employer

---

40 Equality Officer's decision DEC-E2003-035.

was unable to back up its assertion that appointments had been made on a meritorious basis on the day of the interviews. They were not therefore able to rebut the prima facie case established by the complainant and were ordered to pay her back pay (she had subsequently been promoted) and give her €10,000 as compensation for distress suffered.

EARLY RETIREMENT[41]

Mr McLoughlin worked for Bus Éireann as a bus driver for 23 years. He successfully applied for a voluntary severance package which was on offer from the employer. Before he left he asked to be considered for any part-time work vacancies that might occur. After he had left he again applied, but was told that it was not company policy to re-employ people who had taken early retirement. Statistics, subsequently requested by the Equality Authority, showed that over 96 per cent of those who took advantage of the voluntary severance scheme were over the age of 50 years. The Equality Officer found that the claimant had been indirectly discriminated against on the ground of age and awarded him €3,000 as compensation. She also ordered the employer to treat any future application from Mr McLoughlin in the same manner as any other candidate.

RECRUITMENT

Hughes v Aer Lingus concerned a 53-year-old applicant for a cabin crew position. She was experienced in the job, having worked for another airline for some years. Aer Lingus held preliminary walk-in interviews in which the claimant participated. She received a favourable report and progressed to the second interview stage where she was questioned about how she would cope with younger people being in charge and how, being older, she would feel about starting again on the bottom rung of the ladder. She was subsequently turned down and complained that she had been turned down because of her age. The employer responded by rejecting this and said that it was because she had so much experience that the interviewers had concluded that she would have difficulties taking a much more junior post than she was used to. In the event the employer was able to show that it had employed three people over the age of 50 years in the recruitment exercise, albeit out of 150 successful applicants. The Equality Officer accepted that there was not a blanket policy on not considering older applicants for cabin crew positions and concluded that she had failed to establish a prima facie case that she was not recruited because of her age.

---

41 *Brian McLoughlin v Bus Éireann.*

However, the Equality Officer then went on to conclude that the claimant was subject to a discriminatory line of questioning in the second interview. As a result the Company was held to have discriminated on the grounds of age. They were obliged to pay €3,000 as compensation and to give the claimant a further interview by a different interview board within 12 weeks if they had not offered her a post within the same time period.

One further example, cited in the Equality Authority Annual Report 2004 was about a claimant who went for an interview for a position as a legal secretary with a firm of solicitors. During the interview she was asked her age and whether she was married. She responded by saying that the first question was not relevant and that she did not think it correct to ask the second. At that point the potential employer terminated the interview and subsequently agreed to mediation. The result was that the firm of solicitors apologised to the claimant and paid her compensation.

ADVERTISING

Ryanair published an advertisement in the *Irish Times* for a Director of Regulatory Affairs.[42] In the advertisement the Company stated that they needed: 'A young and dynamic professional' and also that, 'the ideal candidate will be young, dynamic ...'. The complaint was that this was in breach of Section 10(1) of the Employment Equality Act which provides that a person must not publish, or cause to be published, an advertisement, relating to employment, which indicates an intention to discriminate or might reasonably be understood as an indication such an intention. The respondent claimed that it was not in contravention of the Act because it did not advertise a particular age or age range and that the word 'young' was always used in conjunction with the word 'dynamic'. They stated that they wanted to attract not only experienced candidates but also those who might have less experience. In the event the respondent said that 30 candidates had applied, and of those that gave the information, their ages were between 25 and 38. The successful candidate was 32. The Equality Officer found the complaint to be justified and stated:

> *In my view many people who are older rightly regard themselves as young or young at heart. However, most people in that situation recognise that others may not, necessarily, regard them in the same light. In my opinion, people in such a situation seeking employment*

---

42 *Equality Authority v Ryanair.*

would feel rejected and excluded when they see an advertisement which specifies 'young' as a requirement for a job.

The Equality officer awarded £8,000 in compensation and also that the respondent carry out a full review of its equal opportunities policies to ensure compliance with the Act.

Other cases concerning advertising were also summarised in the 2004 Equality Authority's annual report: 'A newspaper published a recruitment agency advertisement for 'young and dynamic' people for jobs in telesales. Subsequently the newspaper and the agency apologised for the mistake and agreed to re-advertise the jobs as well as reviewing their own policies with regard to proof reading of advertisements.'

An advertisement appeared in a newspaper in 2004 stating: 'My client is seeking an enthusiastic young person looking to springboard their career.' The Equality Authority requested the re-advertisement of the position and that no appointment should be made as a result of the original advertisement.

United States of America

One report for the US government defined age discrimination as the rejection of an older worker because of assumptions about the effect of age on the worker's ability to perform, regardless of whether there was any factual basis for the assumptions.[43]

During the debate on what was to become the Civil Rights Act of 1964, the US Congress rejected attempts to amend the Bill[44] by adding age discrimination to the others being considered at the time, such as race, colour, sex and religion. Instead it directed the Secretary of Labor to investigate the issue and make recommendations for future action.[45] The result of this investigation was a report to Congress entitled 'The older American worker-age discrimination in employment' in June 1965. It stated that:

Collectively, the leading studies on various aspects of the effects of aging document the conclusion that chronological age is a poor indicator of

---

43 Gregory (2001).
44 See Eglit (1999).
45 The House of Representatives rejected the amendment by 123–94 and the Senate by 63–28.

working ability. Health, mental and physical capacities, work attitudes, and job performance are individual traits at any age. Indeed, measures of traits in different age groups usually show many of the older workers to be superior to the average for the younger group and many of the younger ones inferior to the average for the older group.[46]

The report concluded that many employers adopted specific age limits and that these limits had a marked effect on the employment of older workers. This arbitrary age discrimination caused harm by firstly depriving the economy of the productive labour of millions as well as adding substantially increased social security costs, and secondly, it inflicted economic and psychological injury on those affected. It stated that age discrimination was rarely based on the rationale that motivated racial discrimination, but that it was still based on stereotypes which had no basis in fact. The report stated that: 'We find no significant evidence of … the kind of dislike or intolerance that sometimes exists in the case of race, color, religion, or national origin, and which is based on considerations entirely unrelated to ability to perform a job.'

It did go on to say, however, that: 'We do find substantial evidence of … discrimination based on unsupported general assumptions about the effect of age on ability … in hiring practices that take the form of specific age limits applied to older workers as a group.'[47]

There had been a history of legislation at State level to outlaw age discrimination in employment. Indeed, in 1965, there were 20 States that already had such legislation, including Colorado which had introduced such a law as far back as 1903. The majority of these laws outlawed discrimination against older workers (those between 40 and 65 years), although Colorado, Idaho, Louisiana, New Jersey and Oregon had either lower minimum ages or none at all.

In 1964 also, the President[48] issued an Executive Order[49] establishing a policy against age discrimination in employment by federal contractors and sub-contractors. The Order provided that contractors and sub-contractors could not discriminate on the basis of age in hiring, promotion, termination or

---

46   p. 81.
47   See Eglit (1999).
48   Lyndon B. Johnson.
49   Order No 11141, February 12 1964.

terms and conditions of employment. It also barred age limits in recruitment advertising.

The outcome of these measures and this debate was the Age Discrimination in Employment Act 1967 (the ADEA).

AGE DISCRIMINATION IN EMPLOYMENT ACT 1967

The ADEA is only concerned with older workers, in contrast to the UK Regulations which cover all ages. It applies to workers who are least 40 years' of age.[50] The Act also only applies to those employers who had at least 20 employees for 20 or more calendar weeks in the preceding year.[51] The ADEA requires the employer to ignore an employee's age (absent a statutory exemption or defense); it does not specify further characteristics that an employer must ignore.[52]

The Act itself has been amended on a number of occasions. Most notably this included the Age Discrimination in Employment Act Amendments of 1978 which increased the upper age limit (from 65 years imposed when the Act was originally adopted) to 70 years for non-federal employees and removed it altogether for federal employees. It also stopped mandatory retirement prior to the age of 70 years. In 1986 this was further amended so that the upper age limit of 70 years for protection was effectively removed for all workers. There were also further substantial amendments brought about by the Older Workers Benefit Protection Act of 1990 and the Civil Rights Act of 1991.

The purpose of the ADEA is described in Section 2(b) as threefold:

1.   To promote employment of older persons based on their ability rather than age.

2.   To prohibit arbitrary age discrimination in employment.

3.   To help employers and workers find ways of meeting problems arising from the impact of age on employment.

---

50   ADEA, Section 12(a).
51   ADEA, Section 11(b).
52   *Hazen Paper Co v Biggins.*

The Act applies to labour organisations and employment agencies as well as to employers in general.

Section 4(a) states that: 'It shall be unlawful for an employer:

1.   To fail or refuse to hire or to discharge any individual or otherwise discriminate against any individual with respect to his compensation, terms, conditions, or privileges of employment, because of such individual's age.

2.   To limit, segregate, or classify his employees in any way which would deprive or tend to deprive any individual of employment opportunities or otherwise adversely affect his status as an employee, because of such an individual's age.

3.   To reduce the wage rate of any employee in order to comply with this chapter.'[53]

Thus discrimination on the grounds of age is unlawful in hiring and firing; compensation, assignment, or classification of employees; transfer, promotion, layoff, or recall; job advertisements; recruitment; testing; use of company facilities; training and apprenticeship programs; fringe benefits; pay, retirement plans, and disability leave; or other terms and conditions of employment.[54]

There are, however, two general exceptions to the protection offered. The first is where 'the differentiation is based on reasonable factors other than age' and the second is for a bona fide occupational qualification (BFOQ) reasonably necessary to the normal operation of the particular business.[55] Some cases in the Supreme Court have highlighted how these exceptions can be used to treat discrimination on the grounds of age differently to other grounds such as race and sex (see later).

There are a number of specific exceptions where it will not be unlawful for an employer, employment agency or labour organisation to take action that might otherwise be prohibited.[56] These are to take any action:

---

53 ADEA, Sections 4(b) and 4(c) apply similar provisions to employment agencies and labour organisations.
54 List taken from EEOC's website (see later) at <www.eeoc.gov>.
55 ADEA, Section 4(f)(1).
56 ADEA, Section 4(f).

- To observe the terms of a bona fide seniority system that is not intended to evade the purpose of the legislation.

- To observe the terms of a bona fide employee benefits plan.

- To discharge or otherwise discipline an individual for good cause.

There is also a specific exception for 'highly compensated people'.[57] Similarly there is an exception to the retirement provisions of the higher paid. Section 12(c)(1) states that: 'Nothing in this chapter shall be construed to prohibit compulsory retirement of any employee who has attained age of 65 years … and for two years prior has been a bona fide executive or in a high policy-making position and can receive a pension of at least $44,000 per annum.'

ESTABLISHING AGE DISCRIMINATION

An individual claiming unlawful age discrimination will need to show disparate treatment. Disparate treatment requires it to be shown that the employer intentionally treated an individual less favourably because of their age. The onus is first on the plaintiff to establish a prima facie case of discriminatory intent. The employer is then able to argue a permissible non-discriminatory justification, thus leaving the plaintiff with the opportunity to argue that this non age-based justification is false. This no longer seems to apply in some situations making it much more difficult to bring age claims (see later – 'Supreme Court limits the effects of ADEA').

In *Woroski v Nashau Corporation*[58] the Court accepted that a prima facie case had been indicated when two plaintiffs complained of age discrimination after losing their jobs in a 'reduction in force' exercise. The employers, however, were able to show a proper business motivation for large-scale downsizing and that there was a lack of evidence that the operation was 'infected by age bias'. In order to establish a prima facie case of age discrimination a plaintiff needed to show that:

- They were in the protected age group.

- They were qualified for the position.

---

57 ADEA, Section 4(5); highly compensated employee within the meaning of Section 414(q) of title 26 – the Internal Revenue Code of 1986.
58 *Woroski v Nashau Corp* citing *Spence v Maryland Casualty Co; McDonnell Douglas Corp v Green.*

- They were adversely affected.

- The discharge occurred under circumstances giving rise to an inference of age discrimination.

Disparate impact, on the other hand, would require an apparently neutral employment policy that in fact has an adverse impact on older workers, but cannot be justified by any sort of business necessity justification. Traditionally this had not been possible under ADEA, but in March 2005 the US Supreme Court handed down a judgment stating that age discrimination may be shown using the disparate impact approach.

Smith v City of Jackson, Mississippi concerned a group of older police officers. The City had pay increases to all its police officers, but had given more to those with less than five years service, in order to make their pay more competitive. As older officers tended to have more service, then they claimed that this policy had an adverse impact upon them because of their age. A majority of the Court held that ADEA allowed disparate impact claims, although not all for the same reason. The application of disparate impact to age was limited by the Court, for example if the employer was able to show that the prohibited practice was based on reasonable factors other than age (see later), such as seniority. Unfortunately for the plaintiffs, although the Court had made this important judgment, it also concluded that the police officers had not shown a specific practice which resulted in the alleged effect. This inclusion of disparate impact has, however, been considerably weakened by Court decisions which have used the RFOA defence to justify some apparently discriminatory practices by showing that they are 'reasonable'.

Unlike in the UK, where all are covered by the legislation, the US has a protected class – those aged 40 years and over. This may aid the judgment as to whether there has been discrimination on the basis of age. Discrimination against someone in the protected class in favour of someone from the unprotected class might infer age discrimination. This is not conclusive, however, as discrimination can take place between two persons within the protected class.

Because the ADEA prohibits discrimination on the basis of age and not class membership, the fact that a replacement is substantially younger than the plaintiff is a far more reliable indicator of age discrimination than is the fact that the plaintiff was replaced by someone outside the protected class.[59]

REASONABLE FACTORS OTHER THAN AGE

An employer may be permitted to take actions against an older worker for reasons other than age,[60] and seems to be considered on a case-by-case basis. The employer, however, cannot rely on stereotypical images of a decline in abilities with age. On the other hand, Congress made it plain that the age statute was not meant to prohibit employment decisions based on factors that sometimes accompany advancing age, such as declining health or diminished vigor and competence.[61]

One issue is how to distinguish between discrimination on the basis of age and treatment resulting from certain characteristics that come with age. In the UK there will clearly be an important overlap with the Disability Discrimination Act 1995. Dismissals for capability in such circumstances may end up being tested both under the Age Discrimination Regulations and under the Disability Discrimination Act.

In *Beith v Nitrogen Products Inc* an employer dismissed a 55-year-old employee because of back problems. He had been taken on as a temporary operator pending a physical examination. Mr Beith's examination revealed that he had some degenerative disc disease and some osteoarthritis. As a result it was recommended that he did not regularly lift weights over 20 lbs. On the basis of the report his employers decided that he was at high risk of being injured and claiming compensation. His employment was therefore terminated.

Mr Beith also happened to be the oldest employee in his department. He obtained a second medical opinion stating that there was no reason why he should not continue working as his medical condition was normal for a man of his age. He lost his appeal because, firstly, according to the Court, he did not manage to show that he had been replaced by a younger person. This is also an issue in the UK. The US legislation has a protected class of all those of 40 years and over and it is therefore possible to look at treatment of those in the protected class and compare them with treatment of those outside the class (those under the age of 40 years) in order to try to establish a prima facie

---

59 *O'Connor v Consolidated Coin Caterers Corp* at 313; see also *Metz v Transit Mix Inc.* which concerned the dismissal of an older worker with 27 years service in favour of a much younger worker who would be paid considerably less. See also Weber (1998).
60 See generally Mitchell (2001).
61 *Holley v Sanyo Manufacturing Inc.* quoted in *Beith v Nitrogen Products Inc.*

case of age discrimination. When everybody is protected such a comparison is much more difficult. Secondly, the Court also rejected Mr Beith's argument that because his back condition was an ordinary and natural consequence of ageing, then, by inference, he was really dismissed because of his age. Because such back conditions are more common in older persons, it did not follow that a dismissal because of the back condition was an age-based decision.

One commonly accepted pretext for turning down older candidates for positions is that they are over-qualified. Because an older person may have a curriculum vitae which shows longer experience and perhaps more qualifications than younger candidates, employers may be able to cite 'over qualification' as a reason for turning down an application for employment. This may, at times, be a genuine reason of course, but there will also be occasions when this is just a pretext for turning down an application from someone who is, in the employer's eyes, too old to be considered. This was the claim in *E.E.O.C. v Insurance Co. of North America*. The employer placed an advertisement in a Phoenix newspaper for a 'loss control representative'. The advertisement described the ideal candidate as someone with a degree, or equivalent professional experience, two years loss control experience, verbal and communication skills, the ability to travel and who is a self-motivated professional. Mr Pugh, who had over 30 years relevant experience, applied. He did not obtain an interview, all the short-listed candidates were younger than him and, in the event, a 28-year-old, with no loss control experience, was recruited. During the EEOC's (see later) investigation of the recruitment process it was stated on a number of occasions that Mr Pugh was held to be over-qualified.

There were other reasons given for not short listing him. These included the unprofessional nature of his application (hand-writing on his CV and no covering letter) and the fact that he might consume too much working time in investigating uncomplicated accounts as a result of all his experience. The Court did not find that the phrase 'over qualified' in this case was a pretext for age discrimination. Indeed if the employer's rejection was based on a genuine belief that he was over qualified, that belief did not violate the ADEA. Other courts had shown scepticism about the use of the term 'over qualified',[62] but in this case the evidence was that the assertion that Mr Pugh was over qualified was not a mask for age discrimination. This case perhaps illustrates some difficulties with proving discrimination at the application stage. At what stage does the experience that an individual candidate has become too much for the

---

62   *Taggart v Time Inc* was cited.

job in question? Maybe an experienced older worker applies for positions that are at a lower level than that at which they have been operating just in order to get back into the workforce. Does an employer's rejection of an older candidate on these grounds amount to age discrimination in employment? Is it valid to argue that a less-experienced person will be more suited to the role?

BONA FIDE OCCUPATIONAL QUALIFICATION

In *Western Airlines Inc. v Criswell* it was held that an employer can show age as a BFOQ by proving that some members of the age-defined group cannot perform the job safely and efficiently and that they cannot be identified by any means other than age. The airline operated a policy of retiring its pilots at the age of 60 years and such pilots were denied re-assignment as flight engineers because such posts also had a mandatory retirement age of 60 years. In theory a flight engineer could be called upon to fly an aircraft if both the pilot and the co-pilot were incapacitated. The issue was whether the retirement age of 60 years for flight engineers could be a genuine BFOQ.

The airline argued that the retirement age was a BFOQ 'reasonably necessary' to the safe operation of the airline, or the essence of the airline's business. The essence of the airline's business was the safe transportation of its passengers and that it could show that it was highly impractical for them to deal with each flight engineer over the age of 60 years on an individual basis to decide if that particular engineer could perform the job safely. In addition the airline asserted that some flight engineers over the age of 60 years would possess psychological and physical traits which would affect the safe performance of their duties, and that these traits could not be ascertained other than by knowing their age. There is a two-stage approach:

1. The employer must establish that there is a potential for unacceptable risk to the employer or third parties that older workers are more likely to impose.

2. The employer must prove that it is impracticable to perform individual evaluations that could identify which of these older workers pose that risk.

The Court considered that: 'Throughout the legislative history of the ADEA, one empirical fact is repeatedly emphasised: the process of psychological and physiological degeneration caused by ageing varies with each individual.'

It is not enough to make generalised assumptions and the BFOQ exception is construed narrowly. The safety of passengers is a priority that may justify the use of age-discriminatory measures such as a mandatory retirement age. Here the essence of the employer's business was the safe transportation of passengers. The employer then has two options: they can establish that there is an unacceptable risk associated with all employees over a certain age, or alternatively, that it was impossible or impracticable to deal with older employees on an individual basis.[63]

Similar arguments were raised in *Mahoney v Trabucco*. This case concerned a mandatory retirement age for all state uniformed police officers in Massachusetts. The plaintiff was a uniformed police officer but was normally employed in a desk-bound capacity as a communications person. In emergencies, however, he might be called upon to take up more strenuous conventional duties carried out by other police officers. The issue therefore was whether a generalised retirement age applying to all police officers, regardless of their individual duties, could be a genuine BFOQ. The Court held that the state had failed to justify this generalised treatment:

> *To evaluate the state's BFOQ defense against the more demanding requirements of the typical member of the uniformed branch would only serve to perpetuate the stereotyping and labelling that the ADEA was designed to prohibit, and would ignore the Act's instruction to treat older Americans on the basis of individual ability.*[64]

SUPREME COURT LIMITS EFFECT OF ADEA

Although legislation concerning discrimination on the grounds of age was contained in a different statute than that which applied to race and sex, there had been a common assumption that a similar approach would be taken in each when a complainant wanted to show that discrimination had taken place. This has been limited by the decisions of the Supreme Court in a number of cases. In *Gross v FBL Financial Services*[65] the Supreme Court appears to have denied that there was a shared approach and made it much more difficult for plaintiffs to show age discrimination in 'mixed-motive' cases. In this case Mr Jack Gross claimed that he had been demoted because of his age and he claimed a violation

---

63   The case used to illustrate this was *Usery v Tamiami Trail Tours Inc*. This concerned a company which had a policy of not hiring anyone over the age of 40 years as inter-city bus drivers.
64   At 961.
65   129 S. Ct. 2343 (2009).

of his rights under ADEA. At the District Court the jury was instructed by the Court to enter a verdict for him if he proved that he was demoted and that his age was a motivating factor in the decision to demote him. In the event the jury found for Mr Gross. On appeal this decision was reversed and the Court held that the jury had been incorrectly instructed as to when an employee alleges that he or she has suffered adverse treatment because of a mixed-motive case, that is, when there are a mixture of permissible and impermissible reasons. The Supreme Court subsequently held that a plaintiff bringing such a claim must prove that age was the 'but-for' cause of the action. The burden of proof does not switch to the employer to show that it would have taken the action regardless of age, even if there is evidence that age was a factor.[66] The ADEA was to be treated differently to the other grounds of discrimination such as race and sex because the plaintiff now had to show that age was the reason the employer decided to act. It appears subsequently that some lower courts have interpreted this to mean that age must be the sole cause of the discriminatory action. Thus it becomes almost impossible to bring an age related mixed motive claim, considerably weakening the scope of the ADEA.

Kentucky Retirement Systems v EEOC[67] concerned a claim of discrimination in relation to a disability related pension plan that, it was claimed, discriminated on the grounds of pension eligibility, even though that eligibility was based on age because the employer was not actually motivated by age. The Court relied upon *Hazen Paper v Biggins*[68] and decided that the differences in treatment were not actually motivated by age. Age and pension status were analytically distinct concepts and that here pension status did not serve as a 'proxy for age'.

It is clear that both of these cases place a severe restriction on the ability of employees to claim discrimination under the ADEA in some circumstances. At the time of writing the US Congress was considering the 'Protecting Older Workers Against Discrimination Act' as a means limiting the effects of these cases and ensuring the application of Title VII standards to the ADEA.

EQUAL EMPLOYMENT OPPORTUNITY COMMISSION (EEOC)

In 1978 the ADEA was amended to transfer responsibility for conciliation, investigation and record keeping to the EEOC. The EEOC is an independent federal agency originally set up in 1964 to enforce Title VII of the Civil Rights

---

66 See <http://www.law.cornell.edu/supct/html/08-441.ZS.html>.
67 128 S. Ct. 2361 (2008).
68 507 U.S. 604.

Act of that year. It is composed of five commissioners and general counsel in addition to a chair and vice-chair appointed by the President. There are some 50 area offices situated throughout the country. It has responsibilities that cover discrimination on the basis of race, sex, national origin, religion, disability and equal pay, as well as age.

Any charges under the ADEA must first be filed with the EEOC, subject to a time limit of between 180 and 300 days after the event complained about. The EEOC will inform the employer and may then carry out an investigation and also attempt conciliation between the parties, unless it dismisses the charge. If at any time the Commission decides that the charges will not reveal a violation of federal law, then it will be dismissed. When a charge is dismissed, this will be explained and a notice is issued which gives the complainant 90 days in which to file a lawsuit. If the investigation establishes that discrimination has occurred both parties will be informed and the EEOC will make a further attempt at conciliation, mediation or some form of settlement. If the Commission fails in this then it has 90 days in which to bring the matter to Court. If it decides not to sue, then it will issue a notice to the complainant giving him or her 90 days in which to file charges themselves.

The remedies available include back pay, hiring, promotion, re-instatement, other pay lost as a result of the discrimination plus legal fees. Compensatory and punitive damages are available.

The EEOC handles a significant number of age discrimination complaints each year, the majority of which are held to have no reasonable cause. The figures for 2004–2009 are shown in Table 6.3.

Table 6.3   EEOC statistics

Year	2004	2005	2006	2007	2008	2009
Charge receipts filed	17,837	16,585	16,548	19,103	24,582	22,778
No reasonable cause	9,563	8,866	8,746	10,002	11,124	12,788
Reasonable cause	515	583	612	625	678	614
Monetary benefit* ($ millions)	69	77.7	51.5	66.8	82.8	72

* Not obtained through litigation

The balance is made up of various withdrawals, conciliations and so on.

In the fiscal year 2009, EEOC received 22,778 charges of age discrimination and resolved 20,529 age discrimination charges in recovering some $72 million in monetary benefits for charging parties and other aggrieved individuals (not including monetary benefits obtained through litigation). The numbers are significant, making up almost 25 per cent of all charges on all grounds of discrimination.

7

Retirement

There have perhaps traditionally been a number of types of retirement age. These are the pensionable retirement age, the contractual retirement age and the actual or normal retirement age. These may all take place at the same time, or they may occur at different times.

Pensionable retirement age is that established by the pension scheme to which an individual belongs. This may range from 55 years upwards, but may be lower for particular occupations, where there may be objective justification. The state pension retirement age is being equalised so that by 2020, it will be the same (66 years) for men and for women. In order to eliminate the contractual retirement age, the link between it and the pensionable retirement age needs to be broken.

It is interesting to speculate as to why a retirement age exists at all. It appears, historically, to be a relatively recent innovation. There are differing views about its origins (Sargeant 2010).[1] One view is that there has been a decreasing demand for older workers; another is that it results from the introduction and establishment of old age pensions.[2] This first view traces retirement at the age of 65 back to the late-nineteenth and early-twentieth centuries when British and US industry went through a period of structural change and retirement became an accepted method for removing what were seen as obsolete workers from the workforce.[3] There appeared to be an increasing view that people were worn out by this age. For a period, also, early retirement was seen as a way of reducing employee numbers. This was illustrated in the Cabinet office report *Winning the Generation Game* (2000) which stated that at age 50, almost 90 per

---

1   Sargeant ILJ DRA.

2   J. Macnicol, *The Politics of Retirement in Britain 1878–1948* (Cambridge: Cambridge University Press, 1998).

3   J. Macnicol, *Age Discrimination: An Historical and Contemporary Analysis* (Cambridge: Cambridge University Press, 2006).

cent of men in the UK were in the workforce, and that by the age of 60 this had fallen to some 48 per cent.

A good example of the use of retirement as a way of reducing the workforce is illustrated in the case of *Taylor v Secretary of State for Scotland*.[4] This concerned a Mr George Taylor who was a prison officer in the Scottish Prison Service. The service had a minimum retirement age of 55 years, but at its discretion the employer could allow the employee to continue working until a maximum age of 60 years. Mr Taylor was allowed to continue to work after 55 as long as he carried out the full range of duties and provided he maintained an acceptable attendance record and satisfactory performance. Three years later, after a review, the employer decided to give notice to all those over the age of 55 years in order to recruit a younger workforce. The Employment Tribunal found that: 'The change in the retiring arrangements was part of a policy to bring about the loss of 1000 staff for the purposes of bringing in younger employees with different skills who could be paid less.'

Pensions

The alternative approach is to blame the development of old age pensions as a reason for having a cut off between working life and retirement. Until quite recently, it was suggested that more than three-quarters of men had a retirement age which was the same as the state pension age. Prior to 1989, retirement was a prerequisite of receiving the state pension, but this is no longer so: 'Many people see state pension age as the point at which society as a whole regards it as reasonable that they should stop working.'[5]

The first universal system of state old age pensions took place in 1908 with the adoption of the Old Age Pensions Act,[6] which received the royal assent on August 1 1908 after rapid progress through Parliament. Old age pensions systems had already been initiated in Germany (1898), Denmark (1891) and New Zealand (1898).

The Prime Minister, H.H. Asquith, first introduced the measure in a budget speech on 7 May 1908. He stressed the importance of having a non-contributory

---

4   [2000] IRLR 503.
5   P. Meadows, *Retirement Ages in the UK: A Review of the Literature*, Department of Trade and Industry Employment Relations Series No 18 (2003).
6   Consolidated by the Old Age Pensions Act 1936.

system and how a contribution-based one would have missed out on the most deserving:

> We have had to consider this matter very carefully, and the first conclusion at which we arrived was that all so-called contributory schemes must be ruled out. They do not meet the necessities of the case. If the contribution which is to be the condition of a pension were left to the option of the would-be pensioner, the assistance of the state might be confined to a comparatively small class, and that not by any means necessarily the most necessitous or the most deserving class.[7]

When the bill reached its second reading on June 15, Lloyd George, Chancellor of the Exchequer, stated that a contributory scheme was impossible because it would, amongst other matters, practically exclude all women from its benefits.[8]

Section 1 of the Act provided for a right to an old age pension to people provided that they fulfilled certain criteria, which were set out in Section 2. These criteria were that the individual:

- Must have attained the age of 70.

- Must satisfy the pensions authorities that for at least 20 years before receipt of the pension he or she had been a British subject.

- His or her 'yearly means' do not exceed £31.10s.[9]

Section 3 further disqualified a person from receiving a pension if he or she had been in receipt of poor law, detained in an asylum or had been convicted of an offence. It also excluded those over 60 who have been convicted under the Inebriates Act 1898! The penalties for fraudulent application were severe, with Section 9 of the Act providing for a penalty of 6 months with hard labour. The actual pension awarded was graded according to income. In order to receive the full amount, the individual's previous earnings were not to exceed £21 per annum. The age of 70 was chosen as a cost-cutting measure as the cost of granting a universal pension to all over 65, it had been estimated, would

---

7   William A. Casson (1908) Old Age Pensions Act 1908 Chas. Knight & Co, London.
8   William A. Casson, ibid.
9   10s means 10 shillings, or 50p in decimal currency; according to MeasuringWorth.com £31.10s in 1908 would be worth £2,261.17 in 2006, using the retail price index.

have been £27,508,000, compared to £16,302,000 for those aged 70 plus. The important features, in a more historical sense, of the 1908 Act were that:

- It provided an age-related pension.

- It applied equally to men and women.

- It was a subsistence pension.

- It was non-contributory.

Although it applied equally to men and women, more women potentially benefited. In 1907 there were more women than men in the ratio of 1.27:1 for the over 65s and 1.37:1 at the age of 75 plus. Not all would qualify however. A select committee in 1899 had estimated that in 1907, out of a total population aged over 65, of 2,116,000, about 686,000 would qualify for a pension. These numbers decreased by half for the population aged 70 plus.[10]

The subsistence level pension was introduced to help the very poor and it has been accurately described as: 'Hardly a pension scheme at all. Rather it was a mechanism for delivering poor relief to the destitute old provided out of the benevolence of taxpayers'.[11] It was important, in this regard, that it was non-contributory. There was no requirement to be anything but a British resident who had reached the age of 70 years. There was no rule which required a contribution from the individual over a period of time in order to qualify for a pension. It was the subsequent introduction of this contribution requirement which helped to condemn many women to retire into poverty in the succeeding century.[12]

The non-contributory principle with regard to state retirement pensions did not last long. In 1925 the Widows' Orphans' and Old Age Contributory Pensions Act introduced a compulsory scheme of contributory pensions between 65 and 70 years of age. It applied to all persons, male or female, who were employed under a contract of service, earning £250 per annum or less (unless employed in manual labour). A wife aged 65, who was not herself insured, only became entitled to a pension if her husband was already receiving one.

---

10 William A. Casson *supra*.
11 Martin Sullivan (2002) What to do about retirement ages; paper at conference on ageing populations, Institute of Actuaries, Edinburgh 2002.
12 During this period occupational pensions also increased in numbers and, in 1921, the Finance Act introduced tax relief on pension scheme contributions and investments.

Nevertheless an important principle had been established. An 'intergenerational' arrangement was entered into where the present generation agree to pay more for the past generation's pension, on understanding they will be aided by a newer generation.[13]

The Inter-Departmental Committee on Social Insurance and Allied Services[14] was appointed, according to its terms of reference: 'To undertake, with special reference to the inter-relation of the schemes, a survey of the existing national schemes of social insurance and allied services, including workmen's compensation, and to make recommendations.' All the members of the Committee, apart from the Chair, Sir William Beveridge, were civil servants. The report itself was a significant survey of the state of pensions and insurance provision at the time and made detailed recommendations for the future. In its analysis of the 'problem of age' the report stated that there were two particular issues.[15] The first, which was a reflection of the debate leading up to the adoption of the Equal Employment (Age) Regulations in 2006, was the increasing number of pensioners in relation to the numbers of young people and those working. The second was that the consequences of retirement and old age were not uniform in all cases. For some it might be poverty, but not for others.

One of the consequences was the future cost of pensions. Individuals, therefore, were to be encouraged to make their own provision rather than relying on the state provision alone. Additionally pensions were not to be paid to those that continued working after the pensionable ages of 65 for men and 60 for women. Old age pensions were only to be paid to those that were past work and had actually retired.

Beveridge felt, presumably reflecting a wider belief, that pension provision should not only be provided by the state, but also by the individual. The report stated that 'social insurance should aim at guaranteeing the minimum income needed for subsistence'.[16] An underlying assumption to the recommendations in the report was that the plan for social security would contain three elements. These were social insurance for basic needs, national assistance (means tested) for special cases and voluntary insurance for additions to the basic provision.

---

13 Martin Sullivan (2002) *supra*.
14 Inter Departmental Committee: *Social Insurance and Allied Services* Report by Sir William Beveridge 1942 Cmd. 6404.
15 See Section 2 of the Report entitled 'The problem of age'.
16 p. 14.

A second issue was that the contributions (and the benefits from) to the schemes were to be of a flat rate in nature, thus imposing a proportionately higher burden on the poor in order to secure the benefits. The report justified this by stating that those with larger means would be paying more as tax payers to the Exchequer.[17]

A third issue was the abandonment of the non-contributory part of the current pension arrangements. Those over 70 years, the majority of whom were women, were entitled, subject to a means test, to receive a pension regardless of any contributions. The post war system that was to emerge from Beveridge was one based on contributions. In particular, married women were able to rely on their husbands' contributions, rather than building up a pensionable service in their own right.[18] This meant that such women would not be entitled to any pension until their husband retired.

The National Insurance Act 1946 subsequently established the foundations for, amongst other matters, post war policy towards old age pensions. Section 1(2) of the Act divided insured persons into three categories: employed persons, self-employed persons and non-employed persons. It did not include a fourth category, which Beveridge had recommended, of married women.[19] All insured persons, with the exception of those unemployed or incapable of work, or drawing pensions or in full-time education,[20] were to be paying insurance contributions. Thus a universal and comprehensive system of national insurance was introduced.

It is interesting how the legislation on employment protection mirrored closely the state pension age and, perhaps, historically reflected an expectation that employees will retire from work at the state pension age. Prior to the Age Regulations 2006, the Employment Rights Act 1996 had, for example, excluded employees from protection against unfair dismissal (Section 109) or the right to redundancy payments (Section 156) if they had reached the employer's normal retirement age or 65 years. This exclusion had been in existence for some time. The Industrial Relations Act 1971, which introduced the concept of unfair dismissal, contained such an exclusion in Section 28(b). This referred to the

---

17 p. 121.
18 p. 120.
19 The Act was preceded in September 1944 by Part One of a White Paper on Social Insurance Cmd 6550; Part Two was published in the same month Cmd 6551. The White Paper divided everyone into six classes: employees, self employed, housewives, adults who did not earn, children, and people over working age.
20 Section 5 National Insurance Act 1946.

employer's normal retirement age or an age of 65 for men and 60 for women, thus depriving women of this protection at an earlier age. An even earlier piece of legislation, the Redundancy Payments Act 1965, which first introduced statutory redundancy payments, contained a similar provision.

One of the consistent themes of responses to government consultation on age discrimination has been that of the trade unions who have been concerned that an abolition of the mandatory retirement age, or any change to the retirement age, should not be at the expense of an individual's right to a decent retirement pension. There has been a suspicion that measures affecting the retirement age are really intended to reduce the current pension entitlement of workers at a certain age. One trade union, Amicus, for example, declared that it was against setting a default retirement age at 70[21] because this would encourage employers to reduce pension benefits currently available at state pension age. Creating an opportunity for the minority who wish to carry on working must not be at the expense of others. One way for employers to reduce costs is for there to be a later retirement age with reduced benefits for those who retire earlier; Amicus believed that: 'The government should seek to protect the current right of those employees who are contractually entitled to retire on full pension not later than 65.'[22]

Britain's trade unions have been campaigning firstly for a retirement pension, and secondly, for a reasonable level of income, since the latter part of the nineteenth century. The assumption behind the trade union campaigns has, of course, been that those who retire at the end of their working life are entitled to a reasonable income in their retirement. This may be the approach in some other EU member states but has not been the case in the UK. The only purpose of the state pension seems to be to prevent poverty. The Pensions Commission in its first report summed this position up:

> *Among the rich, developed countries the UK is therefore in a specific*
> *group with Ireland, New Zealand and Canada, where the state pension*
> *is primarily designed to prevent poverty rather than to provide income*
> *replacement. In these systems, replacement rates for those on half*
> *average earnings during working life are not far below continental*
> *levels but they are much lower for the average earner.*[23]

---

21 This was a proposal in 2003 consultation.
22 Amicus response to the 2003 DTI consultation exercise, published in 2005.
23 'Pensions: challenges and choices. The first report of the Pensions Commission' (2004).

Given this situation it seems rather strange to force people to give up work and enter into near poverty. Many people have some alternative income to add to the state pension, but many do not. Some 59 per cent of employees work for a firm with a fixed retirement age – 68 per cent men and 48 per cent women.[24] More than twice as many professional men (76 per cent) are members of an occupational pensions scheme compared to unskilled workers (34 per cent); for women the figures are 71 per cent and 27 per cent. One particular group at a disadvantage are part-time women employees, 28 per cent of whom are in occupational pension schemes compared to 55 per cent of full-timers.

An acceptance that state pension provision in the UK is actually about the alleviation of poverty, rather than about replacement of income from work, might affect the argument about the mandatory retirement age, contained in so many contracts of employment, and the so-called default retirement age. If the reality is that for many pensioners the objective of the state pension is the alleviation of poverty, then it does not seem sensible to argue for a mandatory retirement age. The logic of the argument for the stipulation of this age is that it is intended to drive many into poverty and then give them the minimum financial help contained in the state retirement pension. One argument for retaining flexibility is to enable some people to work their way out of poverty. The second report of the Turner Commission on pensions argued for more flexibility around retirement. It said, of the state pension system, that: 'Given demographic trends, either the average generosity of this system (relative to national earnings) or pensionable ages must rise, or the tax/national insurance contributions devoted to pensions must rise as a percentage of GDP.'[25]

Not only was the old system unfair it was also unsustainable given the change in the demographic make-up of the population.

Most other unions supported this call for flexibility, such as the GMB which stated that some members look forward to a fixed retirement age and others wanted more flexibility: 'The GMB wants to see a framework which enables employers and trade unions to come together to develop a flexible approach to retirement. This would enable older workers to scale down their activity gradually by working part-time.'

---

24 'Ageing and employment policies UK' (2004).
25 'A new pension settlement for the twenty-first century: The second report of the Pensions Commission' (2005).

Why Have a Retirement Age?

It is projected that there will be one million fewer working-age people under the age of 50 and three million more aged over 50 by 2022.[26] Older workers will play an increasingly important part in the economy, so it does seem strange that the government still insisted in 2006 on allowing the practice of compulsory retirement by employers which means ending the contribution of many millions of workers to the economy. There is now enough evidence to show that for many the leaving of the workforce means entering poverty. The government elected in 2010 is phasing out the default retirement age (see later) but there remains the possibility of employer justified retirement ages, allowing them to continue to discriminate against older workers.

The arguments set out in this book are not arguments in favour of employers conducting an age-neutral policy in the workplace or that age is not an issue for workers of different ages. Workers in their 50s and 60s may experience a wide range of personal circumstances which are not necessarily experienced by younger workers and a failure to take these other factors into account may end up amounting to age discrimination at work. One study suggests that there are a number of issues that can play a major part in work decisions of older workers, especially with regard to when they might decide to retire:[27]

- Health and fitness issues – many people may live and work longer, but for a substantial minority, health issues will have an important effect on their working lives, for example the large numbers of people who retire for reasons of sickness and disability.

- Having caring responsibilities – about one in five people in their 50s has responsibility for care in relation to older relatives and to grandchildren.

- Peoples' views and outlook may change as they get older – work may become less important than roles in the family or the community, especially, for example in relation to partners who may retire or have health or other problems. The conduct of a sensible policy requires an appreciation of this rather than a strictly neutral policy which tries to ignore age altogether.

26 Whiting (2005); the figures come from projections by the government Actuary's Department.
27 Hirsch (2003).

There are almost 850,000 people aged 65 plus who are in employment in the UK.[28] This is made up of 506,000 men and 340,000 women. This represents an employment rate of some 8.6 per cent in total; 11.5 per cent for men and 6.2 per cent for women. Both men and women who continue to work are more likely to be self-employed and/or working part-time than other groups. Thus some 37.4 per cent of all workers in work over the age of 65 years are self-employed (46 per cent of men and 23.1 per cent of women) compared to the 50–54 age group which had 15.1 per cent who were self-employed. Some 73.9 per cent of over-65s, in work, are part-timers (66.6 per cent of men and 86.2 per cent of women) compared to the 50–54 age group where 23 per cent worked part-time.[29]

These figures do not necessarily suggest that there is anything wrong with working part-time or being self-employed, but are perhaps a reflection of the wish for flexible forms of working for this age group. It is interesting that the research also suggests that the older a person was when leaving full-time employment the less likely they were to make the transition to retirement through flexible employment, or 'bridge employment'.[30] 'In some cases bridge employment represents a positive choice, giving older workers the opportunity to undertake new and challenging work on their own terms; in other situations it is merely a downgrading of people's previous working conditions.'[31]

Research suggests that about one-third of all those who begin to draw their pensions are aged 54 years or less and about two-thirds are aged 59 years or under.[32] A DTI survey showed that only 43 per cent of the male respondents and 40 per cent of the female ones expected to retire at the state pension age, although one in three would like to retire earlier.[33] According to the government Green Paper 'Working and saving for retirement' the mean age for men retiring in the UK is 62.6 years and for women 61.1 years. Amongst those already retired and who had retired early, the survey found that 33 per cent had retired because of illness or disability, 16 per cent were made redundant and 17 per cent had their workplace closed or changed. Perhaps not surprisingly, given these figures, some three-quarters of all firms have no employees over the age of 60 years.[34]

---

28   Figures from Labour Market Statistical Bulletin October 2010; Office for National Statistics.
29   Whiting (2005).
30   Ibid. Drawing upon research by Lissenburgh and Smeaton (2003).
31   Ibid.
32   'Early retirement schemes still the norm in final salary schemes' (2002).
33   See DTI report on the Code of Practice.
34   Grattan (2002).

What is clear is that many people retire early out of choice. It would be wrong to argue that a compulsory retirement system which may breach individual human rights is not welcomed by many. Retirement offers many opportunities for people and for many it must be an exciting and challenging new chapter in their lives. It is seen as a reward for a lifetime of work. It is a strange concept, however, that says that we should all have the same retirement age regardless of our wishes or needs. Surely the only sustainable argument in favour of retirement must be an argument in favour of a variable and flexible retirement age. Otherwise it becomes coercive and unwelcome to many.

Making Way for Younger Workers

Retiring older workers to make way for new workers entering the workforce has always been an argument by both employers and trade unions in favour of making people retire at a certain age. On a global scale this approach assumes that there are a finite number of jobs available and if older workers did not leave the workforce, then there would be few jobs for young people eager to enter the workforce. On a smaller level, it provides a simple means for employers to carry out workforce planning as older (and more senior) workers retire they can be replaced by suitably trained and promoted or recruited younger employees.

The global argument has a simplistic charm but is clearly nonsense. It assumes a static society and a static economy. It is termed the 'lump of labour fallacy'.[35] The lump of labour fallacy ignores the fact that, in a flexible labour market, wages can and do adjust. More people competing for jobs means that people are less keen to demand wage increases. This reduces inflationary pressures and allows interest rates (and higher non-inflationary growth) than would otherwise be the case. A large number of new jobs are created in the UK economy each year. These are not jobs held by older workers denying a place to younger ones. There is no evidence that a lack of a mandatory retirement age would stop younger people entering the job market, as there is no evidence that the existence of a contractual retirement age would do so either.

The employer argument is seen as a means of enabling employers to plan their workforce, so that perhaps they can recruit, retain and train younger people to take over the positions of those that leave through retirement. This may be the effect in some organisations, but again it assumes a static workforce and an ordered procession in and out of organisations. Most HRM people will

---

35 See 'Winning the generation game' (2000).

know that this is not the reality within organisations. Even the contractual retirement age cannot be relied upon to make this model of workforce planning happen. As has already been shown, most people retire at a different time to the expected retirement date, sometimes through ill health and sometimes for other reasons. It is difficult to see how this helps workforce planning.

There is no evidence to support the view that older workers are inherently less productive than younger workers, except in a limited range of jobs requiring rapid reactions or physical strength, and people tend to move out of these as they become harder for them. Only where older workers do not receive the same level of training as younger workers doing the same kind of work does their performance show differences.[36]

There are two aspects to this reason for keeping a mandatory retirement age. Firstly, there is the one which is really about having stereotypical views about older and younger workers: older workers are slower, more resistant to change and so on. Hopefully, by the time you get to this part of the book you will have seen enough evidence to show that such generalisations should be unacceptable. The second factor is an important one: it is the likelihood that older workers, or those nearing retirement, earn more than younger workers for apparently doing the same or similar jobs. If one measures productivity as a return on costs, then it might be possible to argue the productivity point based on the lower wages of younger workers. An example of this in action is the *Taylor v Secretary of State for Scotland* case discussed above, where some 1,000 prison officers were retired in a deliberate policy to recruit younger and less expensive workers. This is a reflection perhaps of having long salary scales which of course employers and trade unions have argued in favour of being retained. The longer scales are a combination of reward for service and a reflection of extra skills and knowledge attained by older workers. Regardless of whether there is truth to the argument, however, the outcome is that older and more expensive employees can be removed because of their age and replaced by younger, cheaper employees, giving the employer a gain financially and perhaps managerially. This situation is not changed by the Age Regulations 2006, where the employer will be able to continue to do this.

It is worth contemplating whether having a mandatory retirement age is of benefit to employers. A survey[37] of 198 HR Directors and senior managers found that 85 per cent reported that their organisation had a mandatory retirement

---

36 'Retirement ages in the UK: a review of the literature' (2003).
37 'Is mandatory retirement really helping business? A survey report by TAEN and EFA' (2009).

age (MRA), 98 per cent said that the MRA was 65; and 95 per cent said that this applied to all employees. Some 10 per cent always agreed to employee requests to continue work; 84 per cent said sometimes and 7 per cent never did so. They were asked a number of specific questions:

Do you believe there are any of the following disadvantages in having a mandatory retirement age?			
	Yes	No	Total
• Loss to the organisation of knowledge and talent?	106 (64%)	59 (36%)	165
• Risks from demographic factors?	60 (37%)	101 (63%)	161
• Harder to maintain performance when experienced workers retire?	42 (26%)	120 (74%)	162
• Lost opportunity to be employer of choice among older and mid-life workers?	74 (45%)	89 (55%)	163
• Adverse impact on employees who would prefer to work on?	120 (74%)	43 (26%)	163
• Adverse impact on company's image?	48 (30%)	110 (70%)	158
Do you believe your organisation derives any of the following benefits from having a mandatory retirement age?			
	Yes	No	Total
• Ease of succession or manpower planning?	128 (81%)	31 (19%)	159
• Creation of headroom for younger people coming up?	129 (80%)	32 (20%)	161
• Improved performance in some way?	49 (32%)	104 (68%)	153
• Underperforming employees can be moved without disciplinary or competency procedures being used?	75 (47%)	83 (53%)	158
• Positive impact on your organisation's image?	28 (19%)	119 (81%)	147

In contrast to these views, of the 29 respondents without an MRA, 93 per cent said this was as a result of a formal policy decision. Respondents were asked to indicate whether an absence of the MRA had presented difficulties in a number of suggested ways. Only eight out of 28 (29 per cent) said it had presented problems in succession or manpower planning; nine (32 per cent) said it had created a lack of headroom for younger people coming up in the organisation, though 68 per cent disagreed that this was the case. Just five (19 per cent) said it had contributed to a decline in performance in some way and eight (30 per cent of respondents) said it had made for difficulties in managing underperforming employees though 70 per cent of the group said this was not the case. Ninety-six per cent said there had been no adverse effect on their organisation's image from abolishing the MRA.

The debate about the default retirement age seemed to be between those that have a positive view of ageing and those who are worried about the negative consequences, resulting from a decline in competency and capability traditionally associated with the ageing process.[38] This certainly showed itself in the responses of many employers to the government's consultation on the subject.[39] Most of the employer responses supported the introduction of the DRA. The employers were concerned with how to end peoples' careers with dignity, rather than through disciplinary procedures. There was a general assumption that older workers would decline in competence and capability as they aged, but would nevertheless wait to be dismissed or retired rather than leave voluntarily. One employer stated that:

> We would not want to resort to using our capability/competence procedure for long serving loyal employees who chose to stay on to a point where it affects their ability to do the job effectively. The effect would be very negative on staff morale generally if this were to happen in organisations. This is in contrast to a view which celebrates the increase in the number of older workers as an achievement for society.

EARLY RETIREMENT

Early retirement policies have been a means of encouraging older workers to exit the workforce. It is a contributory cause for there being almost three million people aged between 50 and state retirement age who are outside the labour market. The change in the workforce after the age of 50 years is quite staggering. The Cabinet Office report 'Winning the generation game' (2000) stated that at age 50, over 90 per cent of men are in the labour force in France and almost 90 per cent in the US, Sweden and the UK. By the age of 60 years this had fallen to:

France	40 per cent
US	67 per cent
Sweden	70 per cent
UK	48 per cent

---

38 D. Hirsch, *Crossroads after 50: Improving Choices in Work and Retirement* (York: Joseph Rowntree Foundation, 2003).

39 'Department of Trade and Industry, equality and diversity: coming of age' (2006).

Interestingly, in the UK, only one in ten of the 50–65 year age group were looking for work, but only 18 per cent classified themselves as retired. The same report tried to categorise these 'missing people' into five groups:

1.   Early retired, affluent professionals – some 12 per cent of the total; they have retired voluntarily and have good occupational pensions and savings, as well as being home owners.

2.   Occupational pensioners with changed expectations – homeowners with low mortgages who took early retirement because there was little alternative to this; having to adjust lifestyle to new income level.

3.   Displaced workers on invalidity benefit – former skilled manual workers who had been in a previous job for over ten years; made redundant due to company closure with small occupational income; have tried to get work again but have been unsuccessful; now de-motivated and health has suffered, so are now on invalidity benefit; wary of taking work now because of the effect on state income.

4.   Family carers – some 85 per cent of these are women; not looking for work and supported by low-paid partner; not been in full-time employment for some time and now caring for elderly relative and maybe grandchildren.

5.   Job seekers – unskilled men with few educational qualifications; have some temporary jobs but money is tight and health beginning to fail.

It is possible to argue that early retirement is a voluntary process and that, often, workers will volunteer for early retirement. It is also possible to argue that early retirement policies are a manifestation of how age discrimination became an acceptable method of reducing the size of a workforce. It is older workers who qualify for early retirement and who, often, at least historically, with the agreement of the trade unions, are selected for exiting purely because of their chronological age. It is an example of indirect discrimination, which has its major impact on older workers. One report claimed:[40]

---

40 Drury (1993).

> *Trade unions often appear to condone these practices, on the basis that redundancy and unemployment is more acceptable for older than for younger workers. In the UK, for example, trade unions sometimes campaign for 'voluntary' redundancy measures, in practice targeted at older workers, in order to avoid compulsory redundancies spread across all age groups.*

It is not possible to say how many of these 'voluntary' schemes are really voluntary (although the European Commission estimated that some 40 per cent of early retirees felt that there was an element of coercion in their decision)[41] or what proportion of affected workers feel under pressure to accept enhanced benefits, which might not be available in a situation of compulsory redundancies. The practice is seen as an acceptable way of dismissing older workers in order to avoid dismissing workers in other age groups.

In the past, UK governments have encouraged policies of early retirement. Insufficient is known about the effects on individuals who are 'early-retired', although one French study suggested:[42] 'After an explosion of initial optimism, early retirees are quickly faced with a change in the reality of their lives, in a society which has not yet developed honourable alternative roles which could be taken on by young, active and healthy retirees.'

The study suggested that many such people refuse to join organisations for older people or find an alternative role for themselves outside work. They are also likely to find it more difficult to return to work and, in the words of the French study: 'Their standard of living will also fall'.

Early retirement on enhanced packages was an attractive way for employers to reduce the size of their workforces, not least because such schemes could often be funded by the pension scheme rather than by the employer. The enhanced packages are now less common, but there remains pressure on older employees to consider such retirement.

---

41 'Towards a Europe for all ages' (1999).
42 Gaullier (1988).

Replacing the Mandatory Retirement Age

It has been suggested that retirement is: 'Both the leading form of age discrimination and the driving force behind the wider development of ageism in modern societies'.[43]

The contractual retirement age, and the default retirement age contained in the Age Regulations 2006, is an event where an employee is treated less favourably than other employees because of their chronological age. At this age, the employee is dismissed from their employment. In the Age Regulations 2006 the government took the retirement age issue from the contract of employment and enshrined it in statute.

According to the 2005 Consultation document the Framework Directive: 'Allows age discrimination if it can be objectively justified'.[44] The government was obviously convinced that the national default retirement age could be so justified. The opportunity to do this arose in the Age UK case.[45] Here it put forward its justification for introducing a default retirement age:

> *The government's labour market objectives include encouraging the recruitment, training, retention and proper remuneration of workers, and ensuring proper pension provision for them when they retire. There are a number of factors which are required to support those objectives and to ensure that employers are most likely to behave in a way which is consistent, rather than inconsistent with them.*

One of those factors is that employers have confidence in the labour market. This means, for example, that they are optimistic about future prospects and trust that the labour market will not be unduly affected by external factors over which they have no control and which will have a detrimental impact on them. In general, business prefers to operate in a climate of certainty and any factors, including labour market factors that increase uncertainty may have a detrimental effect on confidence. Significant new legislation which affects all employees will inevitably reduce the confidence of some employers because of fears about the impact, which will be uncertain at least until the case law has clarified its effect. If the government failed to consider the impact

---

43 See Walker (1990).
44 Paragraph 6.1.3.
45 The Queen on the application of *Age UK v Secretary of State for Business, Innovation and Skills and the Equality and Human Rights Commission*, HM Attorney General [2009] IRLR 1017.

of new legislation on business, employers would fear that the impact could be significant. The government's policy in regulating, therefore, is to ensure that the impact of new measures on business is always taken into account. Levels of employer confidence affect their investment and business decisions, which encompasses their decisions about employees. Without confidence then they are less likely to take the risks which are necessary to ensure increasing recruitment, training, remuneration and proper pension provision.

According to the case report, the Secretary of State took the decision to provide for a default retirement age in pursuit of two aims. These were workforce planning and avoiding an adverse impact on the provision of occupational pensions and other work-related benefits. The government also considered that other benefits would flow from the default retirement age and that these supported the aim of workforce planning. These benefits included the protection of the dignity of workers at the end of their working lives; improving the participation of workers in the 50–64 age group; and encouraging culture change.

The claimants were sceptical of most of these arguments but, in particular, were concerned at the government's motives:

> ... the Defendant did not reach the conclusion that it was justifiable to permit retirement ages above 65 (on the basis of the aim it cites) as a result of objective consideration of legitimate employment policy aims. Instead ministers determined policy on the basis of intense pressure from lobby groups. The decision reached was to adopt the policy preferred by certain employer representatives, and essentially to maintain (and not improve) the law on retirement for people over 65. The objective justification that the Defendant has offered is essentially a post-facto rationalisation of a decision made outside the framework of the test for justification.

Thus, 'the process of objective justification was made to fit the demands of changing policy, rather than policy development being constrained within parameters set by the legal test.' The government did not, of course, accept this view and stated in the second witness statement given by senior civil servant Ms McCarthy-Ward that it had carried out an 'an assessment of the relative merits of the arguments and views put forward'. Generally, the Court stated that: '... in the light of changed economic circumstances and the generally recognised problems that a longer living population creates for the social security system the case for advancing the DRA beyond minimum age of 65, at least would seem compelling.'

It was therefore a limited and conditional acceptance of the government's case in showing that the DRA of 65 was a proportionate means of achieving the legitimate aim of market confidence. What appeared to save the day for the government was the imminent review of the DRA. Indeed, the judge stated that if regulation 30 had been adopted for the first time in 2009, or if there had been no imminent review, he would have considered the selection of age 65 not to be proportionate. He stated that:

> It creates greater discriminatory effect than is necessary on a class of people who both are able to and want to continue in their employment. A higher age would not have any general detrimental labour market consequences or block access to high level jobs by future generations. If the selection of age 65 is not necessary it cannot therefore be justified. I would, accordingly, have granted relief requiring it to be reconsidered as a disproportionate measure and not capable of objective and reasonable justification in the light of all the information available to government.

European Court of Justice

Apart from the Age UK case there have been a number of other cases concerned with the ending of employment at a particular age. These include: *Félix Palacios de la Villa v Cortefiel Servicios SA*[46] where the Spanish Court asked whether the prohibition on discrimination precluded a national law allowing compulsory retirement clauses to be included in collective agreements; also, *Gisela Rosenbladt v Oellerking Gebäudereinigungsgesellschaft mbH*[47] where the German Court asked whether a national rule that a contract which specified the automatic termination of an employment relationship upon reaching a specific fixed age (in this case 65) contravened the prohibition on age discrimination; in *Vasil Ivanov Georiev v Tehnicheski Universitet*[48] the Bulgarian Court asked whether the Directive precluded provisions of a national law which did not permit indefinite contracts with professors who had reached the age of 65, and which provided that professors who had reached the age of 68 were to be compulsorily retired; and, finally, in *Reinhard Prigge v Deutsche Lufthansa*

---

46 Case C-411/05; [2007] IRLR 989.
47 Case C-45/09.
48 Case C-250/09.

AG^{49} the German Court asked whether the Directive precluded rules of national law which recognised an age limit of 60 for pilots established by collective agreement for the purposes of ensuring air safety.

In *Palacios de la Villa* the Court did not consider the general issue of whether a mandatory retirement age was compatible with a Directive aimed at tackling, among other matters, age discrimination in employment and occupation, but only looked at the particular circumstances raised by the reference. Law 14/2005 permitted collective agreements to contain clauses providing for the termination of employment at the retirement age stipulated in Spanish social security legislation, provided that, firstly, such a measure was 'linked to objectives which are consistent with employment policy and are set out in the collective agreement'; and, secondly, that the worker 'must have satisfied the conditions laid down in social security legislation for entitlement to a retirement pension under his contribution regime'. A further special measure, the Single Transitional Provision (STP), was adopted to deal with those collective agreements already in force. Under the STP, collective agreements which already provided for the termination of contracts of employment where workers had reached normal retirement age, would be lawful provided that the collective agreement stipulated that the workers concerned had: 'Completed the minimum period of contributions and that they [had] satisfied the other requirements laid down in social security legislation for entitlement to a retirement pension under their contribution regime'. There was no requirement here for a link to objectives consistent with employment policy.

Mr Palacios claimed age discrimination as a result of his dismissal at the age of 65. The issue referred was whether the STP was compatible with Community law. All parties, except Mr Palacios, argued that the principle of non-discrimination did not apply to the STP, and relied upon recital 14 for this. Recital 14 states that: 'This Directive shall be without prejudice to national provisions laying down retirement ages.' Alternatively, it was argued, that the setting of a retirement age could be justified under Article 6(1).

The Court stated that Recital 14 merely provided that the Directive did not affect the competence of member states to determine retirement ages, but the Directive did apply to national measures, 'governing the conditions for termination of employment contracts where the retirement age, thus established, has been reached'. The issue was whether the measure could be justified under Article 6(1). The fact that it was contained within a collective

---

49   Case C-447/09 *Reinhard Prigge, Michael Fromm and Volker Lambach v Deutsche Lufthansa AG.*

agreement between the social partners was not decisive. The Court accepted that the aim was legitimate (the aim being to check unemployment and promote employment) and the means were also judged to be appropriate and necessary. Compulsory retirement could be a proportionate means of achieving the aim, particularly taking into account the, 'fact that the persons concerned are entitled to financial compensation by way of a retirement pension at the end of their working life, such as that provided for by the national legislation at issue in the main proceedings, the level of which cannot be regarded as unreasonable.' Thus, it is important to see the rule within the context of national legislation, part of which ensures that the individual has achieved a not unreasonable level of pension.

One further case about maximum recruitment ages, but also having an impact on retirement, is the judgment in *Petersen*.[50] The German equality law[51] did not amend the age limits applicable to 'panel dentists' which provided for a maximum age of 68. Ms Petersen's authorisation to operate as a dentist therefore expired when she reached this age. The questions from the national court concerned whether this maximum age limit was an objective and reasonable measure to achieve a legitimate aim. The legitimate aim was the health of patients as, 'based on general experience', 'a general drop in performance occurs from a certain age'. Thus although the question is about a maximum recruitment age, it really aligns itself with those cases concerning a mandatory retirement age. The Court considered the aims put forward by the German government and concluded that Article 2(5) precluded a national measure setting a maximum retirement age for practising as a panel dentist where the aim was 'the protection of patients from the effects of the decline in performance of dentists after the age of 68'. The reason for not accepting this as a legitimate aim was that it only applied to panel dentists and there was no age limit for non-panel ones. In terms of Article 6(1), however, where the aim was 'to share out employment opportunities among the generations', the measure was not precluded. The outcome of this case is therefore that, in certain situations, it seems to be acceptable to discriminate against older members of a profession in order to facilitate new members entering.

---

50 Case C-341/08 *Dr Dominica Petersen v Berufungsausschuss für Zahnärte für den Bezirk Westfalen-Lippe.*
51 General Law on Equal Treatment (Allgemeines Gleichbehandlungsgesetz) of 14 August 2006.

The End of Mandatory Retirement?

In 2010 the coalition government announced that the default retirement age would be abolished from October 2011. On the face of it this is a great victory for those, including the Age NGOs who had been campaigning for such a change. It will still be open for employers to have an 'employer justified retirement age' (EJRA). The Framework Directive still allows for the possibility of justifying a mandatory retirement age on the basis that it is for a legitimate aim and that the means of achieving that aim are appropriate and necessary. A good example of this was in the case of *Rosenbladt*[52] where a part-time cleaner in Hamburg was forced to retire when she reached the age of 65 years. This was as a result of a collective agreement for employees in the commercial cleaning sector. The test was whether there was a legitimate aim and whether retirement was an appropriate and necessary means of achieving that aim. The 'legitimate' aims put forward in this case included giving 'priority to appropriate and foreseeable planning of personnel and recruitment management over the interest of employees in maintaining their financial position'.[53] There was also the aim of 'facilitating the employment of young people, planning recruitment and allowing good management of a firm's personnel, in a balanced manner according to age'.[54] This was despite the Advocate General in the case pointing out that the national referring court had stated that the collective agreement in question did not actually provide any obligation on employers to recruit any workers, let alone young ones, to replace those that are forced to retire.[55] Thus it is apparently possible for an employer to have a notional justification for retiring older workers without any requirement for them to show that the practice outlined in the justification actually occurs.

In the UK the case of *Seldon v Clarkson Wright*[56] concerned the retirement of an equity partner in a firm of solicitors. Mr Seldon was forced to retire at the end of the year following his 65th birthday. The Court of Appeal stated that it was, of course, for the employer to show that the enforced retirement age was for a reason which was a legitimate aim and that the retirement was a proportionate means of achieving that aim. There were a number of aims put forward in the case to justify the action in accordance with the government's overall social policy. These included the need to provide promotion opportunities for younger solicitors and that people should be able to retire with dignity. The

---

52   Case C-45/09 *Rosenbladt v Oellerking Gebäudereinigungsges mbH.*
53   Paragraph 59 of the Court's judgement.
54   Paragraph 60.
55   Paragraph 137 of the Advocate General's Opinion.
56   *Seldon v Clarkson Wright & Jakes* [2010] IRLR 865.

Court also held that having a 'cut off' age of 65 was a proportionate means of achieving this.

That this is possible is a reflection of the weakness of European Community and British law. That it is possible to eject individuals from the workforce to make way for other individuals (possibly) who in turn will also be ejected when they reach a certain chronological age. There is no consideration of an individual's abilities or personal situation. An artificial 'cut off' appears to be acceptable depending upon the needs of employers rather than individuals.

8

Multiple Discrimination

The Equality Act 2010 contains nine 'protected characteristics'. These are the grounds on which one can be protected from discrimination. The protected characteristics are: age, disability, gender reassignment, marriage and civil partnership, pregnancy and maternity, race, religion or belief, sex, and sexual orientation. The Act replaced a number of important pieces of legislation, such as the Equal Pay Act 1970, the Sex Discrimination Act 1975, the Race Relations Act 1976 and the Disability Discrimination Act 1995. It also replaced a number of Regulations dealing with discrimination on the grounds of age, religion or belief, and sexual orientation.

Prior to the Equality Act 2010 it was possible to bring a complaint only on a single ground of discrimination. Thus it was possible to bring complaints about sex discrimination or race discrimination or disability discrimination individually under different statutes. It was not possible to bring complaints of multiple discrimination under one statute. They needed to be addressed as separate complaints using the different pieces of statute. This is despite the fact that it was clear that there is a substantial overlap in some cases, for example, between racial and religious discrimination and between discrimination on the grounds of sex and sexual orientation.

A further issue was, and is, that there was no opportunity for other forms of discrimination, or multiple discrimination, to be identified. The potential grounds are those contained within the legislation or regulation. All other grounds are excluded by omission. This, of course, is a reflection of the approach of the EU, which also has Directives concerned with gender, race and a variety of other grounds contained within the Framework Directive. According to a review of the European Network of Legal Experts, there are a number of countries within the EU that do have a non-exhaustive list and allow for the possibility of other grounds.[1]

It is clear, however, that with the increasing number of grounds for complaint that there are more likely to be a growing number of complaints that do not fit neatly into one or other of the categories. As one report for Age Concern England stated:[2] 'Many older people experience disadvantage and discrimination not just because of their age, but for other reasons as well – because they are black or disabled or from a religious, cultural or linguistic minority, for example.'

The same report also points out that many people suffer from discrimination throughout their lives, for example, on the grounds of sex or race, and that becoming an older worker adds to the level of discrimination suffered. The Equality Act 2010 has recognised this in a limited way and will hopefully provide the opportunity to bring claims on a combination of two grounds. Section 14 provides:[3]

Combined discrimination: dual characteristics:

1. A person (A) discriminates against another (B) if, because of a combination of two relevant protected characteristics, A treats B less favourably than A treats or would treat a person who does not share either of those characteristics.

2. The relevant protected characteristics are –

    a. age
    b. disability
    c. gender reassignment
    d. race
    e. religion or belief
    f. sex
    g. sexual orientation.

---

1   'European anti-discrimination law review no. 2' (2005); it also contains a piece by Sandra Fredman titled 'Double trouble: multiple discrimination and the law', which makes this point.
2   Age and ... multiple discrimination and older people (2005).
3   At the time of writing (December 2010) the government had yet to bring this Section into effect.

3. For the purposes of establishing a contravention of this Act by virtue of Subsection (1), B need not show that A's treatment of B is direct discrimination because of each of the characteristics in the combination (taken separately).

As a result of this legislation it is now be possible to bring a claim for discrimination based upon a combination of age and one of the other characteristics mentioned.

Additive and Intersectional Discrimination

Two types of multiple discrimination that have been suggested[4] are 'additive discrimination' and 'intersectional discrimination'. The first consists of a situation where the person complaining of discrimination belongs to two separate groups, both of which are affected by discrimination legislation, for example, a lesbian woman or a disabled black man. This is where a person may be able to justify individual claims under different statutes and they are essentially additive in nature.

The second type consists of intersectional discrimination where the multiple discrimination cannot usefully or effectively be broken down into its component parts. It is where the sum of the parts is something more than the constituent elements. Thus a young black woman may suffer discrimination in a way that an older black woman does not. The grounds for complaint should be that she is young and black and a woman, not necessarily three different complaints under firstly, age regulations, then racial discrimination and then sex discrimination. Intersectional discrimination is where the different forms of discrimination meet but result in a form of discrimination that is not covered by any of the individual statutes or regulations. An example of this is occurred in *Burton v De Vere Hotels*.[5] Two young Afro-Caribbean women were amongst the casual staff waiting at tables during a dinner attended by 400 men. There was an after dinner speaker, described as a 'blue comedian', who was a guest at the dinner. During his after dinner performance the two waitresses were clearing the tables. When spotted by the speaker, he made sexually and racially offensive remarks. The two waitresses brought a complaint against the hotel

---

4   See, for example, Hannett (2003).
5   The decision in this case was held, by the House of Lords, to have been wrongly decided in *MacDonald v Advocate General for Scotland; Pearce v Governing Body of Mayfield School* it is the facts of the case that are used here for illustrative purposes.

that employed them under the Race Relations Act 1995. They complained that they had been unlawfully discriminated against on the grounds of their race by their employers. The reason that this unpleasant experience is related here is that these two waitresses were actually picked on because they were young, black and female, yet they brought a claim for racial discrimination. In a different legal system, which recognised intersectional discrimination, they perhaps should have been able to bring a complaint of being discriminated against because they were young, black women and not just because they were black.

This may be an argument in favour of a rights-based approach to discrimination. Rather than focussing on the difference which has resulted in the discrimination, it might be more worthwhile to focus on the fact that an individual has a right not to be discriminated against. The right comes not from some category of discrimination such as race, sex or age but from a recognition that irrational discrimination breaches a fundamental human right.

The issue has been recognised in other jurisdictions. Madam Justice L'Heureux-Dubé stated in the Canadian Supreme Court:

> *Categorising such discrimination as primarily racially orientated, or primarily gender orientated, misconceives the reality of discrimination as it is experienced by individuals. Discrimination may be experienced on many grounds, and where this is the case, it is not really meaningful to assert that it is one or the other. It may be more realistic to recognise that both forms of discrimination may be present and intersect.*[6]

Canada (see Chapter 6) has an anti-discrimination programme that is human-rights based and it might be easier to do a contextual analysis, focusing on society's response to the individual and its construction of identity, that includes examination of historical disadvantage, social, political and cultural context and socio-economic issue.[7] A report for the Ontario Human Rights Commission (OHRC) stated:[8] 'Persons with disabilities may experience particular barriers when they identify by other grounds. For example, during the Commission's consultations on age discrimination, the Commission was

---

6   An intersectional approach to discrimination addressing multiple grounds in human rights claims (2004); *Canada (A.G.) v Mossop*.

7   Ibid.

8   Ibid.

told that for persons with disabilities, ageing can result in a disproportionate impact or unique experiences of discrimination.'

The same Commission has also produced a report which includes age and intersectionality.[9] This included issues related to age and gender, age and disability, and age and sexual orientation. The strongest argument for a human rights approach to age is so that it can be combined with other areas of discrimination with which it overlaps. An example of where this happens is Ontario, Canada.

Age and Gender

One report for the Equality Authority in Ireland stated:

> *Older peoples' experiences have been acquired through living within a particular set of social, economic and cultural circumstances. So, the experience of an older professional man can be quite different from the experience of an older woman in the home. Within the group of older people, there are people who suffer and/or have suffered discrimination on other grounds. The discrimination problems faced by the current generation of older women largely arise from past discrimination on the grounds of gender, in particular exclusion from the labour market, arising from the 'marriage bar' and caring responsibilities, and the consequent exclusion from independent pension arrangements.*[10]

Older women may suffer from disadvantages compared to older men. This is because they tend to live longer, although the gap between the sexes has narrowed in recent years. There were 28 per cent more women than men over the age of 50 years in 1961. This difference had narrowed to 18 per cent in 2002. Projections suggest a further narrowing with the difference in numbers being reduced to 14 per cent by 2031.[11]

Older women are often poorer because of this relative longevity and for a number of other reasons, which may include:

---

9   'Time for action: advancing human rights for older Ontarians' (2004).
10   'Implementing equality for older people' (2004).
11   'Focus on older people' (2004).

•   Women on average receive a much lower occupational pension income partly because they were dependent upon male pension-holding partners. Some indication of this is shown on an EU-wide basis in the following table, where there is a clear pattern of large numbers of women who do not take up paid employment and are therefore likely to be reliant on their male partner's income.

Table 8.1   Employment rates by age in the EU[12]

Age	Females	Males
15–24	34.6	40.4
25–54	72.3	86.9
55–64	36.9	55.0

The result of this is that, on average, women's income during their lifetime is some £250,000 less than men's, with an income in retirement that is some 57 per cent of men's.[13]

•   Older women will have a broken work history as a result of the traditional caring role adopted by women.

In 1984, for instance, when today's 72-year-old pensioner was aged 45, the employment rate for 35–49-year-old women was 65 per cent versus 88 per cent for men, and 55 per cent of these women were employed as part-timers compared to 1 per cent of men. Lower overall employment meant fewer opportunities to accrue pension rights; and part-time employment, until the early 1990s, very rarely involved pension scheme membership.[14]

Women in the UK have suffered from inequalities in pensions because of this. The pensions credit system is designed to improve the lot of low-income pensioners. According to government figures, since 1997 some 1.9 million people in retirement have been lifted above the absolute poverty level, but two-thirds of this total have been women. Altogether some 3.3 million people have received pension's credit of which some 2.18 million have been women. There

---

12   Employment rate is the percentage of the population of that age group in work, the figures are for 2008, taken from 'Employment in Europe 2009' European Commission.
13   'Age and ... multiple discrimination and older people' (2005).
14   'Pensions: challenges and choices', p. 262 (2004).

are historical reasons for this, of course. At the time of the Beveridge Report at the end of the Second World War there was an assumption that women would not normally work and that they would be dependant upon their husbands as the breadwinner. This, of course, is changing. The employment rate for women in 2010 was some 69 per cent, compared to 55 per cent in 1983.[15]

In the UK research has also shown that, taking all forms of inactivity together, the chances of men leaving inactivity for paid work were sharply reduced after the age of 50 years 'and were close to zero for those over 60'. For women the chances of moving out of inactivity were much reduced after the age of 40 years and 'was particularly uncommon for those older than their late 50s'.[16]

- Older women are more likely not to be in paid employment.

In March 2000 the EU Council of Ministers agreed at the Lisbon Spring Council Meeting to adopt a strategy aimed at raising the rate of growth of employment. There was a particular concern about the poor performance of the EU economy compared to the US as well as a concern with the emerging economies of Asia. The targets set included increasing employment rates for women to 70 per cent and for older people (50–64) to 50 per cent. The total employment rate had risen from 62.5 per cent in 1999 to 64.6 per cent in 2009.[17] The rate for women had risen to 58.6 per cent and for older workers to 46 per cent, also for 2009.

It is interesting that the two groups who need to have their employment rate increased in order to meet the Lisbon targets were older workers and women. How much more difficult is it then if the individual is both a woman and an older worker? Indeed, the employment rate for older women (50–64) in the EU in 2009 was 37.8 per cent, compared to 54.8 per cent for men. The highest employment rate for older women in the EU27 was Sweden with a rate of 66.7 per cent. The lowest was Malta with 11.2 per cent and Slovenia with just over 24 per cent.

In the UK some 26 per cent of all women between 16 and state pension age are economically inactive, compared to 17 per cent of men. This gap is at its widest between the ages of 25 and 34 years when some 23 per cent of such

---

15 Women and pensions the evidence (2005); Employment Statistics 2010 <www.statistics.gov.uk>.
16 'Characteristics of older workers' (1998).
17 The 2009 figure is for the EU27 which of course did not exist in 1999; figures from EU Labour Force Survey 2009 Eurostat.

women are economically inactive, compared to just over 7 per cent of men.[18]
If one also looks at the reasons for inactivity amongst those over 50, then the
caring role of women becomes clear. Just over 6 per cent of men gave 'looking
after family/home' as the reason for their inactivity. This contrasts with some
43 per cent of women.

- Older women are more likely to work part-time and, as a result,
  have lower average earnings.

Figures published by the European Commission show that this is a pattern
of employment that is continuing. In 2009, some 31 per cent of employed
women in the EU27 worked part-time, in comparison to just 18 per cent of male
workers.[19] These figures, however, hide differences related to age and gender.
One report concluded:[20]

> *There is a clear gender distinction in the occurrence of part-time work
> by age. In general, men are most likely to be in part-time employment
> during their youth, while for women it is during the latter stages of their
> working lives. Furthermore, while the share of part-time employment
> for men decreases sharply from youth to prime age, for women the share
> remains roughly the same across these age categories.*

Women are also more likely to be carers of the young and the elderly than
male workers, thus affecting their ability to earn pay and pensions.

Around 90 per cent of all lone parents are women and 24 per cent of all
children living in Great Britain live in lone parent families.[21] It is clear that
the caring duties of women are limited by the lack of available flexible work
practices and that many women end up in low paid part-time jobs because
these are the only ones which allow them to combine work and family
commitments.[22]

- Women are more likely to suffer age discrimination at a younger
  age than men.

---

18 Labour market statistics July 2010; <www.statistics.gov.uk>.
19 'EU labour force survey 2009'; Eurostat.
20 'Employment in Europe 2004'; European Commission.
21 'Women and pensions: the evidence' (2005).
22 Ibid.

Women are perceived as being 'older' at a much younger age than men and a greater proportion are likely, therefore, to suffer from age discrimination related to their sex. One survey showed a respondent employer stating that women who returned to work in their mid-thirties after a career break to raise children were regarded as older workers.[23] Another survey concluded that: 'The disadvantage incurred in being "too young" or "too old" was found to impact more on women than men, suggesting that in these age ranges at least, being female acted to intensify age prejudice.'[24]

There have also been surveys about the effects of physical attractiveness on decisions concerning recruitment and promotion and one study did show that there was a relationship between physical attractiveness[25] and promotion. There has been also research showing that women are perceived to decline in attractiveness as they age far more than men. Thus women are more likely than men to suffer from these prejudices as they age.[26]

Age and Ethnicity

Unemployment rates generally for black and minority ethnic groups tend to be higher than for the white population. According to one report by the House of Lords Select Committee on Economic Affairs this problem is exacerbated by age:[27]

> *However, this disadvantage appears to be compounded by age. In the late 1990s, the unemployment rate for whites was 5 per cent for both 35–44-year-olds and for people aged between 45 and state pension age. For blacks it was 12 per cent among 35–44-year-olds, and 16 per cent among those aged between 45 and state pension age, and for members of the Pakistani/Bangladeshi communities it was 13 per cent among the 35–44 age group, but 26 per cent among persons aged between 45 and state pension age.*

---

23 'Older workers: employers' attitudes and practices' (1990).
24 Duncan and Loretto (2004).
25 This is a difficult issue because of course there is no absolute standard of what is meant by physical beauty. What is meant here I think can be better described as youthful beauty; or maybe just a male stereotype of such a thing.
26 Hurley and Giannantonio (1999); see also Ashiagbor (2000).
27 'Aspects of the economics of an ageing population', Paragraph 4.29.

A Commission for Racial Equality representative, speaking to the Select Committee,[28] stated that it appeared that many black and minority ethnic persons aged between 45 and state pension age suffered both an 'ethnic penalty' and an 'age penalty' in the labour market. The Select Committee noted that the government's initiatives in this field appeared to be directed at young people and new entrants to the labour market[29] and recommended that more attention should be given to those over the age of 50 years.

The comparison of employment rates between various ethnic minorities and the white population are revealing (Table 8.2). It appears that with some groups such as the black or black British group, discrimination takes place against both young people and older workers.

Table 8.2   Employment rates by ethnicity and age (per cent)[30]

Ethnic group	16–24	25–44	45–59/64	All ages
Asian or Asian British	42	69	55	59
Black or black British	35	69	63	60
White	67	83	74	77

This is illustrative of the fact that there may be a particular issue with younger people and race discrimination. Whilst all ages have much lower employment rates than the white population, the gap is greater with older people and younger ones, notably amongst the black or black British group. Older people from ethnic minority groups are more likely to be living in poverty than pensioners in general.[31] This may be a reflection of the discrimination in employment that they have faced during their lifetime.

It is really interesting when one looks at the breakdown of statistics for those over the age of 65 years. There are much greater numbers of over-65s in the white population in Great Britain than in the ethnic minority population. Thus 14.9 per cent of white British people and 22.9 per cent of white Irish people are aged between 65 and 84 years. This contrasts with a figure of 5 per cent for all Asian or Asian British people; 6.2 per cent of all black or black British people

28 Ms Maureen Fraser, Paragraph 4.30.
29 'Ethnic minorities and the labour market' (2003).
30 Taken from the CRE website <www.cre.gov.uk>; original source Labour Force Survey.
31 'Age and ... multiple discrimination and older people' (2005).

and 4.8 per cent of Chinese ethnic people in Great Britain.[32] The reasons for this are probably too complex to be discussed here, but it may indicate that a different priority needs to be given in relation to age and ethnic minorities. It may be that discrimination against young people is proportionately more of an issue than that against the old.

Age and Sexual Orientation

There are large numbers of people who are lesbian, gay, bisexual and transgender (LGBT). The statistics are estimates because of the perceived difficulty in asking people about their sexual orientation. It is estimated that, in the UK, some 5–7 per cent of the population is LGBT.[33] This results in a figure of up to some four million people. Projections of growth in the older population also suggest that, by 2031, there will be one to 1.4 million people over the age of 60 who are lesbian, gay or bisexual.[34] All the figures are, however, only estimates with various surveys giving a range of from 0.3 to 7 per cent of the population.[35] In the US it is estimated that there are some three million LGBT people over the age of 65 years, and that this will grow to four million by 2030.[36] Other estimates put the number of LGBT older people now at between two and seven million.[37] It appears that lesbians will be 'disproportionately represented in these numbers reflecting both general population trends and the decimation wrought by HIV/AIDS, which disproportionately affected gay men.'[38]

It is clear from the research that has been done that older people are not regarded by many as being sexually active. There is a prejudice that turns

---

32 'Focus on older people' (2004).
33 Figures from the web site of Age Concern, which also states that Stonewall (the main LGB campaigning organisation in the UK) considers this a reasonable estimate: <www.ageconcern. org.uk/AgeConcern/openingdoors_facts.asp>.
34 Musingarimi, Primrose (2008) 'Older gay, lesbian and bisexual people in the UK; a policy brief' International Longevity Centre <www.ilcuk.org.uk>.
35 Mitchell, Martin, Howarth, Charlie, Kotecha, Mehul and Creegan, Chris (2009) 'Sexual Orientation Research Review 2008' Equality and Human Rights Commission, London, UK.
36 Cahill, S., South, K. and Spade, J. (2000). 'Outing age: public policy issues affecting gay, lesbian, bisexual and transgender elders', The Policy Institute of the National Gay and Lesbian Task Force Foundation.
37 Grant, J.M. (2010). 'Outing age 2010'. National Gay and Lesbian Task Force Policy Institute, USA.
38 Improving the lives of LGBT older adults (2010) LGBT Movement Advancement Project (MAP) and Services and Advocacy for Gay, Lesbian. Bisexual and Transgender Adults (SAGE): <http:// sageusa.org/uploads/Advancing%20Equality%20for%20LGBT%20Elders%20[FINAL%20 COMPRESSED]. pdf>.

both heterosexual and homosexual people, as they age, into asexual people. Interviewees in one project described encounters with health professionals where it was just assumed that the older patient was sexually inactive. A difference between older heterosexual and older LGBT people is that whilst the former came up against assumptions that they were sexually inactive, the latter came up against disbelief that they could be lesbian or gay.[39]

OLDER LGBTS AND DISCRIMINATION

To be an older bisexual, gay, lesbian or transgender person is to potentially suffer from multiple discrimination. Terry Kaelbar, Executive Director of SAGE (Senior Action in a Gay Environment) summed up the issues in the US and elsewhere:

> *Aging for GLBT seniors is informed by discrimination and anti gay bigotry, which impacts our ability and willingness to access needed programs and services as we age. It is informed by the fact that we, by and large, age as single people without the traditional familial supports of a spouse or children, supports available to the vast majority of heterosexual seniors, which makes us more reliant on the programs that we are not so willing to access. GLBT aging is informed by ... our invisibility; with care providers who assume that all old people are straight, one of many heterosexist assumptions.*[40]

To understand the discrimination suffered by LGBT elders it is important to consider how recent are many of the changes in Society's attitudes and norms with regard to sexuality. A person who was 85 years old in 2011 was born in 1926. Such a person would have grown up in the 1930s when homosexuality was regarded as a psychiatric disorder which required therapeutic intervention. Methods of treatment included *drugs, aversion therapy, lobotomies and electric shock treatment* (Knauer 2009). Someone who was 65 in 2011 would have been born in 1946 and would have lived as a young person through the 1950s and 60s when homosexuality was still unlawful. It was not until 1967 that the Sexual Offences Act in the UK was adopted. This provided that homosexual acts in private did not constitute an offence, provided that it was consensual

---

39 Bytheway, B., Ward, R., Holland, C. and Peace, S. (2007). *Too Old: Older People's Accounts of Discrimination, Exclusion and Rejection*; Chapter 7 – 'Sexuality and Sexual Orientation' Help the Aged, London <www.ageuk.org.uk>.

40 Presentation as part of 'Make room for all: diversity, cultural competency and discrimination in aging America'. Presentations, testimony, and organisational materials from the National Gay and Lesbian Task Force Summit and Hearing held in Washington D.C. 11 December 2005.

and that the participants were over 21 years of age (Section 1(1) Sexual Offences Act 1967). Not until 1973 did the American Psychiatric Association remove homosexuality from its list of mental disorders and it was only in 1992 that the World Health Organisation declassified homosexuality as a mental illness. Finally it was in 2003 that the UK started to make discrimination against people on the grounds of their sexual orientation unlawful, with the adoption of the Equal Opportunities in Employment (Sexual Orientation) Regulations and it was not until 2007 that this became unlawful in respect of facilities, goods and services (the Equality Act (Sexual Orientation) Regulations).[41]

The significance of all these events is that the current cohort of LGBT elders would have grown up in a time of harassment, illegality and discrimination against LGBT people. There are dangers, of course, in over generalising and it is not argued here that all older people who share common experiences will react in the same way. One important consequence appears to have been that 'coming out' was much more difficult and challenging than it is perhaps today. One elder respondent in a research project stated, for example, that: 'I'm going back quite a long way ... when I was young we didn't have any choices ... we didn't have any choice about whether we would declare we were going to be gay or not, we didn't. You just accepted that fact, and you got on with it ... you know, we were the twilight men then ...'[42]

A survey of LGBTs in the UK found that some 37 per cent of men (particularly older ones) and 23 per cent of women had hidden their sexuality throughout their lives 2003).[43] Heaphy et al.'s research suggests a number of reasons why LGBs were reluctant to come out and declare their true sexual orientation. These were, firstly, employer perceptions, secondly, the fear of 'queer bashing', thirdly, geography as it was more difficult to come out in a small rural community compared to being in a big city.

There is also some evidence that older LGB people suffer from discrimination within the LGB community. The 'gay scene' is said to be youth orientated. The research indicated that 'the pervasive story amongst older gay

---

41 'Both now superseded by the Equality Act' 2010.
42 Heaphy, B. and Yip, A.K.T. (2006). 'Policy implications of ageing sexualities', *Social Policy and Society*, 5:4, 443–51.
43 Heaphy, B., Yip, A. and Thompson, D. (2003). *Lesbian, Gay and Bisexual Lives Over 50* (York House Publications).

men is that visible signs of ageing can mark one as undesirable or unwelcome in gay culture'.[44]

It is the bringing together of the stereotypes for older people and for LGBT people that help create important issues for protection from discrimination and important issues for further research. As one study[45] stated: 'Most people have opinions about aging, and many people have thoughts about homosexuality. But few individuals have considered them simultaneously; many scholars, advocates for older adults, and other individuals consider the terms gay and aging to be incompatible.'

There are many problems, of course, that are common to both LGBT and heterosexual communities in old age. These include concerns about loneliness, ill-health and financial issues. It seems likely, however, that these issues are more prevalent amongst the older LGBT population. Grant[46] describes the position as: 'Recent studies show that lifelong experiences of social and economic marginalisation place lesbian, gay, bisexual and transgender elders at higher risk for isolation, poverty and homelessness than their heterosexual peers.'

There are, however, a number of issues that affect older people and are of particular importance to same-sex families. One issue is in health decision-making, especially when there are accidents and illnesses such as alzheimers. The 'onset of dementia may mean that private matters become public, domestic arrangements and personal circumstances become more evident to outsiders and it is more difficult to keep the information given about oneself secure.'[47] A related issue is the fear of negative responses from institutions such as hospitals and medical professionals. One example of this cited in research is the gay man caring for his dying partner who receives little support from neighbours and has a doctor who asks him if his wife has died (Ward et al. 2008).[48] In a

---

44 Ward, R., Jones, R., Hughes, J., Humberstone, N. and Pearson, R. (2008). 'Intersections of ageing and sexuality', Chapter 4. In: R. Ward and B. Bytheway (eds) *Researching Age and Multiple Discrimination*, Centre for Policy on Ageing London <www.cpa.org.uk>.

45 Grossman, A.H., D'Augelli, A.R. and O'Connell, T.S. (2003). 'Being lesbian, gay, bisexual, and sixty or older in North America. In: L.D. Garnets and D.C. Kimmel (eds) *Psychological perspectives on lesbian, gay and bisexual experiences*, (2nd ed), 629–45 at 629 New York: Columbia University Press.

46 *supra* Ward n44.

47 'Out of the shadows' accessed from the website of the Alzheimer's Society, UK; taken from Community Care October 2003; <www.communitycare.co.uk>.

48 Ward, R., Jones, R., Hughes, J., Humberstone, N. and Pearson, R. (2008). 'Intersections of ageing and sexuality', Chapter 4. In: R. Ward and B. Bytheway (eds) *Researching Age and Multiple Discrimination*, Centre for Policy on Ageing London; www.cpa.org.uk.

further US study, of some 205 older LGBTs, it was said that their greatest fear about growing older was being or dying alone. Some 19 per cent also stated that they had little or no confidence that medical personnel would treat them with dignity and respect as LGBT people.[49] A UK study (River 2006) stated, in respect of care homes, that:

> The older lesbians we talked to said they would be worried how other residents would react. Older lesbians responded with comments such as 'it would be a nightmare' and 'I am hoping never to need one'. The perceptions behind these latter comments are, of course, shared by most heterosexual older people. However, older lesbians have particular concerns over and above the basic fears (amplified by television publicity about appallingly bad practice in some homes).

A UK government report[50] stated that: 'Older LGBT people have told us about fearing responses on the grounds of their sexuality from institutions when life changing events occur, for example, loss of independence through hospitalisation, going into a residential home, or having home-carers.'

In a survey for the UK Commission for Social Care Inspection[51] some 45 per cent of LGB respondents stated that they had suffered discrimination when using social care services. In addition only 9 per cent of service providers in the sample had carried out any specific work to promote equality for LGB people, and only 2 per cent had done this for transgender people. The LGBT community is itself diverse and there were further issues related to this shown in this survey, for example, a disabled lesbian who stated that she had black lesbian friends who had stopped using services for fear of having a carer from the same community who will 'out' them; and the Asian gay man who was also a family carer and who thought it unthinkable that he would tell staff about his sexuality.

---

49   'Out and aging: the MetLife study of lesbian and gay baby boomers'. November 2006, MetLife Mature Market Institute.
50   Department of Health and Department for Work and Pensions (2006). 'A sure start to later life: ending inequalities for older people'. A social exclusion unit final report.
51   Commission for Social Care Inspection (2006). 'Putting people first: equality and diversity matters; providing appropriate services for lesbian, gay and bisexual and transgender people'.

Age and Disability

The likelihood of disabilities and chronic conditions increases with age.[52] Older workers with disabilities are more likely to lose their jobs in workplace re-organisations as a result of fewer opportunities to train and upgrade their skills. Age and disability are a barrier when trying to get a job, according to the OHRC.[53] The number of people aged over 50 years who are long-term sick or disabled has been increasing. This is somewhat paradoxical because there has also been a continuing increase in life expectancy and in the health position of older people.[54] There is a concentration in sickness-related benefit claims in areas of declining industry. It was suggested to the House of Lords Select Committee that this was because: 'As the structure of the economy has changed, some workers from old industrial sectors, have seen themselves as unfit for different types of jobs in the service sector, and employers have also seen them as unsuitable.'[55]

Thus an individual's perception of their health status may have more effect than any objective medical opinion. The answer for the Select Committee was for the government to disseminate best practice with regard to job and workplace design to facilitate the employment of older workers who might have health problems which limit their employment.

In the EU some 16.4 per cent of the population state that they have a long-standing health problem or disability (LSHPD). The proportion varies amongst member states (Table 8.3).[56]

Table 8.3   **Percentage of the working population with LSHPD**[57]

EU15	16.4
Belgium	18.4
Denmark	19.9
Germany	11.2
Greece	10.3

---

52 See Sargeant (2005b).
53 See <www.ohrc.on.ca>.
54 'Aspects of the economics of an ageing population' (2003). Paragraph. 5.3.
55 This point was made by Mr David Coates of the TUC.
56 Eurostat news release 142/2003, 5 December 2003; the figures were provided for the closing ceremony of the European Year of People with Disabilities 2003.
57 Those aged 16–64 years.

Table 8.3   *Concluded*

Spain	8.7
France	24.6
Ireland	11.0
Italy	6.6
Luxembourg	11.7
Netherlands	25.4
Austria	12.8
Portugal	20.1
Finland	32.2
Sweden	19.9
UK	27.2

If one translates this into age ranges there is a clear pattern suggesting that the older a person becomes the more likely it is that a person will have a long-term health problem or be disabled (Table 8.4).[58] This is true of all countries in the EU.

Table 8.4   **Age-specific percentages of people reporting disability**

Age	Germany	France	Italy	Spain	UK	EU
16–19	7.0	7.6	3.3	2.6	12.4	6.6
20–24	8.5	7.5	1.9	1.9	8.7	6.1
25–29	8.6	8.1	2.4	3.2	11.1	7.2
30–34	8.0	9.6	3.4	4.8	13.8	8.3
35–39	11.1	12.7	3.9	6.1	15.2	10.5
40–44	12.9	13.3	6.1	8.2	15.5	12.1
45–49	16.8	17.5	7.1	9.6	20	15.5
50–54	25.4	20.9	13.0	15.7	24.9	21.1
55–59	33.5	31.1	15.6	24.5	35.7	28.9
60–64	35.1	34.3	22.5	32.2	32.6	31.7

These figures are perhaps reflected in the employment rate for older workers. If one looks at the figures for all countries in the EU, there are only five out of the twenty-five member states where the majority of people in the

---

58 'Disability and social participation in Europe' (2001). These are different figures to Table 7.4 and are not meant to match, but are merely used to illustrate the point that older people are more likely to be disabled than younger people.

55 to 64 years age band are in employment. These are Denmark (60.2 per cent), Estonia (52.3 per cent), Portugal (51.1 per cent), Sweden (68.6 per cent) and the UK (55.5 per cent). The lowest figures are for Slovenia (23.5 per cent), Slovakia (24.6 per cent), Poland (26.9 per cent) and Belgium (28.1 per cent).[59]

One paper by the European expert group on employment for disabled people reported that:[60]

> *Disability is much more prevalent among older people: 63 per cent of people with disabilities are older than 45. For non-disabled people the corresponding percentage is only 34 per cent. So the disabled population is relatively old. This is particularly so in Germany, Greece, Italy and Spain. This pattern is mainly due to individuals' health condition deteriorating with age. Furthermore, many impairments leading to disability are acquired during a person's life. There may, in addition, be a 'generation factor', insofar as younger age groups experience better health and working conditions in their early working life and better health care and rehabilitation provisions, than their predecessors in older generations.*

UK figures reflect a similar pattern. According to figures from the Disability Rights Commission[61] (DRC) some 19 per cent of the labour market population are long-term disabled (6,860,000 people) compared to 81 per cent not disabled (29,342,000). Of the disabled work population only some 49 per cent (3,389,000) are in work, compared to 81 per cent of the not disabled (23,847,000).

The prevalence of disability also increases with age (Table 8.5), so that some 10.3 per cent of working age men in the 20–24 years age band, for example, are disabled compared with 33.9 per cent of men in the 50–64 years age group, suggesting a high correlation between age and disability.[62]

---

59 Eurostat news release 142/2003, 5 December 2003.
60 'The employment situation of people with disabilities in the European Union' (2001).
61 Disability Briefing – January 2004; figures available from the DRC's website <www.drc-gb. org>; the figures are based on the DRC's estimates from the summer 2003 Labour Force Survey for Great Britain.
62 Smith and Twomey (2002), 415–27.

Table 8.5   People of working age with disabilities (per cent)

Age	Disabled
16–24	9.4
25–34	13.2
35–49	33.8
50–59/64	43.6

In the case of disability generally, it is suggested that factors affecting a disabled individual's ability or willingness to work are likely to include the severity of the disability, access to and within a potential workplace, beliefs on the likelihood of facing discrimination or the availability of suitable jobs and the trade-off between employment income and benefit receipt.[63]

Disability and age are two areas of discrimination that are closely linked and stand apart from the other grounds because perhaps there is sometimes a need to positively facilitate equal participation. There is a close correlation between age and disability and it can be argued that, because of this, age discrimination should be treated in a similar way to disability discrimination rather than, as proposed, adopting a similar approach to sex and race discrimination. This is because at a certain point there is a very high probability that disability and age merge or intersect and the discrimination takes place against an older worker who is, or is likely to become, disabled.

It is true that the older a worker becomes the more likely it is that the individual will be disabled. The employers' response is to have a default age at which an employee can be removed from the workforce without any of the related problems (for the employer) of any potential unfair dismissal claims, discrimination claims and so on. The alternative approach posited here and elsewhere in this book is that it would be more appropriate to extend to older workers the duty of employers to make reasonable adjustments. Thus, if a person has a genuine impairment to their health, mental or physical, then the employer should be required to treat them in the same way as a disabled employee. If a worker does not have a mental or physical impairment, then the only reason for adopting the CBI approach is to dismiss them because they are likely to have such an impairment in the future. This in itself, it could be argued, may be enough to justify further protection for older workers.

---

63   Ibid.

The Ageing Process[64]

Reading about getting older or old can be a depressing experience. With age comes an increasing likelihood of both physical and mental ill health.

CONSIDER SOME OF THE POSSIBILITIES[65]

Vision

Blindness and impaired vision become more common as we get older. In the UK 42 per cent of people over 75 will develop cataracts, almost 50 per cent will have age-related macular degeneration and 7 per cent will be affected by the most common form of glaucoma. Significant numbers of people will suffer from more than one condition.

Hearing

More than half of people over 60 have a hearing loss and 30 per cent of them have to use a hearing aid. The most common cause of age-related hearing loss is through disease or damage to the hearing organ in the inner ear, or the nerve which carries hearing information to the brain.

Dementia, Depression and Mental Health

Up to 700,000 people are estimated to be suffering from dementia in the UK. It becomes much more common as we get older, with nearly one in every 20 people over the age of 65 being affected. Depression affects about one person in eight over 65.

Osteoporosis and Bone Disease

Osteoporosis is a condition characterised by a thinning of the bones. As a result of hormonal changes after the menopause, the majority of women will develop osteoporosis to some extent and 50 to 70 per cent of women will suffer an osteoporotic fracture at some time. One in 12 men will also suffer significant bone loss. Thin bones are more likely to fracture, with the spine, hip, thigh, wrist and forearm being most at risk.

---

64 First discussed in Sargeant (2005b).

65 I took this list and the data in Table 7.7 from the website of the national medical research charity 'Research into Ageing' <www.ageing.org>.

Stroke and Heart Disease

Cardiovascular and circulatory problems, such as stroke, blood pressure problems and heart attacks, are the commonest causes of death and disability for older people. There are over 100,000 first strokes every year in the UK, 90 per cent of these affect people over 65 years.

This is not the happiest of lists and, of course, is not a comprehensive one. The word disability covers a wide range of impairments and the employment rates vary for those with different disabilities (Table 8.6). Those with a mental illness or with learning difficulties have a much lower employment rate than others.

In this chapter, I have tried to show that age discrimination is often not a simplistic judgement about whether an individual or a group have suffered detriment on the grounds of their age. Sometimes it is the combination of apparent disadvantages that can lead to discrimination. Older people with a disability and older women will suffer discrimination in a different way compared to their younger counterparts. The UK Equality Act 2010 may go some way in recognising this with the introduction of the possibility of claiming for 'combined discrimination'. This is an important development but it is limited to only two characteristics and will not directly assist the black disabled older woman, for example, who is likely to suffer discrimination as a result of a combination of these factors.

Table 8.6   Employment rate by type of disability (per cent)

Musculo-skeletal problems	45.6
Difficulty in seeing	44.3
Difficulty in hearing	68.1
Skin condition, allergies	69.3
Chest, breathing problems	64.0
Heart, blood pressure, circulation	50.3
Stomach, liver, kidney, digestion	52.0
Diabetes	65.1
Epilepsy	44.0
Mental illness	18.4
Depression, bad nerves	22.2
Mental illness, phobia, panics	10.4
Learning difficulties	21.4
All disabled	47.9

Bibliography

Articles

Bowling, A. (1999). 'Ageism in cardiology'. *British Medical Journal*, 319, 1353–5.

Butler, R.N. (1969). 'Age-ism: another form of bigotry'. *Gerontologist*, 9, 243–6.

David, E. (2001). 'Recent cases affecting the role of ADEA in protecting older workers'. *Duq. L. Rev.*, 39, 437.

Duncan, C. and Loretto, W. (2004). 'Never the right age? Gender and age-based discrimination in employment'. *Gender Work and Organisation*, 11:1, 95–115.

Eglit, H.E. (1999). 'The ADEA at thirty'. *U. Rich. L. Rev.*, 31, 579.

Fredman, S. (2001). 'Equality: a new generation?'. *Industrial Law Journal*, 30:2, 145–68.

Gaullier, X. (1988). 'La deuxieme carriere, Seuill'. Cited in 'Ageing of the working population and employment'. *EFILWC*, 1991.

Grant, P.T., Henry, J.M. and McNaughton, G.W. (2000). 'The management of elderly blunt trauma victims in Scotland: evidence of ageism'. *Injury*, 31:7, 519–29.

Gunderson, M. (2003). 'Age discrimination in Canada'. *Contemporary Economic Policy*, 21:3, 318–28.

Handley, K. (1993). 'The case for legislation on age discrimination'. *Personnel Management*.

Hannett, S. (2003). 'Equality at the intersections: the legislative and judicial failure to tackle multiple discrimination'. *Oxford Journal of Legal Studies*, 23:1, 65–86.

Hepple, B. (2001). 'Age discrimination in employment: implementing the framework directive'. Paper presented to the IPPR seminar, 11 December 2001 at the Nuffield Foundation.

Hurley, A.E. and Giannantonio, C.M. (1999). 'Career attainment for women and minorities: the interactive effects of age, gender and race'. *Women in Management Review*, 14:1, 4–13.

Jolls, C. (1996). 'Hands-tying and the age discrimination in Employment Act'. *Tex. L. Rev.*, 74, 1813–46.

Kee, Y.K., Brooks, W. and Bhalla, A. (2009). 'Do older patients receive adequate stroke care? An experience of a neurovascular clinic'. *Postgraduate Medical Journal*, 85, 115–18.

Lahey, J. (2005). 'Do older workers face discrimination?' Boston College Center for Retirement Research.

Lewis, J. (2001). 'Does the law begin at 40?' *Law Society Gazette*, 98:02.

Marsh, A. and Sahin-Dikmen, M. (2003). 'Discrimination in Europe'. Eurobarometer.

McGregor, J. (2002). 'Stereotypes and older workers'. *Journal of Social Policy New Zealand*, 18, 163–77.

Mitchell, D.E. (2001). 'Recent cases affecting the role of ADEA in protecting older workers'. *Duq. L. Rev.*, 39, 437.

Musingarimi, P. (2008). 'Older gay, lesbian and bisexual people in the UK; a policy brief'. International Longevity Centre. <www.ilcuk.org.uk>.

Robinson, T., Gustafson, B. and Popovich, M. (2008). 'Perceptions of negative stereotypes of older people in magazine advertisements: comparing the perceptions of older adults and college students'. *Ageing and Society*, 28, 233–51.

Sargeant, M. (2004). 'Age discrimination in FE and HE'. *Education Law Journal*, 5:2, 91–7.

Sargeant, M. (2005a). 'Age discrimination: equal treatment with exceptions'. *International Journal of Discrimination and the Law*, 6, 251–66.

Sargeant, M. (2005b). 'Age discrimination: multiple potential for discrimination'. *International Journal of Sociology of Law*, 33, 17–33.

Sargeant, M. (2005c). 'For diversity: against discrimination – the contradictory approach to age discrimination in employment'. *International Journal of Comparative Labour Law and Industrial Relations*, 21:4, 627–42.

Sargeant, M. (2006). 'The employment equality (age) regulations 2006: a legitimisation of age discrimination in employment'. *Industrial Law Journal*, 35, 209–27.

Sargeant, M. (2008). 'Age stereotypes and the media'. *Communications Law*, 13:4, 119–24.

Sargeant, M. (2009). 'Age discrimination, redundancy payments and length of service'. *Modern Law Review*, 72:4, 628–34.

Sargeant, M. (2010a). 'Age discrimination and the national minimum wage'. *Policy Studies*, 31:3, 351–64.

Sargeant, M. (2010b). 'Young workers and age discrimination'. *International Journal of Comparative Labour Law and Industrial Relations*, 26:4, 467–78.

Schiek, D. (2002). 'A new framework on equal treatment of persons in EC law?'. *European Law Journal*, 8:2, 290–314.

Schmidt, D.F. and Boland, S.M. (1986). 'Structure of perceptions of older adults: evidence for multiple stereotypes'. *Psychology and Ageing*, 1:3, 255–60.

Smith, A. and Twomey, B. (2002). 'Labour market experiences of people with disabilities'. *Labour Market Trends*, Labour Market Division Office of National Statistics, 415–27.

Taylor, P. and Walker, A. (1994). 'The ageing workforce: employers' attitudes towards older people'. *Work, Employment and Society*, 8:4, 569.

Weber, B.M. (1998). 'The effect of O'Connor consolidated coin caterers corp on the requirements for the establishing of a prima facie case under the age discrimination in employment act'. *Rutgers Law Journal*, 29:3.

Whiting, E. (2005). 'The labour market participation of older people'. *Labour Market Trends 2005*, Office for National Statistics.

Whittle, R. (2002). 'The framework directive for equal treatment in employment and occupation; an analysis from a disability rights perspective'. *European Law Review*, 27:3, 303–26.

Books and Pamphlets

Arber, S., Davidson, K. and Jay, G. (eds) (2003). *Gender and Ageing*. Maidenhead: Open University Press.

Cormack, J. and Bell, M. (2005). *Developing Anti-discrimination Law in Europe*. European Commission.

Dine, J. and Watt, B. (1996). *Discrimination Law*. Longman.

Drury, E. (1993). *Age Discrimination Against Older Workers in the European Community*. Eurolink Age.

Fredman, S. and Spencer, S. (eds) (2003). *Age as an Equality Issue: Legal and Policy Perspectives*. Oxford: Hart Publishing.

Friedman, L.M. (1984). *Your Time Will Come: The Law of age Discrimination and Mandatory Retirement*. New York: Russell Sage Foundation.

Ginn, J. (2003). *Gender, Pensions and the Lifecourse*. Bristol: Policy Press.

Grattan, P. (2002). *Short Guide to Pensions, Retirement and Work*. Third Age Employment Network.

Gregory, R.F. (2001). *Age Discrimination in the American Workplace: Old at a Young Age*. New Brunswick: Rutgers University Press.

Hirsch, D. (2003). *Crossroads After 50: Improving Choices in Work and Retirement*. York: Joseph Rowntree Foundation.

Hornstein, Z. (ed.) (2001). *Outlawing Age Discrimination: Foreign Lessons, UK Choices*. Bristol: The Polity Press in association with the Joseph Rowntree Foundation.

Lissenburgh, S. and Smeaton, D. (2003). *Employment Transitions of Older Workers: The Role of Flexible Employment in Maintaining Labour Market Participation and Promoting Job Quality*. Bristol: The Polity Press in association with the Joseph Rowntree Foundation.

McEwen, E. (ed.) (1990). *Age: The Unrecognised Discrimination*. Age Concern England.

Morris, A. and O'Donnell, T. (eds) (2000). *Feminist Perspectives on Employment Law*. Cavendish Publishing.

O'Cinneide, C. (2005). *Age Discrimination and European Law*. European Commission.

Sargeant, M. (1999). *Age Discrimination in Employment*. London: Institute of Employment Rights.

Thane, P. (2002). *Old Age in English History*. OUP.

Wedderburn, Lord (1986). *The Worker and the Law*. Penguin Books.

Book Chapters

Ashiagbor, D. (2000). 'The intersection between gender and race in the labour market: lessons for anti-discrimination law', in Morris and O'Donnell.

Evans, J.G. (2003). 'Implications of the ageing process', in Fredman and Spencer.

Gunderson, M. (2001). 'Age discrimination legislation in Canada', in Hornstein.

Henwood, M. (1990). 'No sense of urgency: age discrimination in healthcare', in McEwen.

Price, D. and Ginn, J. (2003). 'Sharing the crust? Gender, partnership status and inequalities in pension accumulation', in S. Arber, K. Davidson and J. Ginn.

Robinson, J. (2003). 'Age equality in health and social care', in Fredman and Spencer.

Schuller, T. (2003). 'Age equality in access to education', in Fredman and Spencer.

Walker, A. (1990). 'The benefits of old age? Age discrimination and social security', in McEwen.

Reports

'A literature review of the likely costs and benefits of legislation to prohibit age discrimination in health, social care and mental health services' (2007). Centre for Policy on Ageing on behalf of the Department of Health.

'A new pension settlement for the twenty-first century: the second report of the Pensions Commission' (2005). TSO, Norwich.

'A profile of older Americans: 2009 administration on aging'. US Department of Health and Human Services.

'Action on age: report of the consultation on age discrimination in employment' (1998). Department for Education and Employment (DfEE). HC 4 November 1993.

'Advancing women in the workplace: statistical analysis' (2004). Lewis, M., Miller, L. and Neathey, F., IRS Research Working Paper Series No. 12. Women and Equality Unit, Equal Opportunities Commission.

'Age discrimination is alive and well' (1999). Submission to the House of Representatives Standing Committee on Employment, Education and Workplace Relations Inquiry into issues specific to workers over 45 year. Drake Personnel Limited, available at <www.aph.gov.au/house/committee/eewr/OWK/subslist.htm>.

'Age discrimination in employment' (2001). House of Commons Education and Employment Committee Seventh Report Session 2000–01, HC 259.

'Age discrimination in employment: survey of retired members of NATFHE and PCS' (2003). Sargeant, M., Centre for Legal Research, Middlesex University Business School.

'Age discrimination in health and social care' (2000). Roberts, E., Kings Fund Briefing Note at <www.kingsfund.org.uk>.

'Age matters: a report on age discrimination' (2000). Human Rights and Equal Opportunity Commission (Australia).

'Age discrimination at work survey report' (2001). Chartered Institute of Personnel and Development.

'Age and ... multiple discrimination and older people' (2005). Age Reference Group on Equality and Human Rights, Age Concern England.

'Age at work: the definitive guide to the UK's workforce' (2005). Employers Forum on Age.

'Ageing and employment policies: United Kingdom' (2004). OECD.

'Ageing and the labour market: policies and initiatives within the European Union' (1998). Report of a European conference at the University of Twente, Netherlands. Eurolink Age.

'Ageism: attitudes and experiences of young people' (2001). Department for Education and Employment.

'An intersectional approach to discrimination addressing multiple grounds in human rights claims' (2004). Ontario Human Rights Commission.

'Aspects of the economics of an ageing population' (2003). House of Lords Select Committee on Economic Affairs, 4th Report, Session 2002–03, HL Paper 179–1.

'Casualty watch 2001' (2001). Association of Community Health Councils for England and Wales and Help the Aged.

'Changing priorities, transformed opportunities?' (2005). Parry, J. and Taylor, R., Policy Studies Institute, London.

'Characteristics of older workers' (1998). Researchers: McKay, S. and Middleton, S. Centre for Research in Social Policy, Loughborough University. Research Report RR4 and RR45, DfEE.

'Confronting demographic change: a new solidarity between generations' (2005). COM (2005), 94, Green Paper.

'Critical review of academic literature relating to the EU directives to combat discrimination' (2004). Bell, M. and Kjellstrand, S., European Commission.

'Demographic ageing: consequences for social policy' (1988). Maria, M., OECD.

'Demography report 2008: meeting social needs in an ageing society' (2009). European Commission.

'Disability and social participation in Europe' (2001). European Commission, Eurostat.

'Discrimination in Europe' (2003). Marsh, A. and Sahin-Dikmen, M., Eurobarometer.

'Discrimination in the European Union: perceptions, experiences and attitudes' (2008). Special Eurobarometer, 296, European Commission.

'Early retirement schemes still the norm in final salary schemes' (2004). IDS Pensions Bulletin 160.

'Employment in Europe' (2004). European Commission.

'Employment in Europe 2009' (2009). European Commission.

'Entry in the legal professions' (2000). Research Study No. 39, The Law Society, cited in occupational age restrictions sector review: Law (2001). DWP.

'Equality authority annual report' (2004). Equality Authority Ireland.

'Equality bill' (2009). Vincent Keter, House of Commons Research Paper, 09/42, 7 May 2009.

'Equality and diversity: age matters' (2003). Department for Trade and Industry.

'Equality and diversity: age matters. Age consultation 2003: summary of responses' (2005). DTI.

'Equality and diversity: coming of age' (2005). Department of Trade and Industry.

'Equality and diversity: coming of age report on the consultation on the draft equality (age) regulations 2006' (2006). Department of Trade and Industry.

'Equality in later life: a national study of older people's mental health services'. Healthcare Commission March 2009.

'Equality and non-discrimination in an enlarged European Union' (2004). Green Paper, European Commission, Brussels.

'Ethnic minorities and the labour market' (2003). Cabinet Office Strategy Unit.

'EU proposals to combat discrimination' (1999). House of Lords Select Committee on European Union, Ninth Report Towards a Europe for all Ages. Communication from the Commission, COM 221.

'Europe 2020: a European strategy for smart, sustainable and inclusive growth' (2010). Communication from the Commission COM(2010).

'Europe's demographic future: facts and figures on challenges and opportunities' (2007). European Commission, Luxembourg.

'European anti-discrimination law review no. 2' (2005). European Network of Legal Experts, produced by Human European Consultancy on behalf of the European Commission.

'Evaluation of the code of practice on age diversity in employment' (2000). Interim Summary of Results. Jones, D., DfEE.

'Evaluation of the code of practice on age diversity in employment final report' (2001). Department for Work and Pensions.

'Facing the challenge: the Lisbon strategy for growth and employment' (2004). Report from the High Level Group chaired by Wim Kok, November, European Commission.

'Factors affecting the labour market participation of older workers' (2003). Humphrey, A., Kostigan, P., Pickering, K., Stratford, N. and Barnes, M., Department for Work and Pensions, Research Report No. 200.

'Facts about women and men in Great Britain' (2005). Equal Opportunities Commission.

'Financial exclusion among older people' (2006). Research carried out by Andrew Irving Associates; Help the Aged.

'First annual report on migration and integration' (2004). COM (2004) 508.

'Focus on older people' (2004). Office for National Statistics.

'Government evidence to the low pay Commission on the economic effects of the national minimum wage Department for Business Enterprise and Regulatory Reform' (2007).

'Green Paper on an EU approach to managing economic migration' (2004). COM (2004) 811.

'How ageist is Britain?' (2005). Age Concern.

'Immigration, integration and employment' (2003). COM (2003), 336.

'Implementing equality for older people' (2004). Equality Authority of Ireland.

'Increasing labour force participation and promoting active ageing' (2002). COM (2002) 9.

'Insurance and age: exploring behaviour, attitudes and discrimination'. A report for Age Concern and Help the Aged.

'Live longer, work longer' (2006). OECD.

'National adult learning survey' (2002). Fitzgerald, R., Taylor, R. and Lavalle, I. National Centre for Social Research, Research Report 415, Department for Education and Skills.

'National service framework for older people: interim report on age discrimination' (2002). NHS.

'Non-discrimination and equal opportunities: a renewed commitment communication from the Commission SEC' (2008). 2172.

'Not because they are old: an independent inquiry into the care of older people on acute wards in general hospitals' (1998). Health Advisory Service, London.

'Occupational age restrictions sector review' (2001). Department for Work and Pensions.

'Older people inside and outside the labour market: a review equality and human rights commission' (2009). Smeaton, D. and Vegeris, S., London.

'Older workers: employers' attitudes and practices' (1990). Metcalf, H. and Thompson, M. Institute of Manpower Studies Report No. 194.

'Older workers; statistical information booklet' (2004). Department for Work and Pensions.

'Ontario human rights commission year-end results 2002–2003'. Ontario Human Rights Commission.

'Opportunity age' (2005). Department for Work and Pensions; Vol. 1 – Meeting the challenges of ageing in the 21st century, Vol. 2 – A social portrait of ageing.

'Part-time working is no crime – so why pay the penalty' (2005). Equal Opportunities Commission.

'Pensions: challenges and choices' (2004). Pensions Commission, HMSO.

'Pensions: challenges and choices. The first report of the Pensions Commission' (2004). TSO, Norwich.

'Pensions at a glance: public policies across OECD countries' (2007). OECD.

'Phasing out the default retirement age consultation document' (2010). Department for Business, Innovation and Skills plus the Department for Work and Pensions <http://www.bis.gov.uk/Consultations/retirement-age>.

'Policy on discrimination against older persons because of age' (2002). Ontario Human Rights Commission.

'Policy statement on age discrimination in facilities, goods and services' (2007). Help the Aged (2007).

'Protecting young workers: the national minimum wage' (2004). Low Pay Commission Report Cm6152.

'Replacement migration: is it a solution to declining and ageing populations?' (2000). Population Division, Department of Economics and Social Affairs, New York, United Nations.

'Retirement ages in the UK: a review of the literature' (2003). Meadows, P., DTI Employment Relations Series No. 18.

'Significance of age in the workplace' (2001). South London Training and Enterprise Council.

'Simplicity, security and choice: working and saving for retirement' (2002). Department for Work and Pensions.

'Simplicity, security and choice: working and saving for retirement' (2004) DWP.

'Stereotyping' (1995). Jelking, R. and Sajous, E. Public Services Commission of Canada (monograph).

'Survey of employers' policies, practices and preferences relating to age' (2006). Metcalf, H. with Meadows, P. Research Report 325, DTI Employment Relations Research Series No 49, Department for Work and Pensions.

'Tackling age bias: code or law?' (1998). EOR No. 80, July/August.

'Tackling age discrimination in the workplace' (2005). Chartered Institute of Personnel and Development and the Chartered Management Institute.

'The age dimension of employment practices: employer case studies' (2005). McNair, S. and Flynn, M., Centre for Research into the Older Workforce; Employment Relations Research Series No 42, Department of Trade and Industry.

'The demographic situation in the European Union' (1995). European Commission, Brussels.

'The dynamics of retirement' (1997). Disney, R., Grundy, E. and Johnson, P. Department of Social Security Research Report 72.

'The employment situation of people with disabilities in the European Union' (2001). Executive Summary of Research Paper, written by European Experts Group on employment for disabled people, commissioned by the DG Employment and Social Affairs.

'The equalities bill: making it work – ending age discrimination in services and public functions: a policy statement government equalities office' (2010).

'The national committee of inquiry into adult education report 2' (1997). The
    Dearing Report.
'The older American worker-age discrimination in employment' (1965). Report
    to the US Congress.
'The social situation in the European Union 2009' (2010). European Commission.
'The use of age-based practices in financial services' (2009). Prepared for the
    Government Equalities Office by Oxera Consulting, Oxford.
'Time for action: advancing human rights for older Ontarians' (2004). Ontario
    Human Rights Commission.
'Towards equality and diversity: implementing the employment and race
    directives' (2001). Department for Trade and Industry.
'Towards equality and diversity: report of responses on age' (2003). Department
    for Trade and Industry.
'Uncovered: workers without pensions' (2002). TUC.
'Winners and losers in an expanding system' (2001). Aldridge, F. and Tuckett,
    A., NIACE survey on adult participation in learning.
'Winning the generation game' (2000). Performance and Innovation Unit,
    Cabinet Office, April.
'Women and pensions the evidence' (2005). Department for Work and Pensions.
'Working and saving for retirement' (2002). Department for Work and Pensions.

Law

CASES

Agco Ltd v Massey Ferguson Works Pension Trust Ltd [2003] IRLR 783
Application by Badeck and others Case C-158/97 [2000] IRLR 432 ECJ
Banks v Ablex Ltd [2005] IRLR 357 CA
Beith v Nitrogen Products Inc. 7 F.3d 701 (8th Cir. 1993)
Bentley v Secretary of State for Trade and Industry [2002] IRLR 768 Employment
    Tribunal
Brian McLoughlin v Bus Éireann Equality Officer Decision No: DEC-E2004-059
Burton v De Vere Hotels [1997] ICR 1 [1996] IRLR 596
Canada (A.G.) v Mossop [1993] 1 S.C.R. 554 at 645–6
Carroll v Monaghan Vocational Guidance Education Committee DEC-E/2004/003
Case C-229/08 *Colin Wolf v Stadt Frankfurt am Main*
Commission v United Kingdom [1984] IRLR 29
Commonwealth of Australia v Human Rights and Equal Opportunity Commission
    [1999] FCA 1524
Cross v British Airways [2005] IRLR 423

Dr Dominica Petersen v Berufungsausschuss für Zahnärte für den Bezirk Westfalen-Lippe Case C-341/08

EEOC v Insurance Co. of North America 49 F.3d 1418 (9th Cir. 1995)

Equality Authority v Ryanair Equality Officer Decision DEC – E/2000/14

Félix Palacios de la Villa v Cortefiel Servicios SA Case C-411/05

Gillen v Department of Health and Children DEC-E2003-035

Greater Vancouver Regional District Employees' Union v Greater Vancouver Regional District [2001] BCCA 435

Gross v FBL Financial Services 129 S. Ct. 2343 (2009)

Hazen Paper Co v Biggins 113 SCt 1701, 16 FEP 793 (1993)

Hughes v Aer Lingus Equality Officer's Decision No: DEC-E2002-49

Hütter v Technische Univerisät Graz Case 88/08 [2010]....

Igen Ltd v Wong [2005] IRLR 258 CA

James v Eastleigh Borough Council [1990] IRLR 288 HL

Kentucky Retirement Systems v EEOC 128 S. Ct. 2361 (2008)

Kücüdeveci v Swedex GnbH & Co. KG Case C-555/07 [2010] ....

Loeb v Textron Inc. 600 F.2d 1003 (1979)

Loxley v BAE Systems Ltd [2008] IRLR 853

MacCulloch v ICI plc [2008] IRLR 846

MacDonald v Advocate General for Scotland; Pearce v Governing Body of Mayfield School [2003] IRLR 512

McDonnell Douglas Corp v Green 411 US 792

McKinney v University of Guelph [1990] 3 SCR

Mahoney v Trabucco 574 F.Supp. 955 (1983)

Majrowski v Guy's and St Thomas's NHS Trust [2005] IRLR 240

Mangold v Helm Case C-144/04 [2006] IRLR 143

Marschall v Land Nordrhein-Westfalen Case C-409/95 [1998] IRLR 39 ECJ

Massachusetts Board of Retirement v Murgia 427 US 307 (1976)

Metz v Transit Mix Inc. 828 F.2d 1202 (7th Cir 1987)

Nash v Mash/Roe Group Ltd [1998] IRLR 168

O'Connor v Consolidated Coin Caterers Corp 517 U.S. 308 (1996)

O'Flynn v Adjudication Officer Case C-237/94. [1996] ECR 2617

Pearce v Governing Body of Mayfield School [2003] IRLR 512

Quantas Airways Ltd v Christie [1998] HCA 18

R v Secretary of State for Employment, ex parte Seymour-Smith and Perez (No 2) [2000] IRLR 263 HL

Reinhard Prigge, Michael Fromm and Volker Lambach v Deutsche Lufthansa AG Case C-447/09

Rolls Royce v Unite the Union [2009] IRLR 576

Rosenbladt v Oellerking Gebäudereinigungsges mbH Case C-45/09

Rutherford v Secretary of State for Trade and Industry (no. 2) [2004] IRLR 892

Seldon v Clarkson Wright & Jakes [2010] IRLR 865

Smith v City of Jackson, Mississippi 544 U.S. (2005)

Spence v Maryland Casualty Co 995 F.2d 1147 (2d Cir 1993)

Stanley Edward Griffin v Australian Postal Corporation. Industrial Relations Court of Australia 980001, 15 September 1998

Superquinn v Barbara Freeman AEE/02/08 Determination No 021

Taggart v Time Inc 924 F.2d 43 (2d Cir. 1991)

Taylor v Secretary of State for Scotland [2000] IRLR 503

The Queen on the application of Age UK v Secretary of State for Business, Innovation and Skills and the Equality and Human Rights Commission, HM Attorney General [2009] IRLR 1017

Trans World Airlines v Thurston 469 US 111 (1985)

Usery v Tamiami Trail Tours Inc. 531 F.2d 224 (1976)

Vasil Ivanov Georiev v Tehnicheski Universitet Case C-250/09.

Venebles v Hornby [2004] 1 All ER 627

Waite v Government Communications Headquarters [1983] IRLR 341

Western Airlines Inc. v Criswell 472 U.S. 400, 105 S.Ct. 2743, 86 L.Ed.2nd 321 (1985)

Woroski v Nashau Corp 31 F.3d 195 (2nd Cir. 1994)

X v Department of Defense [1995] EOC 92-715

Zafar v Glasgow City Council [1998] IRLR 36 HL

DIRECTIVES

Council Directive 94/33/EC concerning certain aspects of working time OJ L216/12 23-11-1993

Council Directive 97/80/EC on the burden of proof in cases of discrimination based on sex OJ L14/6, 20 January 1998

Directive 76/207 EEC on the implementation of the principle of equal treatment between men and women; subsequently amended by Directive 2002/73/EC

Directive 2000/43/EC of 29 June 2000 which concerned the principle of equal treatment between persons irrespective of racial or ethnic origin

Directive 2000/78/EC OJ L303/16 of 27 November 2000 establishing a general framework for equal treatment in employment and occupation

Proposal for a Council Directive on implementing the principle of equal treatment between persons irrespective of religion or belief, disability, age or sexual orientation. COM(2008) 426

STATUTORY INSTRUMENTS

Part-time Workers (Prevention of Less Favourable Treatment) Regulations 2000 SI 2000/1551
The Employment Equality (Religion or Belief) Regulations 2003 SI 2003/1660
The Employment Equality (Sexual Orientation) Regulations 2003 SI 2003/1661
The Employment Equality (Age) Regulations 2006 SI 2006/1031
The National Minimum Wage Regulations 1999 SI 1999/584
Transfer of Undertakings (Protection of Employment) Regulations 1981 SI 1981/1794
Working Time Regulations 1998. SI 1998/1833

LEGISLATION

Age Discrimination in Employment Act 1967 (USA)
Age Discrimination Act 2004 (Australia)
Anti Discrimination Act 1977 (New South Wales)
Canadian Charter of Rights and Freedoms 1982
Civil Rights Act of 1991 (USA)
Disability Discrimination Act 1995
Disability Rights Commission Act 1999
Employment Equality Act 1998 (Ireland)
Employment Rights Act 1996
Equality Act 2004 (Ireland)
Equality Act 2006
Equality Act 2010
Equal Pay Act 1970
Equal Status Act 2000 (Ireland)
Equal Opportunity Act 1984 (South Australia)
European Communities Act 1972
Further and Higher Education Act 1992
Licensing Act 1964
National Insurance Act 1948
National Minimum Wage Act 1998
Old Age and Widows Pensions Act 1940
Old Age Pensions Act 1908
Older Workers Benefit Protection Act 1990 (USA)
Protection from Harassment Act 1997
Race Relations Act 1976
Sex Discrimination Act 1975

Social Security Act 1975
Trade Union and Labour Relations (Consolidation) Act 1992
Widows, Orphans and Old Age Contributory Pensions Act 1925
Workplace Relations Act 1996 (Australia)

Index